Are You <u>SURE</u> God's Not Talking?

(Or Are You Just <u>NOT</u> Listening?)

John Dennis Maher

Copyright © 2019 by John Dennis Maher

Published by: John Dennis Maher

Updated and expanded from the 2017 edition.

All rights reserved. No portion of this book may be reproduced, stored in a retrieval system, or transmitted in any form or by any means—electronic, mechanical, photocopy, recording, scanning or other—except for quotations in critical reviews or articles, or page copying for group study, without the prior written permission of the publisher.

Scripture quotations marked NKJV are from THE NEW KING JAMES VERSION. Copyright © 1979, 1980, 1982, Thomas Nelson, Inc., Publishers.
Scripture quotations marked HCSB are from the Holman Christian Standard Bible®, Copyright © 1999, 2000, 2002, 2003, 2009 by Holman Bible Publishers. Used by permission. Holman Christian Standard Bible®, Holman CSB®, and HCSB® are federally registered trademarks of Holman Bible Publishers.
Scripture quotations marked NIV are from The Holy Bible, New International Version® NIV® Copyright © 1973, 1978, 1984, 2011 by Biblica, Inc. ™ Used by permission. All rights reserved worldwide.
Scripture quotations marked TNIV are from the Holy Bible, Today's New International Version™ TNIV. ® Copyright © 2001, 2005 by International Bible Society®. All rights reserved worldwide.
Scripture quotations marked KJV are from the King James Version of the Bible.
Scripture quotations marked NLT are from the *Holy Bible*, New Living Translation, copyright © 1996, 2004, 2007. Used by permission of Tyndale House Publishers, Inc., Carol Stream, Illinois 60188. All rights reserved.

NOTICE: Only those names indicated by the Holy Spirit are part of the text of this book. Occurrences and conversations spoken of in this book are from recorded events, prayer gatherings, and meetings. Those not recorded are from both journal entries and personal recollections, as prompted and guided by the Holy Spirit.

ISBN-13: 978-0-999-2699-1-6
ISBN-10: 09992699-1-7

**Available in book form on Amazon.com or through local bookstores.
Watch for the upcoming release in eBook format.**

Contents

Preface	7
Dedication	10
Introduction	11
Acknowledging the "I" in Sin	15
Gaining a New Perspective	23
Called to Be a Vessel	33
A House Divided	47
Learning to War	51
Drawn Aside	59
Facing the Truth	71
Observing the Battle	81
Personally Impacted	89
Coming Alongside	95
Laborer vs. Co-Laborer	101
Multiple Personality Disorder	109
After-Effects	117
Are You Here For You or Me?	123
Gone Away Backward	133
Isolation and Intimacy	147
Let Me Re-Mind You	159
Positioned to See	167
Evidence of Love	179
Holding On, While Letting Go	187
Confusion, Confirmation & Change	199
Broken Stallions Carry Kings	211
Uncovered and Exposed	223
The Spirit of Reconciliation: Grace to Forgive	229
If You Would Be My Voice	241
Everything Matters, However…	253
Burden-Lifting Revelation	269
Scripture, Book & Song References	281
About the Author	282

"...recall the former days, in which, after you were illuminated, you endured a great struggle with sufferings."

Hebrews 10:32 (NKJV)

What Others Have Said About This Book

"I've watched this man for many, many years as he developed into a mighty writer for God. He writes what God tells him, in the exact way that God gives it to him. As a result, he has blessed many. The greatest value of this book is in its revelation of a man surrendered to and directed by the Lord God Almighty. That is what true Christian life is. I encourage you, as you read this book, to consider how these many lessons might apply to YOU. Ask yourself, 'Through which part of this book is He speaking to ME right now?' Then, each time you reread it, allow His Spirit to take you even further in Him, as He pours out His love to you. I've watched this occur in the man who wrote this book, and seen how it changed his heart, his life, and his entire family."

(Byron Huff)

"This book is about a very personal journey with the Holy Spirit and the omnipresence of God. It makes me desire more of a personal relationship with the Father. As God showed the author, 'Everything Matters' in the realm of the Spirit. It was a good read and kept my interest. I looked forward to getting back to it each time I put it down. This book will lead you to a closer walk with the Father." (Steve Ward)

"I very much enjoyed this book. I found it to be intriguing, and it held my attention through the entire book. The building of the story from chapter to chapter painted a picture of the events that the author experienced. I would highly recommend this book to anyone who is seeking in-depth insight into walking with the Spirit."

(Kevin Garrett)

"Going into the book, I wasn't sure what to expect. After digging in, I can honestly say it has provoked my walk with the Lord. Watching a man humble himself and be completely transparent about the struggles of life, and how that affected his family and relationship with God, was eye-opening. I found myself relating on so many levels. The book clearly showed the Father's way of dealing with one of His sons, the heavenly 'adoption process' into His family, and the eventual maturing into a man of God. It was encouraging to read how hearing from the Spirit can indeed affect your life, and how living a life of following His voice is so unique compared to one of simply following your vision." (Mark Campbell)

"This book is powerful! It compels you to search your heart to make sure you are following Christ and letting Him lead you as He guides your steps, thoughts, and actions. It's very uplifting!" (Amazon Customer)

"An encouraging book! It inspired me to pursue hearing the Holy Spirit for myself."
(Amazon Customer)

"To anyone who wants to go deeper or come closer, allowing yourself to break free from where your spiritual journey slowed, this is a 'MUST READ.' Prepare to be stirred deeply while you read as the author humbly and transparently allows the reader to share in his journey with the Lord." (Susan Brumer)

"I have striven in my might for many years to become something my Heavenly Father would be proud of, only to find myself frustrated with my failings. I finally feel set free from myself after reading the interactions between the author and the Holy Spirit. Renewed hope and joy have sprung forth from the realization of the power that is in His name alone." (Frances Gulley)

"This book's insight into yielding to the Holy Spirit is amazing! It will affect your life, as well as the lives of others, far beyond your understanding. The Holy Spirit never leaves or forsakes you during any valley or period of despair. He is always faithful!"
(Ken Wade)

"This book is one of the best books I have ever read. It so enlightened me regarding the ways of the Holy Spirit. I use this book as a guide for understanding how the Holy Spirit is working on me. It has provided great insight." (Loretta Phillips)

"This book tells it like it is. God loves us and wants us both healed and whole. He frees us from the hurts that have plagued our lives. If we listen, the Holy Spirit WILL direct us. The author was very transparent in putting it all on the table, with the Holy Spirit guiding him as he did so. These are incredible 'life lessons' of a wonderful loving God who said He would never forget us or forsake us."
(Amazon Customer)

To be notified of future releases of books, blog postings or podcasts, email your request to John.Dennis.Maher@gmail.com

Preface

Someone I much respect once counseled me, "If you want to know how to live the Christian life, you need to study God's book of directions and guidelines. However, if you are unwilling to be faithful to apply what you learn, do not waste your time studying them. If you are serious though about Christ moving through you, things **must** change. You **must** die that He might live as the 'Christ **in** you, the Hope of glory.' There **must** be a transformation."

Since that conversation, I have come to understand that this transformation begins with **listening** for the Voice of the Living God—with the soul and spirit, not the ears. Although the Spirit of Christ welcomes and encourages our petitioning prayer, **conversation** with us is what He desires most. Understand, therefore, that conversation, by its definition, involves listening and talking, **by both parties**.

Allow me also to clarify upfront that this is NOT an instructional book on how to understand the Voice of the Lord. Likewise, it is NOT a guide on how to stay free from what separates you from God or keeps you from hearing. Even so, over several decades, both of these have come to fruition in my life in varying degrees.

The truth is I struggled unsuccessfully for many years to "easily hear" His Voice. Those were times of great frustration and learning. I had the mistaken understanding that every Christian automatically heard Him all the time after the "born again" experience. However, I did not. The more I spoke with others, including those who claimed to be longtime Christians, the more individuals I discovered experiencing what I was. Dissatisfied, I prayed even more.

Eventually, I learned of the Baptism in the Holy Spirit. In my ignorance, I attempted to receive it through my intellect and understanding. For many years, I read testimonies and listened to others testify and talk about "tongues" or "having a prayer language." My increased pleas to God for "my prayer language"—but **not** for the fullness of, or control by, His Spirit—brought no results. In resignation, three years later, I admitted my foolishness to Him and asked for forgiveness. Immediately, I burst forth speaking fluently in a new language that I had never before heard or spoken and felt indescribable joy surging through my being. At the same time, I clearly "heard" His Voice speaking *conversationally* to my soul and spirit for the first time, and wept with joy.

Soon after that day, a friend suggested I begin journaling my conversations with the Holy Spirit. Purchasing a blank, lined journal and some black and red pens, I awoke early that next morning and began praying in my new spirit language. Once more, an incredible joy welled up inside of me, followed by His Voice telling me to pick up my pen and begin writing what was on my mind. I wrote out each of my questions using a black or blue ink pen and was pleasantly surprised to "hear" an immediate answer or explanation from Him, spoken to my inner being. These, I recorded in red ink. This new experience became a source of great ecstasy in my life and that which I anticipated daily, as our conversations grew more and more detailed and, for me, exciting. Throughout nearly four decades of my journaling, He has covered a multitude of subjects in-depth, teaching me many valuable lessons.

Finally, the day came when He told me to compose the book that follows—with His guidance. Writing, rewriting, and editing the contents of this book took more than five years. Several times, the Holy Spirit instructed me to go back and delete large segments of previous chapters. When I asked, in frustration, the reason for His request, He explained.

"These were points at which you took it upon yourself to expound on what I had already stated with clarity. Remember, son, that your thoughts are not My thoughts. Realize also that your words, created in your mind and imagination, will never surpass the truthful simplicity of Mine."

In other instances, He asked me to elaborate on sections in which I had stated what He said, but did so in a more generic way, using my words, and not His. Obedience to His request to elaborate required my exposing many things about which I had previously been unwilling to speak. Initially, this was quite painful. After I fulfilled His exact instructions and read the reworked sections, I realized how much my previous generalizations of His truth had tainted its potential value to others. Once again, the Spirit explained His reasoning. "Son, My Word declares:

*'...they overcame him [Satan] **by the blood of the Lamb and by the word of their testimony,**'"*

*"You have come to believe that much of what you experienced in your more distant past is of little value to others today. The worth of My shed blood has not changed since the day I presented it as a full atonement to the Father. Remember this! Your testimony only loses its significance when you stop proclaiming it for all to hear. Never forget! It's the two—**COMBINED**—that annuls the fallen one's actions against you and your household."*

"Son, I have reminded you time and again that My sheep hear My voice. They recognize it and have no reason to doubt it. You are one of My sheep, and you hear My voice. There is no need to apologize for what I stated would occur when you became

Mine. There will always be those who are uncomfortable with and unwilling to accept what I have spoken to you as truth. Allow Me to defend you against those who would use My Word to justify their personal beliefs, opinions, and teachings derived through their own intellect. Likewise, take care that you not fall into that same trap, then being guilty of that very sin."

As His child, the Lord only asks that we be faithful to obey what the Spirit of God asks of us. As I discovered many times through my resistance, stubbornness, or outright disobedience, failure to follow what He asks often became an obstruction to future conversation. The Lord impressed this upon my mind one day, when He explained, **"The vine that strangles one's ability to hear My Spirit roots itself deep in the soil of a disobedient heart."**

Included in this book are hundreds of valuable "**life lessons,**" explained to me by the Holy Spirit. Some seemed quite elementary at the time and came through prayer and enjoyable **conversation** with Him. Others were extremely challenging and often bitterly painful. Every **conversation** and **lesson** contained nuggets of pure wisdom from Heaven. Some I understood and applied. Others I feigned confusion and ignored, much to my detriment.

As a result, the progress made by the Holy Spirit in purging and reshaping my soul progressed at the rate in which I was willing to trust Him and release control to Him. Only when this surrender had genuinely occurred did the Spirit move unhindered in and through me to fulfill the Heavenly Fathers' will.

Throughout this book, I freely describe my shortcomings and backsliding, including how these affected my relationship with the Holy Spirit, my family, and my friends. I do so with the hope that the reader might learn from my transparency, thereby avoiding the same delays, hurdles, and sins. My ultimate prayer is that, through these related experiences, many others may enter into a life filled with joyous *conversation* with the Spirit of the Living God.

Therefore, I offer this work for God to use to your benefit. I do so, with no excuses or apologies. I pray that by laying bare my life, I encourage you to invite the Lord God Almighty to help you do likewise. Ask Him to open up your spiritual ears to **HEAR** His Voice, and to free you as He did me. He is longing to heal and release each of us from the hurt, pain, suffering, hindrances, and distractions that He alone knows have shackled our bodies and souls. Through my obedience in writing this book, He delivered, healed, restored, and blessed me. As you read, I pray that He will also lead you to an ever-deepening intimacy with Him during which you participate in endless *conversations* with the Holy Spirit of the Living God who longs to communicate freely with ALL of His children.

DEDICATION

To Patricia: For more than forty-five years, you have been and still are my best friend, wife, and the love of my life. I extend my deepest affection and gratitude for how you have blessed me. You pray for and encourage me, and you never stop believing that God has His hand on me. The evidence of this was most apparent in those times when I struggled to be sure of that myself. You are always ready to celebrate with me in times of great rejoicing. Despite spiritual and physical struggles that threatened to destroy both this work and us, you still stood by my side. You have believed with me that His Spirit is continuing to guide us, as He promised. Thank you for never doubting that He will be faithful to complete that which He began—in both of us. When the Father brought you to me, I knew then that He had given me one of His most precious gifts. I love you!

Introduction

They had all arrived at the agreed-upon place just before eight on that first Saturday morning. The men exchanged greetings, then settled onto an assortment of old chairs set up in a truck service bay. The bay was part of a pole barn structure from which one of the men—the property owner—had once operated his business. Some attendees had come anticipating whatever direction the Spirit might lead. However, the majority had attended out of mere curiosity. Nonetheless, as was later discovered, the unspoken question on the minds of many that morning had been the same. *How long will it be before most—who had enjoyed the comfort and anonymity of our previous hotel environments and large crowds—would find an excuse to stop participating?*

All the men had fellowshipped for years at various churches and Christian groups. Those times had always involved food and good conversation. After the meal, guest speakers would testify of God's working in their lives and place of work. The format was unique, and the Spirit of God often moved in unexpected ways. He prompted men to consider areas of their lives not yet surrendered to the One they called Lord. Even so, many in attendance found it too easy to ignore His invitation time after time.

A few of the men now here on this first morning had fasted for many days and prayed for guidance about the purpose of this new gathering. The Spirit's direction had been clear. It was time to transition from fellowship into discipleship. There was to be no comfortable hotel environment, no food or drink to entice attendees, and no servers to wait on them. Even the building in which we were to meet had been the Lord's choice. That decision made many of the men immediately uncomfortable. Still, the Holy Spirit's hand in the arrangements was undeniable as He explained His desire to a few who were willing to hear.

"This new gathering will be an arena of change and spiritual growth. In My venue, you will come to understand that **'becoming a disciple' involves learning to permit Me to do the work in your heart and soul that you have struggled for years to do on your own without success**. *My desire for each of you is that you would welcome, and move into intimacy with, that cross which I'm inviting you, and you alone, to bear."*

Still, the Father also knew every man entering into this new quest would be arriving with baggage. This *baggage* was not limited to religious doctrinal beliefs and personal prejudices. As we found out later, for some, there also were various vices, debilitating insecurities, paralyzing fears, and secret sins. The Lord then spoke through one of the men, encouraging everyone present.

"Much personal battle lies ahead for each of you. The ones who walk in My victory will be those willing to surrender to My Spirit. This surrender is what will allow My love to transform your soul."

† † †

Only forty of the one hundred fifty men invited had responded. Each man introduced himself for the benefit of the few who were not familiar with everyone there. As they did, the men discovered what a cross-section of the Body of Christ the group represented. There were Anglicans, Baptists, and Episcopalians. Some were Lutheran, Methodist, Nazarene, and one was from a Holiness upbringing. However, the majority were Catholic, Evangelical, Pentecostal, Presbyterian, and Non-Denominational.

The occupations of the men were just as varied. The group included small business owners, one retiree, a college student, and an accountant. Some were mechanics, engineers, and factory workers. One was a plant manager, one a janitor, and another a former pastor. Still, others were printers, architects, bus drivers, painters, roofers, and sales representatives. Education levels spanned high school dropout to doctorate level. Their incomes ranged from unemployed to millionaire.

A couple of the men had formal training in, or knowledge of, the Word of God. Most, however, admitted to only a general understanding gained through years of church attendance. All had with them their preferred version of the Bible. A few had brought notes from the study of their favorite Bible-related subjects. The majority had no understanding of how or where the Holy Spirit desired to guide them. As a result, most showed surprise at the Lord's choice of who was to lead the group.

The Father did not look for a confident speaker or someone with a vast knowledge of His Word. Instead, the Spirit had searched for and found a man after His own heart. This middle-aged business owner was the same one who had shown forth generosity by offering the use of his building in which the group now met. More importantly, he had moved beyond deciding to surrender his life to the Lordship of Christ Jesus by acting on what most of the others had only thought or talked about doing. His walk had not been easy, but he had persisted, one day and, often, one decision at a time, no matter what the cost.

Now, he stood before the group, looking at their faces. Doubt besieged his mind, attempting to distract him. In his spirit, he petitioned the Lord for answers to questions that still weighed on his heart.

How can I hope to explain the infinite possibilities that You have only begun to reveal to me in the past few years? Would I have had those experiences if I had not obeyed by secluding myself with You six days a week for that period? How can I make these men understand what awaits those willing to accept Your invitation to commune at a deeper level than most have ever considered possible? What about those intimate with Your Presence until drawn away by the cares and things of this world? How can I encourage them to return to their first love? Holy Spirit, I waited forty-eight years to accept Jesus as Lord and Savior! How can I convince others that unimaginable intimacy with God is attainable and fulfilling beyond anything they've ever known?

He hesitated for a minute or two, anticipating a response from the Holy Spirit, but none came. He proceeded as the Spirit had instructed, despite feeling inadequate to the call. His speech was not eloquent. He read the notes he had written at the Spirit's leading, seldom looking at those observing him. Many of the men grew restless, and their faces showed forth the unease in their souls. Even so, this did not deter or distract him. With apparent brokenness, he conveyed what the Spirit had directed, then stopped.

After a brief group prayer, the men said their goodbyes and departed. The one who had spoken to the group gathered his things together and retreated to his office. As he did, the feeling that he could have somehow done more for the Lord nagged at his heart. When he reached the seclusion of his office, he questioned the Lord aloud.

"Did *anyone* there today receive what You directed me to say?"

Three days passed before the Lord spoke to him about what had occurred the previous Saturday. The Lord reminded him that it was not his responsibility to do what only the Spirit of God could do. He further explained that God alone knew what it would take to reach the heart of each man who was there that morning. He also assured him that the only demand the Lord would ever place upon him would be his willingness to hear and obey.

The man spent extensive periods of each day in prayer. As he did, the Spirit burdened him to intercede for those who would choose to return at the end of the week. When Saturday dawned, twenty of the original forty showed up. Each week after that, another went missing until the group had dwindled to just twelve. Still, the attitude of those remaining had become both hopeful and purposeful. Most did not have the slightest idea about what the Father might ask of them as an individual. Neither did they foresee where His Spirit might lead them as a group. Even so, they were all hungry enough to follow.

"Now," the Spirit declared through one of the remaining twelve, *"genuine discipleship can begin."*

*"Promotion of 'SELF'
will always be the most cunning
means used by your enemy
to fight against
My influence over your soul.
In this case, your enemy wars to
keep you from surrendering to Me.
This 'warring' is much of the
'wrestling' that you will face.
Satan's forces will...tell you
that one's surrender of 'SELF'
is a deception that ends in
a loss of identity.
In this instance, they will have spoken
the truth, but not the whole truth.
You must acknowledge and accept
this surrender of 'SELF' as a
vital part of the 'Divine Exchange.'
I invite you to trade your
'SELF' identity
for one found in Me alone."*

Acknowledging the "I" in Sin

Several months had passed, and the remaining men had moved from the truck bay into a rough office in the same pole barn. The worn industrial carpet glued to the concrete floor emitted a musty odor from decades of foot traffic. Two portable ceramic heaters struggled to warm the frigid October air penetrating the walls.

As the worship music that was playing ended, the twelve men in the room remained still and silent. Several minutes passed with no one feeling compelled to interrupt the peace. The stillness became solemn, at which point one man—a former pastor—reached for his Bible. Rather than reading a favorite Scripture or two, as most had grown used to him doing, he extracted a blank index card and wrote on it with a pen. Rising from his seat, he hung the message he had written on a protruding nail on the one wall. Returning to his chair, he closed his eyes and bowed his head once more in a spirit of silent worship. On the card, he had written a single word…

s I n.

Over the next few minutes, each of the men looked at the card, curious as to what he had written. Although most wondered in their minds about the pastors' actions, they said nothing, and the silence continued. Some in the room grew restless, repeatedly glancing at the word on the card and looking away. That singular word seemed to unsettle their souls. A few others began to weep as the Spirit moved on their hearts with conviction. Eventually, someone asked the pastor to explain his actions.

"The Holy Spirit told me to write out the word 'sIn,' capitalizing the letter 'I,' and to hang the card on the wall."

Everyone waited, expecting a further explanation, but none was forthcoming. Several minutes later, however, the Lord began speaking to me where I sat at the far end of the room.

"Son, do you realize how many who call themselves Mine listen to the enemy of their souls rather than My Spirit within, accepting as true the belief that some sins are worse than others? You learned this same doctrine in your religious upbringing and, from time to time, are guilty of using it to justify your actions as you ignore the truth. Failing to guard your heart, you then listen to your enemy's promptings, considering thoughts that you know are contrary to My Word. Enticed by your enemy into believing that dwelling on these thoughts causes harm to no one, you easily come into agreement

with the Deceiver. Blind then to the fact that YOU are the one most harmed, your mind categorizes, and your heart accepts these 'small, forgivable missteps' as **sin**."

"Next, you rationalize your thinking, comparing these 'harmless' acts of yours with more destructive actions that you, and the world, are quick to classify as **SIN**."

"These more injurious actions—which most are diligent in keeping themselves from—you readily label in your mind as 'significant' SIN. Meanwhile, you allow what you think of as 'harmless little **sins**' to shape your character contrary to My Word. I remind you, it is the little foxes that spoil the vines and, in this situation, the small, 'supposedly insignificant' **sins**—which you've convinced yourself to be of no consequence—that destroy your character."

"As you know, I am both the Redeemer and an ever-merciful Father. My blood sacrifice was full atonement for all sin and all humanity. However, for it to cover your sin, you must first acknowledge that you have indeed sinned. You must then accept that I poured out My blood as a living sacrifice for you, to free you from the wrath of sin and death. Last, you must rest in the assurance that I am faithful to forgive your sins. When this occurs, My blood covers those sins from Our view, as though they never occurred."

"**Then, and only then,** will you understand what follows. When you accepted the Son as your Savior, the Father became your Father, and you became Our beloved child. As such, recognize that you are now accountable for your actions, thoughts, and words. Remember, son, that My Word promises, '*As many as I love, I rebuke and chasten.*'"[1]

"It also states, '**My son, do not despise the chastening of the Lord, nor be discouraged when you are rebuked by Him; For whom the Lord loves He chastens, and scourges every son whom He receives.**'"[2]

"Even so, be assured that, should you stumble and fall, or fall away, I will always be there to lift you, or encourage and welcome your return. I will forgive you once more when you confess your sin. My blood will then cover these new sins also, restoring you unto Me."

The Lord then cautioned me, saying, "Once your spirit has become Mine, what remains to perfect is your soul—your mind, will, and emotions. This soul—which is your SELF—is what makes you unique. Understand then, that it's your soul—your SELF—that your enemy never stops trying to influence and corrupt."

"Victory over SELF is possible only through continual surrender to My Spirit. To share in My victory, you must first surrender your mind. I will align your thoughts with the mind of Christ. The surrender of your will comes next, allowing your will to align with the will and desire of the Father. The final step is the surrender of your emotions, which will permit the Spirit of Christ to guide them. Each day, each minute, with each of your enemy's enticements, a decision point will stand before you, son. Only your genuine willingness to die to self will allow My Spirit to intercede on your behalf,

Acknowledging the "I" in Sin

exposing and rooting out those things that were, in past times, justified, ignored, or hidden away deep within your soul where they wreak havoc."

"Be aware! Your spirit **will** long for your soul to change, even as David's did. However, your heart and mind will resist releasing control, readily justifying SELF-confidence and SELF-esteem, unwilling to acknowledge them as branches blossomed forth from the well-rooted trunk of SELF-determination, nourished by the stream of personal pride. Be cautious also when your spirit yearns for the Potter's hand to transform your soul, but your soul draws instead toward lusting after, and finding pleasure in, the things of the world and the ways of the flesh."

"Remember what My Word says. It is **'...better to trust in the Lord than to put confidence in man.'**[3] This directive applies not only to your placing trust or confidence in another but also counting on your soul to be trustworthy when I have instructed in My Word that **'...the Lord will be your confidence.'**"[4]

"I am **'He who satisfies the longing soul, and fills the hungry soul with goodness.'**[5] My Word also states, **'Trust in the Lord with all your heart, And lean not on your own understanding; In all your ways acknowledge Him, and He shall direct your paths. Do not be wise in your own eyes.'**[6] Finally, My Word promises **'...God shall supply all your need according to His riches in glory by Christ Jesus,'**[7] and **'...He who promised is faithful.'**"[8]

"Promotion of 'SELF' will always be the most cunning means used by your enemy to fight against My influence over your soul. In this case, your enemy wars to keep you from surrendering to Me. This 'warring' is much of the 'wrestling' that you will face— **'...not against flesh and blood, but against principalities, against powers, against the rulers of the darkness of this age, against spiritual wickedness in high places.'**[9] The more you desire to surrender control to My Spirit, to pick up your cross daily and follow Christ, the more intense the resistance and confrontation will be from your enemy. Satan's forces will try to deceive you about this also. They will tell you that one's surrender of 'SELF' is a deception that ends in a loss of identity. In this instance, they will have spoken the truth, but not the whole truth. You must acknowledge and accept this surrender as being a vital part of the 'Divine Exchange.' I invite you to trade your 'SELF' identity for one found in Me alone. This surrender brings you into unity with My Spirit, allowing your blossoming forth as a branch grafted into Me, the heavenly Vine. When this has occurred, you will finally bring forth abundant fruit for the Kingdom of God."

"I desire that each person would find their true identity and completion in Me. What I allowed your friend to declare to those willing to see and understand is that **a cross exists for each to bear**. Your resistance to surrendering 'SELF' is what prevents you from accepting your cross. This resistance to surrender is what I identified to your friend as **sIn**."

*"Anticipating the **'joy that was set before'**[10] Me, I endured **'the cross, despising the shame.'**[11] Upon My resurrection, I **'sat down at the right hand of the throne of God.'**[12] I became for you **'the Author and Finisher of faith.'**[13] It is My deepest desire that each of My children would come and join Me, thereby fulfilling and sharing in My joy."*

When the Spirit had finished speaking to me, I remained immobile. For several minutes, I pondered what He had said. The only response that seemed right was to leave my seat, prostrating myself before the Lord.

The strong presence of the Lord lingered in the room uninterrupted for forty-five minutes. During that time, the Holy Spirit began addressing the hearts of each man present, and many, one by one, slipped from their chairs to the floor.

On my face at the far end of the room, I wept as I asked the Lord to forgive me, and whispered to Him of my love. Minutes later, my soft words intensified and changed in nature. I found myself participating in a surreal conversation with the Lord. The others in the room could hear only my side of that conversation. My whispering changed to repeated loud protests accompanied by periods of equally loud weeping and then transitioned into a heartrending wail that gushed forth from my utter brokenness. That lengthy exchange concluded with me alternating between intervals of uncontrollable laughter and weeping.

When I had finally calmed, I arose from the floor and settled into a chair, drying my face and trying to compose myself. I could see in my peripheral vision others glancing at me. I realized that my unrestrained display of emotions had shattered their complacency. For several minutes, no one seemed eager to speak. Feeling as though an explanation was in order, I finally attempted to relate what I had just experienced.

"I was lying there, telling the Lord how much I loved Him, and thanking Him for dying for my sins. I asked the Holy Spirit to show me any of my ways that did not please the Father. It was a surprise when He responded by instead asking me a question. *'Are you joyful that Jesus died on the cross for your sins?'"*

"I whispered to Him, 'I'm very thankful.' In response, He asked me more questions."

"'I did not ask if you were thankful. Are you able to say that you are ecstatic that Jesus poured out His blood for you on the cross? Are you able to exuberantly rejoice because He allowed His tormentors to shred His flesh, and beat Him beyond recognition? He endured excruciating pain for hours, which ended with His death on the cross—for your sin and your sake, son.'"

Acknowledging the "I" in Sin

"It bothered me when the Holy Spirit asked me that," I confessed to the men. "I told Him again how thankful I was but admitted to having trouble with the idea of 'rejoicing with exuberance.'"

"In the next moment, He showed me the most graphic depiction of what occurred at Golgotha. I found myself kneeling alongside the cross as it lay on the ground."

I paused to calm myself and wipe my face before continuing.

"They were positioning Jesus on the cross. Blood covered His mutilated body and seeped from His many open wounds. I saw the soldiers jerking His arms, stretching them into position to nail. Each time the soldiers pulled His body, fresh blood started flowing from every tear and wound. Watching their actions, I felt anger rise in me, and the one thought on my mind was, *'Why is this being shown to me?'*

Before I realized what I was doing, I found myself yelling for them to stop, but the soldiers seemed unable to hear me. Jesus then turned His bloodied face toward me and smiled. All that pain, and yet He smiled! He looked straight into my eyes and spoke."

"*'I'm doing this for you, son.'*"

"I yelled at Him, 'I don't want them to hurt You!'"

"He looked at me with His swollen, bloody face and said, *'Rejoice, My son. I came for this very purpose. I agreed to give My life that you might live.'*"

"At that moment, a love unlike any I had ever known poured forth from those eyes locked in on mine, then His next words zeroed in on the confusion reigning in my soul."

'Son, like many others, you acknowledge My death as payment for the sins of all humanity. Even so, you have never entered into the joy of My death and resurrection. As a result, you still don't comprehend the magnitude of My victory – a triumph which I long to share with you.'

"Continuing to stare into my eyes, the Lord said, *'Pick up the hammer and drive the nail into My hand, son.'*"

"My heart lurched within my chest, and I heard myself screaming, 'NO, Lord! I can't do that!' I wanted to run, to get away, and be anywhere but there. A second time He smiled, and said, *'Pick up the hammer and drive in the nail, son. I die willingly, joyfully for you.'*"

I paused for an extended period, my muffled sobbing filling the room in which the other men and I gathered. When I had once again regained some semblance of composure, I continued speaking.

"I knew crucifixion was a horrible way to die," I explained to the other men. "Yet, I never had a genuine understanding of the extent of the pain and suffering the individual felt. I know that Jesus carried the sins of the world—past, present, and future—to the cross, as well as all sickness, disease, and infirmity. Still, I had never imagined that the sins I committed were much more than a minuscule part of the accumulated sins of every man and woman throughout time."

"As I continued to look at Him, the love in His eyes drew me closer. He showed me where and how sin had shredded His body. For a third time, He then said, *'Pick up the hammer and drive the nail into My hand, son. Please!'*"

"Struggling to focus despite my tears, I drove the spike through His hand. Blood squirted everywhere! I was shaking, screaming, and crying because of what I had done. When I looked back at His face, He was still staring at me with such compassion. He said, *'I love you, son. Strike it again.'*"

"I was weeping so hard that I could hardly see, but I felt compelled to swing again and again. With each swing, I glanced back to His face. He was still smiling, urging me on despite the pain, saying, *'I love you, son. I do this for you.'*"

"What I'd just done, and the boundless love He extended to me despite that, overwhelmed me. Then He asked me, *'Would you please nail My other hand too?'*"

I stopped explaining myself to the men, unable to speak, my body shaking as raw emotions spilled forth. It took even longer for me to regain control this time, while the other men quietly waited. When I finally resumed my explanation, I did so with utter brokenness.

"When the Lord asked me that, something shattered in the depths of my heart, and I lost all control. I wept and hammered, driving the other spike. Still, He kept telling me, with each vibrating stroke of the hammer, *'Thank you. I love you.'*"

"My mind could not comprehend it. Why did He thank me for murdering Him? I was no longer a distant observer. It was not just the Jews and the Romans who crucified Him. I finally understood deep in my soul and spirit. It was me—my sin—that nailed Him to that cross."

"I dropped the hammer and knelt there near His ravaged body. I covered my face, sobbing and devastated. After a few moments, the Lord spoke again, calling my name to get my attention. When I looked at him, there was such intensity in His eyes—almost a look of absolute desperation. Somehow, I knew this was not desperation over His situation. No! Deep within my spirit, I understood. He was desperate that I never forget that moment. He longed for me to comprehend and wholly accept the merciful love He has for me. It was not just about the horrendous way He had died for me. It was also about His triumph over Satan—for me."

"With a forcefulness contrary to His weakened state, He commanded me, shaking me out of my stupor."

"*'REJOICE, son! Give thanks to the Father in Heaven from the depths of your heart and soul! It was just for this purpose that I was born. REJOICE, son! REJOICE!'*"

"I told the Lord, 'I can't, Jesus! I can't!'"

"Then, the Spirit of the Lord spoke to my spirit with a gentle Voice."

"*'May I break forth in triumph through your spirit, son? May I allow you to know the overwhelming joy of the Father in heaven because of His Son's willing sacrifice?'*"

"My mind was whirling because what He was saying did not seem to make sense. Still, I told the Holy Spirit, 'I don't understand, but please have Your way in me.'"

"Then something rushed through me with the force of water loosed from a dam. One moment I lay there broken and sobbing. In the next, an incredible explosion of joy and laughter erupted in me and then from me. I was laughing so hard that I started crying. I couldn't stop laughing! I tried, but I couldn't stop! It felt so good! So good! I felt the joy of the Father and the Holy Spirit together. Those in heaven were rejoicing! I could hear them!

"As the laughter in me died down, an unbelievably peaceful Presence settled into my heart," I told the men. "And the Spirit of God spoke to me once again in that still, small voice."

"'*I have shown you what the Father desired for everyone here today in this room to understand, My precious one. Sin has no right over you. Jesus' sacrifice revoked your enemy's rights. Jesus' blood hid your sins from Our ability to see them. Only through willful disobedience is it possible for you to step out from under the covering of My blood. Doing so allows your enemy an opportunity to gain a new hold on you. Even so, this too will vanish when you return with a repentant heart and a contrite spirit, laying your new sin at Jesus' feet so that He may cover it with His Blood. Just as the Prodigal himself discovered, forgiveness and restoration are ALWAYS available. The covenant of the Blood is IRREVOCABLE!*'"

"'*So, son, as I told you before, the only thing that remains for you to deal with is SELF. Knowing this, you must understand that with which you are dealing. In its corrupted nature, SELF is rebellious and idolatrous—it is the 'I' in 'sIn'—and if left unchecked, it will always elevate your will and your desires above Ours.*'"

"'*On the other hand, as you diminish, Jesus will exalt Himself more and more in you. As you surrender, as you die to SELF, I will reveal the Spirit of Christ in and through you. I will transform you, renewing your mind and restoring your soul through the washing of My Word. The Word of the Living God is all-powerful, always faithful, and forever sure. Allow Me to complete the work in you that the Father has ordained—* **a work that you are incapable of doing.** *We can then rejoice together endlessly with the same intensity that I allowed you to experience this day.*'"

"The Holy Spirit said… He does <u>NOT</u> want you to read these books or listen to the information on the tapes for entertainment. He said, 'DEVOUR THIS INFORMATION AS THOUGH YOUR VERY LIFE DEPENDS ON IT.' Those were His words, not mine."

Gaining a New Perspective

What occurred that morning in the pole barn affected the hearts, minds, and futures of many of those present. Most of all, it impacted mine, as the Lord allowed me to experience the reality of the crucifixion.

Notwithstanding, this point had not been for me some sudden arrival at a new level of relationship with my Creator. I had advanced and fallen back time after time over the years, but the Lord had never stopped drawing me ever nearer as He stirred my heart. Even so, He did warn me. *"The truth, for you, My son, is that the only assurance of a hopeful future depends on a clean break from your past. The enemy of your soul is attempting to prevent that from occurring. He binds you by keeping you ever mindful of your past fear, shame, doubt, hesitation, and insecurity."*

The possibility of a lasting separation was all that kept me hopeful. At times, the struggle seemed like a pair of insurmountable mountains had been set before me. The Spirit of God identified these hurdles as *Intentional Surrender* and *Absolute Trust*. When I invited Jesus to be my Savior and welcomed the presence of His Spirit, I began to hear His Voice. That day He told me I was His. He further explained that He had placed a seal upon my spirit, awaiting the day of redemption. Nonetheless, an undeniable battle continued to rage in my soul. I felt a strong urging to resist placing complete trust in the One I was willing to call Savior, with this resistance keeping me from also trusting Him to be my Deliverer and Lord of my life.

For too many years, I had struggled daily to control everything in my life, out of fear of losing control to thoughts of doubt, fear, worry, and many other hellish considerations that regularly bombarded my mind. Without even realizing it at the time, I had begun to respond like an abused child. Certain situations or the appearance of a random individual would sometimes trigger a troubling spontaneous reaction in me, and the worst part was I had no understanding of why this was occurring. As a way of protecting myself, I began to develop an overly cautious nature that carried over into many aspects of my life. Many misinterpreted this either as aloofness or arrogance.

As I moved into my middle years, this developed nature caused me, at times, to withdraw. During these periods, I stayed to myself or occupied my mind and time with the things of the world. These distractions became my desperate attempt to stifle the voices and fears that refused to leave me alone.

Even so, the Holy Spirit was not about to give up on me. The Father had a plan for my life that involved far more than just freeing, healing, and restoring me. His desire was always to open my heart, mind, and spiritual eyes. The Holy Spirit's ultimate goal was to bring forth good out of what my enemy had intended for evil. This process the Lord had started, seven years earlier, in a most peculiar way.

† † †

It began early on a Saturday in the fall of 1989. Men of all ages were gathering at a local hotel by the hundreds. It was the day for the monthly Full Gospel Business Men's Fellowship breakfast. The capacity of the three connecting banquet halls was just over three hundred. The only chair not yet occupied was at a table near the back of the room, next to where I was sitting. The chapter president tapped the microphone to get the crowd's attention.

"Everyone, please quiet down and grab a seat, and we'll thank the Lord for the food, so we can get to it before it gets cold."

Just then, an elderly gentleman in his eighties slipped into the room. He settled into the empty chair and slid a large, filled shopping bag under the table by his feet. Everyone at the table knew him well, and we each reached over to greet him before the prayer began. When he turned to me, he said, "Hold back getting into line for the breakfast. I need to talk to you for a minute."

I had known him for several years, having met him a few months after I had begun attending these breakfasts. Since then, I had purposed to sit at the same table with him each month. I had come to respect how eager he was to talk about both the Lord and His Word. I also noticed how seldom he spoke about himself or his business accomplishments, which were significant. As a result, the request he made to me piqued my curiosity. *Why would he want to talk to me alone?*

When the others exited the room to form lines at the buffet table, the two of us remained where we were, as he had requested. We both sat down, and he slid the shopping bag out from under the table.

With a concerned look on his face, he said, "I'll make this brief. In my quiet time the other day, the Holy Spirit spoke to me. He commanded me to do something and to do it today. He said that what I was to do was of great importance, and I pray you will treat it as such too."

He gestured at the large shopping bag. I could see it was full beyond capacity with cassette tape sets and books. "The Lord told me to gather these particular books and tapes together and give them to you. He said you're going to need them for where He's about to lead you."

Many of the Christian testimonies and teachings I had previously read or heard I'd found to be invaluable. I smiled and thanked my friend. Then, with a bit of a laugh, I said, "I hope you know it's going to take me a while to get through these and get them back to you."

The old man shook his head and said, "No. You don't understand. The Holy Spirit said I should '*give*' these to you. They are now yours. He will speak to you about them and through them. Based on what the Lord showed me, there is something extraordinary awaiting you. He does not want you to read the books or listen to the information on the tapes for entertainment. He wants you to study this material, and He gave me specific words to say to you. He said to **'*devour this information as though your very life depends on it.*'** Those were His words, not mine. Questions will arise in your heart as you begin studying. Of this, I am sure. When they do, ask the Holy Spirit, and He will explain all that you don't understand."

"What's all in here?" I asked as I reached for a couple of tape sets crammed into the top of the shopping bag. The older man blocked my hand, pushing the bag back under the table, and said, "It'll keep. Promise me that you'll wait until you get home to look through the bag."

"Sure. I'll wait," I replied.

"Good. Now, let's get some food and enjoy the morning."

We moved to join the end of the buffet line, and neither of us spoke again about the shopping bag. Still, curiosity consumed my mind. *What did You have that man give me, Lord, and what do You have in store for me?*

When I arrived home, I told my wife what had happened. Dropping into a recliner in our living room, I emptied the bag onto the floor. To my amazement, there were several hundred hours of teaching cassettes and forty books. I did not recognize any of the names of the authors and teachers. There was one book by Don Basham, one by Frank & Ida Mae Hammonds, and several by Merlin Carothers. Multiple oversized paperbacks and three sixteen-hour tape sets were by Norvel Hayes. Of the remaining material, six hardbacks were by Lester Sumrall, and more than half of all that he had given me to study was from Derek Prince. It all focused on just two subjects—deliverance and spiritual warfare.

These subjects were not new to me, but I could not recall ever hearing anyone preach at length about either, especially about deliverance. Neither had I ever been a witness to any casting out of spirits in my three years since becoming a Christian. I was familiar with several passages where the Bible had spoken of this. Even so, I wondered why this was such a big deal to the Holy Spirit. Then a sudden thought came to me. *Is there enough in the Bible on these subjects to warrant this many books and tapes?*

It startled me when the Holy Spirit spoke to me, addressing my thoughts.

"That would be a good place to start your investigation. It is not enough to begin by listening to what others have discovered. Pull out your Bible and concordance and see for yourself."

I spent the rest of the day reading one Scripture reference after another and writing each down in a spiral notebook. As I did, I discovered a pattern. Certain things occurred when Jesus or His disciples cast demons out of an individual.

There was always evidence that the spirit or spirits had departed. The evidence was also visible at the moment in which they left or shortly afterward. That visibility came in one form or another. It could be a blatant manifestation in the physical body. Sometimes it was signs of a struggle with an unseen adversary that would stop and never return. In others, evidence of a disease or infirmity that had resisted all treatment and prayer disappeared.

An individual's abrupt change in facial expression and demeanor invariably conveyed that a genuine transformation of a person's nature has occurred. It was an immediate perceivable change in the one who had received help. Sometimes there was a sudden clarity in the person's eyes. It was as though they had come back into their "right" mind, with this transformation most evident to family members and close friends.

The change to the individual's soul always included a new or increased awareness of how much God loved them.

Knowing this, I found one thing both surprising and disturbing about this entire subject. Most often, Jesus and His disciples taught and ministered on this issue to those who were **of the Church**. What was confusing was the way that most of today's preachers confidently taught that Christians are incapable of harboring demon spirits.

With this new insight in mind, I began reading the books my friend had given me. As I read, I checked to see if what I was reading in the books lined up with the Word of God. I also listened as the Holy Spirit explained and added to what I was reading. He spoke at great length about some Scripture passages that I had read many times before. Previously, I had failed to understand the importance of what the Holy Spirit was saying through what those writers of Scripture had recorded. The pages began to fill with underlining, highlighting, and annotations in the borders.

In many of the books, dedicated sections analyzed what Jesus and the disciples taught. The authors also reviewed how Christ Himself acted toward Satan and his demonic host. The detailed accounting by several of the authors gave weight to their conclusions. Jesus spent more than a year of His three-year period of ministry on this earth focused on one thing—teaching about and freeing others from the influence of the demonic realm.

The more I read and listened, the more eager I became to share with my wife what I was discovering. Although interested in the beginning, she soon found these one-sided discussions irritating. Before long, she grew angry and interrupted me as I was talking about the most recent thing I had read.

"I don't want to talk about this anymore, and I don't think our kids need to hear about this stuff either! Can't we talk about something else?"

Her sudden outburst was perplexing to me, for I did not yet understand one thing. Sharing what the Spirit of God was teaching me was riling things up in the spiritual realm. It was affecting each of us as individuals. It was also affecting our marriage relationship and our home environment. Acquiescing to her request, I no longer brought the subject up in our home. Even so, I continued studying the materials and listening to the Holy Spirit.

I mentioned to several Christian friends what the Holy Spirit was revealing to me. Most seemed bothered by the subject and offered no response or ignored what I had mentioned. Many, to cover up their discomfort, began speaking about something unrelated. Some claimed to recall pressing matters needing their attention, as they apologized and unexpectedly departed. A few told me, "You need to get your focus on Jesus and off of this preoccupation with evil." In reprimanding me, they ignored the many references to the Word of God that I had just quoted. One individual even asked me, with declared concern, "Are you sure you are a Christian?"

Each time one of these reactions occurred, I listened to the individual with patience. In the end, I could not get past one irrefutable fact. The Holy Spirit had gone to a lot of trouble to get that specific teaching material into my hands. He had also guided me to many Scriptures to reinforce what each author had presented. I decided then to mention it to no one else in the future. I continued searching, praying, and filling my notebook with the Lord's teachings.

Approximately one month later, all hell seemed to come against my family and me over three consecutive days. On that Friday, my eldest daughter and I were on our way to her afternoon appointment with an optometrist. Traveling over a damp winding country road, I came to a steep downhill grade leading into a sharp bend to the right. As I drew near, a school bus started around the bend heading in my direction. Although I was already moving at a slow rate of speed, I applied pressure to the brake pedal to slow even more, but my new company car—less than two weeks old—did not slow down or stop. Moments later, I came to a screeching stop with my car—up to the front windshield—wedged under the side of the bus, between the front and rear wheels. All the wheels on the driver's side of the bus were off the ground. Even worse, the bus passengers were children in wheelchairs.

I was thankful when we discovered that no one received injuries. Thirty minutes later, a wrecker arrived and removed my car from the scene, which righted the bus.

Using the officer's phone, I called my office general manager about the accident. I explained the condition of the car. I knew my new vehicle was a total loss, and it would be a while before the company could replace it.

The bus driver admitted to the officer that I was going quite slowly down the hill, but appeared unable to stop. Meanwhile, assured of no damage to hinder the performance of the bus, the driver continued on his route. The officer on the scene kept my daughter and me in his vehicle for a long while. When I told him that my car was new, he had his dispatcher place some calls for him. We soon discovered that another accident had occurred earlier that same day in the same location. In checking the asphalt, the officer found a light coating of oil on the road thirty feet up the hill before the bend. That, combined with the light rain, had made it impossible for me to stop. I received no citation for causing the accident, but we still had to wait a while longer for a rental car to arrive.

My daughter and I were hours late in returning home that evening. With my mobile phone hardwired into the towed vehicle, I had no way to check my office voice messages. Meanwhile, my wife had called hours earlier and left a message informing me that she was on the way to the emergency room. Our second daughter had seriously injured her knee during her high school team's volleyball game.

When I finally was able to check my messages, I listened to the one from my wife as well. Two of the other voice mail messages were from my most significant clients. A few days earlier, I had closed on several sales contracts that I had been pursuing for months. The next day, I had calculated the commissions I would receive at the end of the month from the most significant two. It came to a substantial amount. Now, these two clients were calling back to cancel their contracts. Both stated the same reason. Their corporate headquarters had opted to work through a national sales and servicing agency. Doing so would leave me with nothing to show for all of my efforts.

At one point, as my frustration built and my head ached from the accumulating stress, I voiced my frustration aloud saying, "What else can go wrong?"

My wife arrived home near dusk, in a bad mood. She had spent three hours sitting in the local emergency room with our other three children.

After eating dinner, all four of our children went to their bedrooms to complete their homework or play. My wife and I remained at the kitchen table as I explained about the accident. Not knowing how to soften the blow, I also told her about the canceled contracts. I tried to minimize any worry on her part by stating that I did not intend to give up on the deals. In truth, I knew the reality of the situation. If decision authority were in the hands of a national agency, it would leave the local management with no say. It would also leave me with no possibility of changing the situation. We were both counting on those commissions to catch up on accumulated debts, with a part of it to go toward a long-delayed and much-needed family vacation.

After I had finished eating, I turned the television on to get my mind off the events of the day. Even that did not help, so I turned it off. I found my wife brooding in a chair on the front porch. Joining her there, we sat in the dark until bedtime, with neither of us speaking.

The following morning, my wife took our son to his Little League baseball game while I got an early start on the all-day job of maintaining our yard and large garden.

Many hours later, my wife pulled into the driveway and helped our son out of the passenger side of the car. Seeing him on crutches, I stopped what I was doing and hurried to see what had happened. My wife was in an even worse mood than the previous day. We now had two children injured, and the emergency room had been more crowded than on her last visit, which resulted in a much longer wait before seeing a doctor. The rest of the day, I stayed outdoors, occupying myself with completing the yard work.

Sunday morning, we all arose early to take showers before heading off to church. It was then that we discovered that there was no water pressure. Finding no issues inside the house, I went out of the back door of the garage, looking for the source of the problem. As I rounded the side of the house, I saw a geyser shooting up from our front lawn. I realized immediately that the water main had ruptured—on our side of the meter, of course. I rushed to get some pliers to shut off the valve located near the street. I had no idea how long the water had been escaping, but our front lawn and large garden in the adjoining field had flooded.

We skipped church that morning, and I made calls to one plumber after another. I needed to find someone available right away, with a backhoe. Only one had responded. He explained when he arrived in the early afternoon that his backhoe was finishing up at another site, but would be available the following morning. He and his helper did some preliminary exploration with shovels. Two hours later, he gave us a tentative estimate, including time and a half for Sunday. He said that was all he could offer until he could dig the ground up with the backhoe and assess the extent of the problem.

That evening, I sat and talked with my wife. "We need to go to the bank tomorrow morning to tap the remaining funds in our line of credit. It's the only way we can cover these new expenses," I stated. "We don't have a choice. Eighty feet of the pipe may need replacing, and it's not going to be cheap."

This line of credit was the same second mortgage we had talked a month earlier about paying off. That action depended on the anticipated commissions that would now no longer be available.

A heated discussion with my wife transpired that Sunday evening. Frustration and tempers got the best of both of us. Depressed and worried about our financial situation, my wife then lashed out at me in a way I had not expected.

"Everything that's occurred these last few days is due to you pursuing this demon stuff. You may not talk about it anymore, but you're always reading about it, obsessed with it. Don't you see what's happening to our family? What you're doing has to stop! I hope you love our family and me enough to get that stuff out of our house."

I did not expect such an irrational reaction from my wife. I knew the Holy Spirit was still encouraging me in this direction and no longer doubted that the Lord had guided my elderly friend to put the study materials into my hands. Even so, I had to admit to also questioning in my mind what she had voiced. *Was there any truth to what she was saying? Was this the demonic realm's way of reacting to my intense studying of their methods?*

Not wanting this to be a point of contention between us any longer, I gathered everything up, packed it in a couple of boxes, and placed them on a storage shelf in our garage. I was uncertain that I was doing the right thing. Even so, I ignored the nagging feeling inside by assuring myself that I would get back to it in a few months. I hoped that, by then, my wife would calm down, and things would be back under control.

In the months that followed, business flourished. When I was not working at my job, I spent many long weekend hours trying to appease my wife by completing home renovations she had been talking about for years. That left only weeknights to keep up with the yard work and our half-acre garden, while also squeezing in the endless school activities in which our four children participated.

The sudden influx of contracts with new clients appeared to be a great blessing at a time when we needed it. My wife and I gave thanks and praise to the Lord for turning things around. We even testified to others of how the Lord had come through for us.

Nevertheless, it was almost four years later when the Lord said He wanted to reveal something to me. He talked to me about how I had fallen prey to Satan's influence and explained the devil's way of shutting down my progress in the direction the Holy Spirit had been leading me. In accomplishing this, he had eliminated any threat to his kingdom through me.

"Your enemy saw that he could not sidetrack you through accident, infirmity, or disaster. He instead opted to fuel the fire of your pride and greed. He opened up doors of opportunity for which he encouraged you to strive. He knew these would keep you occupied, and you and your family satisfied and distracted. It worked, son. You thanked and praised Me for every blessing that came your way. Some—but not all—were from Me, because I am a Father who blesses His children. Never once, however, did you question whether all that was occurring was, in fact, something other than a blessing. During this same period, your time spent with Me and My Word again decreased. There

was always something or someone demanding your attention. You did not hesitate to respond. I tried to warn you, again and again, but your heart had grown distant to Me about these things, and you could not hear My voice."

The reality of the situation was that I had become quite distracted, and the boxes remained untouched on the garage shelf for more than four years.

Even during that period, the Holy Spirit had not stopped directing my path. He continued to deal with me in other ways. He drew me into meaningful interaction with other men who had a stable Christian walk. I started developing a real servant's heart, as my ministry to others increased. I participated in Fellowship chapter gatherings, as well as in prison and community ministry. For eleven years, I served as a chapter officer, the last two years as the elected president of the chapter.

Without my even being aware of it at the time, the Holy Spirit had once again guided me into the exact position He needed me. He did so with one purpose in mind. It was time for the training I had stepped away from—now more than five years past—to resume.

"Prophecy is not given just to foretell impending events as much as it is given to prepare the church and invoke a response which will affect the events."

The Harvest (Rick Joyner)

Called to Be a Vessel

It was the first day of summer, and the sun was beginning to peek over the horizon. I had set the cruise control on my company car to the posted speed limit. I relaxed and let my eyes scan the scenery on either side of the Interstate as I rode along in silence. On my way to a scheduled early appointment, my thoughts drifted. I thought back to how surprised I had been when the Spirit had spoken to me several weeks earlier.

On that morning, I had also been on the way to an early appointment. Staring at the lush hay fields passing by the side window, I had whispered to the Father. "Lord, those fields are so beautiful!"

As to whether the reply had or had not been audible, I could never be confident. Nonetheless, I could not deny the impact on my spirit when the melodic Voice immediately responded. *"They are, son, but they don't even begin to compare with the beauty I see in you."*

Warmth had engulfed my heart and surged through my being. Tears had streamed from my eyes then, and I had lost total control of my emotions. Simultaneously, an incredible peace had settled over me, lingering in the car for hours. From that day on, at the most unexpected times and places, the Spirit had spoken in such an unexpected way. It was as though He had been wooing back a wayward lover, and His words penetrated like flaming arrows into the very depths of my soul.

Busy as I had become at work, I'd found myself spending less time each day with the Lord, and feeling guilty about it. As many do, I'd promised myself and the Lord that I'd change my ways, only to later berate myself when I didn't. During one of those times of self-condemnation, the Lord had interrupted my thoughts.

"Son, you need to extend yourself some grace—the same grace that I extend when I observe you. I look beyond the surface, beyond the here and now, and when I do, I see a son who loves the Father with a sincere heart, even though your heart is lately too often distracted. Still, you have no reason to feel guilty. Rest in Me, and receive the love I pour out to you, just because I desire to do so."

Upon hearing those words, I had shaken so hard from crying that I had to pull over to the side of the road. There I sat for several minutes reveling in the Father's love. It was a love that I could not begin to fathom in my mind, but the Spirit had known that my heart and soul desperately needed.

† † †

This particular day, though, was much different from that morning several weeks earlier. I had awakened earlier than usual this day with an unexplainable sense of expectation in my spirit. It was as if my inner being was watching, waiting. Although I was not entirely confident that I could have described it to anyone, nonetheless, I knew it existed.

Now, as I continued down the Interstate, my mind wandered once again. This time it was to the words the Holy Spirit had whispered to me two days prior.

"I have called you for a purpose, son, which I will soon reveal. At that time, I'll begin equipping you with what you'll need to fulfill the Father's call."

That was the entirety of it. There was no special feeling, not even a tugging at my heart or an impulse to respond. For days following that moment, my heart and mind dwelt continually on those words.

Even now, as the miles passed by, I tried to imagine what the Holy Spirit might have meant that day. I considered various possibilities, including my frequent petition to the Father in past years. Was the Lord about to grant my request? The more I dwelt on it, the more curious I became, finally voicing it aloud.

"Are You going to allow me to minister full-time through the Men's Fellowship?"

I waited several minutes longer without speaking, but there was no answer. So, I returned to letting my thoughts wander for a while as I drove.

What happened next both shocked me and brought my mind and spirit to a heightened level of sensitivity. Without warning, the windshield of my car seemed to disappear as my eyes stared in disbelief at a vivid scene spread out before me. Not yet aware that I was viewing a vision from God, my foot jerked to the left, pressing hard on the brake pedal. Then, with the same suddenness as it had appeared, the scene was gone, leaving me extremely shaken. I glanced in all directions, in every mirror. The nearest car was a thousand or more yards away.

"What was that?" I blurted aloud, as fear and consternation gripped my being. Moving to the far right lane, I set the cruise control to a lower speed and focused on calming myself.

Had it indeed happened? Yes! I could not deny it. Although the scene was no longer there before my eyes, I could recall every detail with clarity.

"What was that?" I cried out a second time to the Lord. "Please speak to me, Holy Spirit! Was it from You? If so, what does it mean?"

A minute later, the Voice of the Lord interrupted my erratic thoughts.

"Write it down."

Those three words wrapped themselves around me like a blanket of calming peace. At the same time, my spirit remained on alert.

Three exits later, I signaled and took the off-ramp, stopping at the vacant end of a parking area that surrounded a large suburban mall. A heavenly peace filled the car, and then the scene returned, as real as anything I had ever viewed at a theater. This time it was as though I was there in the scene. I observed what was occurring, as well as heard the voices, and even the thoughts of each person.

The picture show exploded with activity, and all focused on a ship. It was a large, older, wooden vessel drifting slowly down the center of a wide river. The sails were down, and hundreds of people filled the main deck where a group of musicians played and sang. Everyone sang along with them. Some even danced, with great enthusiasm, and the atmosphere was exhilarating.

As I watched the scene unfold, I realized I heard worship music. Focusing my attention on the legal pad on my lap, I began noting what I had seen. When I rested my pen, the scene returned, with new activity occurring.

Great exultation consumed the people. Everyone on the main deck seemed given over to worshipping the Lord.

Meanwhile, on the upper deck located closer to the aft, the captain stood at the wheel. He watched over his vessel and the crowd below as he steered on a steady path. Ever so slowly, they drifted past fields filled with feed corn that would soon be ready to harvest. Looking through binoculars, the captain could also see golden wheat fields far in the distance.

A moment later, he felt the floorboards give slightly under his feet as his first mate approached him from behind.

"Captain, I don't know whether you were aware of something. Many of our crew are members of this same church group that chartered our ship for their celebration."

The first mate paused, expecting a response, but the captain said nothing. "Everything is going as it should, sir," the first mate continued. "It's one of the nicest river cruises we've ever made." Still, the captain did not respond or even acknowledge the man's presence. His gaze remained fixed straight ahead.

Pressing on, the first mate blurted out his request to the captain. "Some of the men were wondering, sir. Would it be all right for them to join with their friends in the celebration for a bit?"

The captain did not immediately acknowledge the first mate. Instead, he pondered it in his mind. *His request is a bit unusual. He knows I've never allowed the crew to mingle with the guests. However, the atmosphere of this cruise is far different from the usual drunkenness we have to tolerate.*

The captain remained with his back to the man. His neck continued to swivel slightly left and right as his eyes scanned the river and banks ahead. There was no other vessel anywhere within sight, and he thought to himself, *Why not? Just this once.*

The first mate moved a step closer. He seemed uncertain if the captain had heard him at all, the sound of the celebration below being quite loud.

"Captain?" he prompted.

The captain turned to face him then, his reply indicating that he had heard every word the man had spoken. "We have a long straight stretch of the river ahead. The crew could benefit from your request. Release them to join in—for a short while."

"Yes, sir! Thank you, sir!" the first mate responded.

† † †

Once more, I looked to my legal pad for a short period to record what I had just seen. When I finished writing, the vision returned with unrelenting intensity, as the scene continued to unfold.

† † †

Back on the main deck, the first mate had several of his crew pass the word among the others. Their excitement was evident as they hurried to take advantage of this rare opportunity. The first mate also wandered through the crowd. He paused here and there to observe the celebration, singing along with the others.

"What a beautiful cruise!" he commented to himself as he nodded and smiled to those he passed.

† † †

Again, I paused to note the new details I had seen. When I put down my pen and relaxed, expecting it to continue, there was nothing more to see. As suddenly as the urgency had arrived, it had departed, leaving me a bit befuddled.

"Is that all You're going to show me, Holy Spirit?" I asked aloud.

Although I waited for fifteen minutes longer, there was no response.

That evening at the dinner table, I was quieter than usual, uncertain about whether I should share with my wife what had occurred. If I did tell her, what would she say? The more I dwelt on it, the more uncertain I became. *Maybe I shouldn't mention it to anyone until I have a better understanding of what it was I saw. Was this about me—a warning of some sort, Holy Spirit? If not, then what?*

The following morning, I sat in quiet with my Bible on my lap. I was trying to keep my mind from wandering off to what had happened the previous day. I had told myself that I would wait for God to explain, in His timing, whatever it was that He was trying to reveal to me. The wait was turning out to be a real struggle. Trying to focus my thoughts elsewhere, I turned to Psalms. After the fourth time of reading the same passages, with no inkling as to what I had just read, I stopped fighting it, became still, and asked the Holy Spirit if He would be willing to explain to me what I had seen. I waited for an extended time but heard nothing.

Each day of that week, as I traveled the roads and highways on sales calls throughout the area, I thought about the vision, and even more so when I neared the part of the Interstate where the original incident had occurred. I asked the question of the Holy Spirit every time my mind wandered to it throughout the day. Still, the Lord did not explain.

After several weeks had passed similarly, I began to question if I had somehow imagined it. The longer I dwelt on it, the more thankful I was that I had kept it to myself rather than look like some crazy person. By the end of the fourth week, I only thought about it now and then. My job, family responsibilities, and life, in general, consumed my time, and days passed in rapid succession.

It was late on a Sunday evening, the start of the seventh week following the unexplained event. I lay stretched out on our bed, on top of the covers. The outdoor temperature had climbed into the nineties that afternoon. The ceiling fans and window air conditioning units were straining to cool our brick house. My wife and our children had finally fallen asleep about an hour earlier. The three-way bulb in the lamp on my side of the bed was on the lowest setting. I had my large-print edition of the Bible propped up on my stomach, reading several chapters of the Book of Proverbs.

Without warning, I found myself staring at the same vision I had seen in my car weeks earlier, instead of the print in my Bible. Shocked at the suddenness of what had occurred, I gazed at it. Though the vision lasted for only a few moments in time, it seemed to play out before me at a far greater length. Then, once again, I was looking at my Bible.

Sitting up in bed, I looked at my wife, who had roused from my sudden movement. Still facing away from me, she adjusted her pillow and fell back to sleep. Meanwhile, I sat there for several minutes, shaken to the core. Finally, I whispered to the Holy Spirit.

"What are You trying to tell me, Lord? Is something going to happen? Is there something I'm supposed to do? Is there someone I'm meant to speak to about this?"

For the second time, I heard in my spirit the same three words: *"Write it down."*

Turning off the lamp on the nightstand, I slipped out of bed without disturbing my wife. Shutting all of the bedroom doors, I retreated to the recliner in our living room with a legal pad and pen.

After stilling my mind and spirit, the vision reappeared. It was a panorama bursting with activity. As I watched, the scene progressed with only a few short pauses.

Everyone on the main deck of the ship was now celebrating. The captain remained on watch from his elevated position. He looked away at times, as he studied the fields fronting the left bank of the river. He admired the crops that extended as far as his eyes could see. "It's been an excellent year for the farmers," he commented aloud to himself.

Lifting the binoculars to his eyes once more, he refocused on fields far downriver. Dozens of men worked there in staggered rows that stretched across a vast wheat field. Each swung a scythe, dropping the cut grain in neat rows as they moved down the field in unison. Following a short distance after these men, the captain counted eighteen wagons drawn by draft horses, spaced out equidistant across the acreage. A larger contingent of women and older children gathered and bundled the cut wheat, carried it to the wagons, and passed it up to those waiting in the wagons who added it to ever-growing mounds.

The captain thought about what he was seeing. *What beauty to see how the Amish all work together so well, but there must be a thousand acres or more of wheat to harvest?*

He pulled the binoculars away from his eyes long enough to search the river ahead in all directions. He assured himself that he was still on course, and everything remained calm. The captain glanced at the continuing celebration on the lower deck. His crew mixed with the crowd and seemed to be enjoying themselves.

Lifting the binoculars to his eyes, he again studied the fields far ahead. This time he saw another wagon positioned on the crest of a hill. It overlooked the fields the others were harvesting. An older man with a full white beard stood in the back of the wagon, leaning on a cane, observing the laborers.

"Must be the old man's fields. Or else he's the community elder, and he's overseeing everything," the captain said to himself.

While looking now and then at the river ahead, the captain made minor corrections to his course. As his ship drifted farther downriver, he continued watching the Amish. Moving and adjusting the binoculars a little at a time, he studied each of the harvesting teams at work. Every so often, he looked back to view the older man in the wagon. The third time he focused on him, the captain noticed his demeanor had changed. He seemed agitated, shouting to the men in the fields, waving and pointing with his cane. Studying him further, the captain saw the worry visible on the older man's face as he twice turned his head and stared over his shoulder.

Lowering his binoculars, the captain turned and looked over his shoulder in the direction the older man had looked. To the captain's dismay, black storm clouds filled the sky on the near horizon. They hung ominously close to the earth. Having focused on the harvesting teams, he had not been as observant of his ship. Now, he realized with a start how much their speed had increased.

Multi-fingered lightning split the sky on the far horizon behind them. Moments later, the captain felt the first large drops of rain begin to fall. He looked below at the folks worshipping, not the least bit bothered by the splattering rain. Instead, they laughed as they lifted their hands toward the heavens and continued rejoicing.

The captain looked back to where the worst part of the storm was closing in on them. He felt a sudden gust of wind and looked again at the river. Grave concern etched his face.

I sat in my chair and observed everything the Spirit was showing me. It was as though I was watching a movie on the big screen, and I felt almost let down when it again ended without a climax. For hours, I sat there, begging God to explain what I'd just seen, and why. Pacing the floor, I petitioned the Lord in prayer—in English, and then in my prayer language. As I did, I once more wondered what possible reason God could have for showing me this. Still, there was not a word of explanation. Growing silent, I waited for a response, glancing at the clock every few minutes. I then forced myself to be still before the Lord for another two hours, hoping the Spirit would explain. Even so, no revelation came and just before dawn, I slipped into bed. Thoroughly exhausted, I was desperate for the ninety minutes of sleep I would get before the alarm would rouse me for work.

More confused than ever, my mind remained distracted for days. My thoughts kept returning to what I had experienced. I longed to share it, but this time, I sensed an urging inside to restrain myself until prompted by the Holy Spirit. I promised God that I would wait, no matter how long it took. Weeks turned into months, and that which had seemed urgent became only an occasional source of reflection. I found myself recalling it during worship at church or long periods of driving on the Interstate. Most often, though, these thoughts arose unbidden, as I relaxed on the porch at the end of a busy day.

Summer gave way to autumn, and soon, the outdoor work required less of my time. I spent more early mornings and late evenings sitting on our porch reading my Bible, and the rest of the time quietly puzzling over the matter. *What else could I ask of the*

Lord that I had not already asked many times? Occasionally, I still caught myself recalling what I had seen. As time passed, I had a sense of relief, glad that I had not spoken a word about it to anyone.

Soon, it was mid-October. The morning air was beginning to hint of the coming cold, and when I awoke, I felt a sense of exhilaration in my spirit. I loved the autumn season! The crisp air and changing coloring in the leaves on the hardwoods always stirred me. My mood also changed that time of year to one that was more mellow and contemplative. It was Sunday morning, and I urged my family out the door a little earlier than usual. We got our children settled into their Sunday school classrooms a few minutes early. My wife and I spent that extra time praying in the sanctuary before the service began.

The church filled as people entered and settled into chairs. The worship team started tuning up while folks continued greeting one another. Soon, the pastor and his wife reached their seats in the front row. The music commenced, and the worship team lifted their voices in song with the congregation joining them.

The praise and worship had seemed to grow more spirited and vibrant with each passing week. Over the next forty-five minutes, the music flowed without effort. Our church body reached what my wife and I later agreed was a level never before experienced. The worship team moved from one song to the next without pausing. There then came a noticeable shift in the spiritual atmosphere in the building, from one of praise into sincere worship. The tempo slowed, and the congregation's voices softened to a near whisper. I stood there with my eyes closed, and my hands lifted to heaven. Tears flowed down my cheeks, as my heart and mind longed for Jesus. It was then that I heard the voice speak, as unmistakable as a ringing bell.

"Open your eyes, son."

When I obeyed, I stared in amazement at the *'picture show'* that played out in a rush before me. The vision repeated what I had already seen four months prior and continued from there. In a burst, as though watching a movie at many times its intended speed, I saw the storm sweep in with a fury.

The captain battled the rising and falling waters, fighting to keep the ship on course. When restoring the vessel to her original condition, he had made one invaluable modification, installing a pair of diesel engines to help him overcome unfavorable winds or turbulent waters. At times like this, he was glad he had done so. He started the engines and brought them up to speed. Meanwhile, some of the crew rushed to their assigned positions. Others helped the passengers, now overwhelmed by the storm that had overtaken the ship.

Glancing back to the shore, the captain noticed with alarm how swollen the river had become. With great concern, he watched as it began overflowing its banks. The ship advanced nearer to the farmers harvesting the wheat fields. Only a few minutes earlier, it had appeared as though they were much further downriver. Now, the captain no longer needed his binoculars to see the older man standing in the wagon.

The men, women, and children in the fields were moving at a run. They continued to load the wheat, even as the front end of the storm reached them. All the wagons were nearing the point of overflowing. Still, they piled on more, covering the wheat with large tarps.

While maintaining control of his vessel, the captain glanced again to the fields. He observed several more wagons pulling into the area at a dead run. When they had halted, everyone on the ground worked to fill these also.

The next time the captain looked back toward the land, he saw the overseer wildly signaling. Dumbfounded, the captain realized the older man was beckoning his ship to come and help. Meanwhile, when his vessel had nearly drawn abreast of the wagons, the captain watched in dismay as the river roared over its bank, the floodwaters surging unimpeded through the fields.

The captain reacted by trying to bring his ship closer to shore, although he was uncertain what type of help he could offer. As he did, he noted that his passengers were now all huddled along the port side. They clutched onto the railing, facing the ravaged fields where the Amish families struggled. Everyone aboard the ship watched in astonishment as the floodwaters continued to smash the remaining wheat, flattening it into the earth with a fury, wiping out much of the harvest.

As before, the vision vanished as quick as it had appeared. I closed my eyes and stood still, shocked by a conclusion I had not anticipated. A holy hush had settled over the congregation, and no one made a sound. Then an intense heat began to arise in, and radiate from, my stomach. It moved in waves up into my chest and down my legs that were quivering uncontrollably. At that point, the same clear voice spoke to my spirit once more and commanded: *"Open your mouth, and I will fill it."*

I obeyed, and what came forth was a message in tongues, in a language that I had never before known or spoken. The unknown words went on and on, each word slow and enunciated. It continued for two full minutes. As with the vision, the words then halted. I sat down in my chair and covered my face with my hands. Waiting there, afraid to look around, I sensed that no one else in the church was moving.

I knew what the Bible stated about the act of speaking in tongues in a public setting. It was clear that an interpretation would have to follow if God had indeed initiated it. I waited, yet, no one spoke. Another minute or two passed. Fear, Self-condemnation, and Criticism hounded my mind: *"You messed up bad this time! There's not going to be an* interpretation. Can you imagine what the pastor and others will think of you now? You couldn't keep your big mouth shut, could you?"

I struggled to stay composed, begging God in my mind to give someone the interpretation. The silence became intense, unbearable. I glanced at my watch and saw that another minute had passed.

Then, just as before, the extreme heat returned in my stomach. I heard that same clear voice of the Holy Spirit speaking to my spirit.

"Arise. Open your mouth, and I will fill it."

Standing shakily to my feet, I held onto the back of the chair in front of me. Keeping my eyes closed, I opened my mouth, and the interpretation in English came without hesitation. Once again, the words came forth slowly and very distinctly.

"My children! Hear the word of the Lord and understand. There was a great sailing vessel, with its sails down, drifting down the center of a wide river. On the main deck of the ship, musicians played, while men and women worshipped Me, the Lord God Almighty, with song and dance and great celebration. The worship was glorious and pleasing to My hearing. The ship continued to move slowly downriver, passing vast fields of corn awaiting harvest, and beyond that, broad areas of wheat. At a far distance from the ship, hundreds of people worked to harvest the now ripened wheat as the master stood and observed the progress of the laborers from a high place."

"Meanwhile, those on the ship continued to worship. Exuberance and passion for the Lord consumed them. At the request of the men, the captain had even released his crew to join in the celebration."

"As the ship steadily drifted forward, the captain never stopped shifting his focus. He watched the river ahead, glanced at the festivity on the main deck, and then, lifting his binoculars, studied those busily harvesting the wheat far ahead of them. Unnoticed by all aboard the ship, an unprecedented storm arose quickly behind them, filling the horizon. The clouds overtook them, and the rains began to fall. The guests on the ship ignored the rain as they continued worshipping, hands raised to the heavens. Soon, lightning filled the darkening sky, and the rainfall increased in intensity. The captain became alarmed and took measures to get his ship under control in the rapidly accelerating current and growing waves. For a moment, he glanced again to the fields where he saw the laborers working frantically to cut, gather, and load the harvest into the waiting wagons, while still more wagons arrived to help. Observing the river now overflowing its banks, the captain watched as it penetrated ever deeper into the fields. He looked again to the hill where the master of the harvest stood. He was surprised to see the elderly gentleman beckoning him, as though he wanted him to bring the ship to shore, in what appeared to be an impassioned plea for their help in saving the harvest. However, before the captain

and his crew could respond, the river engulfed the fields. The waters buried the uncut wheat in the wet earth, wiping out a significant portion of the harvest."

"Aboard the ship, the music had stopped. All of the passengers now lined the rails of the ship. They stared in astonishment, as they asked themselves and one another: 'Why would God let something like this occur?'"

"My children, hear and understand what I am about to tell you. This church is that ship, and you—this body of believers—are the people on the ship. Your pastor is that captain. The crewmembers are the associate pastor, elders, deacons, and staff. Your worship has been a source of continual blessing to Me. Your openness to the move of My Spirit in this body has encouraged My visiting you in an ever-increasing capacity. All heaven can testify that your love for me is unwavering. Even so, understand that there is a time to rejoice, and there is a time to work."

"I have brought together in this place a unique and diverse body that ranges from young to old. You are a well-balanced mixture of ethnic and racial peoples. This body includes the wealthy, the middle class, as well as the less fortunate and struggling. I have regularly visited this house with My Presence and anointing. Demonstrating My love, mercy, and grace, I have increasingly poured forth signs and wonders in your midst."

"It was I who moved your pastor's heart to birth this church. I chose this very location, surrounded by grassy fields, for a specific reason. Only I know what is about to take place soon in this location. You do not yet see or understand because you think and plan with your minds. You observe with your eyes rather than with your spirits. You look now in all directions and see little development and few homes. However, I tell you, all around you are fields that are already white unto harvest. Hear Me when I say that I am about to multiply the harvest in this area supernaturally. My children, this is YOUR harvest. Do not stand idly by saying there are yet four months and then comes harvest. Lift your eyes and behold the fields. They are white and ready to harvest. Rise and go forth, gathering that which is available now. Then sharpen your scythes, increase your wagons, and make ready your storehouse for what is soon to come. The time to prepare, the time to labor is now, lest the harvest arrives, and you find yourselves unprepared."

When the interpretation ended, I once again sat down and covered my face with my hands. No one in the church made a sound for several more minutes. The pastor then climbed the stairs to the platform and made his way to the lectern. As though nothing had occurred, he proceeded to preach his sermon. When the service ended, I asked my wife if she would gather our children and meet me in the car. I made a fast retreat down the aisle toward the rear of the church. As I did, I overheard several angry comments from men and women as I passed them.

"Who does he think he is, telling us we need to start working harder? Haven't I already been doing enough around here?" one woman commented, the frustration in her voice evident. Another man added, "Trust me! It didn't sit right with our pastor, or he would have acknowledged it."

As I tried to make my way through the large foyer, another man vented his anger loud enough to be sure I heard him. "That message couldn't have been from God. It was too critical, too judgmental to have been God!"

Hurrying to my car, I closed the door and even lowered the car's sun visors so I would not have to talk to or look at anyone. When my wife and children all loaded into the car, I wasted no time in heading for home.

After we had eaten lunch, and our kids busied themselves elsewhere, I asked my wife to join me on a swing situated under a large shade tree at the rear of our property. She listened as I described all that had been occurring for the previous four months. It was such a relief to share those experiences. We prayed together, asking God to bring His peace and to give us a clear direction for the future.

I was still a bit concerned about the potential reaction of others in our church toward me. The following Sunday, my family and I intentionally arrived several minutes after the service had started. I planned for us to sit somewhere in the back rows, but no seats were available. The usher motioned for the two of us to follow him as he led the way to two places near the front. The worship went on for over one hour, and, as usual, it was glorious. I kept my eyes closed and focused my heart and mind on the Lord. When the music ended, everyone sat down. I picked up the Sunday bulletin as though I intended to read it. I wanted something to focus my attention on as an excuse to not have to look at others sitting around me.

The audience grew still as the pastor climbed the stairs to the platform, after which the associate pastor and all of the church elders followed him. The senior pastor and associate pastor moved to the center of the stage and faced the crowd. The elders continued walking, passing through a gap in the heavy drapes covering the rear wall. A moment later, the pastor began speaking.

"Last Sunday we had a most unusual thing happen. A brother felt led to speak forth a lengthy message in tongues. I felt the Holy Spirit strongly urging me to wait for the interpretation, so we did exactly that. After several minutes, through the same brother, the Holy Spirit also gave an interpretation."

"We recently began recording all prophetic words given in this house. Most of you did not know this. I'm also certain that this brother, who God used to speak to us, was unaware of this. The purpose of recording them is so we may later take them to the Lord in prayer. Our primary aim in doing this is to be sure that what we are hearing is from the Holy Spirit. The leadership prays over them. If the Spirit tells us it was genuine, we wait for Him to give us an explanation, or to elaborate further. We acted similarly toward the message that came forth last Sunday. So, what we're going to do right now is play the entire recording, after which I have something to say."

The prophetic tongue and interpretation replayed for all to hear. I sat there looking down at the floor, feeling embarrassed, mortified, and afraid to open my eyes. In my mind, a thought arose. *Is the pastor about to publicly reprimand me?*

Now and then, I peeked up at the senior pastor and the associate pastor standing on the platform. They stood there, listening to the message and observing the congregation. My stomach was in turmoil, as doubt and worry crowded into my thoughts.

The recorded tongues and interpretation finished playing, and the elders rejoined the pastors on the platform. They were carrying a large object covered with a white sheet. The senior pastor then addressed the audience.

"Six months ago, the leadership of this church prayed at great length. We asked the Lord to show us His purpose for this body of believers. After much prayer, discussion, and more prayer, we agreed as to what God wanted. He told us to do something definite, something symbolic of His stated purpose."

"There is a big wall out in the front foyer visible to everyone who enters this building. We agreed, as individuals and a group, to do what the Spirit of God asked. Therefore, we contracted with a local artist to paint a scene depicting the vision God showed us for this body. The artist just delivered the completed, framed painting two days ago. No one knew about this painting other than the pastoral staff and the board members. We made certain to tell no one, as we wanted it to be a surprise. Now, I have to admit to you that the Holy Spirit grabbed my attention when this brother spoke last Sunday. And, in a moment, I'm sure you'll understand what I'm talking about."

When the pastor nodded his head toward the men standing alongside him, the elders uncovered a large, framed oil painting and held it up for the audience to view. I could hear gasps and exclamations of surprise filling the sanctuary. I sat there and stared in awe. All sense of doubt and fear had fled, as faith rushed in to fill the void they left in my being. At that moment, I did not hold back my emotions, and the tears flowing down my cheeks were evidence of that.

The painting showed the image of a large wooden ship, with its sails down. On the main deck were many people. The captain struggled to maintain control on a raging river, and beyond the river were fields of ripened grain ready for harvest.

At the pastor's request, his secretary had typed up the interpretation. Hundreds of copies were available in the foyer for anyone desiring to pick one up after the service.

The following Sunday morning, the painting was visible for all to view as they entered the church.

*"Always remember, son!
Even as Satan is capable
of deceiving humanity by
appearing as an angel of light,
so also can he mislead
the 'sincerest' of my people
when that claimed sincerity
is born of and undergirded by
a desire for self-determination.
Such a desire is most destructive
when it restricts and supplants
the movement of My Spirit."*

A House Divided

Thanksgiving and the Christmas holidays were drawing near. As usual, I was looking forward to the final two weeks of the year when I would usually schedule any remaining paid vacation, primarily because it also coincided with our school district's winter break. Most years, my children, my wife, and I would spend much of this time outdoors. We made snowmen and staged the occasional snowball fight. My son and I cut down trees in our woods, split firewood, trimmed other trees, and cleaned out the gutters. We also spent many hours together in our garage. It was the perfect time to perform the annual cleaning, sharpening, and maintenance on the mower, tiller, chain saw, brush cutter/trimmer, and wood chipper/shredder.

This year the snow came early, dumping almost ten inches on the frozen ground by Christmas Day. The plummeting temperature that followed caused the snow to freeze and made the unheated garage unbearable, even with portable heaters.

At five in the morning, on December 28, the Holy Spirit woke me from a deep sleep. He directed me to get a legal pad, pen, my Bible, and a concordance, and to meet Him in our living room. After closing the bedroom doors so as not to disturb the rest of the family, I turned on the living room lamp. Settling back in the recliner, I waited for Him to speak. Meanwhile, I began reading passages from the Gospels and various Proverbs. An hour later, the Holy Spirit both startled and confused me. He did not make a statement. Instead, He asked me a question that seemed unrelated to anything I had just read.

"Is the result of division reduction or multiplication, loss, or gain?"

I knew that the Lord was not presenting me with a mathematical challenge or logic problem. So I waited without speaking, hoping He would elaborate. His next words came, not as another question or an explanation, but as a command.

"Study DIVISION. I will guide you."

That was the entirety of the Holy Spirit's directive. Those six words set my heart and mind to work, as I read, listened, and wrote non-stop for the next three days.

I slept little as I worked each day from well before dawn until long after the rest of the family were asleep. My wife sensed that what the Spirit was teaching me was critical. She kept our children occupied with shopping, a trip to the library, playing in the snow, or relaxing in their rooms. Her only interruption to what I was doing was to be sure I ate and drank. Over those three days, I seldom left that chair for anything that would distract me. Before long, I had accumulated many stacks of opened books on the floor around the recliner. These the Spirit had referred me to in His effort to show me a fascinating study in the Word. [He told me at the time that one day He would have me share all that He had revealed.]

Three days after beginning, the Spirit said to send a copy of what He had shown me to the senior pastor at our church. The following day I did as directed, typing it up and mailing it. The attached note stated that the Lord had just spent three full days revealing the included information to me. I also explained to the pastor that the Holy Spirit Himself directed me to postal mail it to him. Although I later asked the Lord for a reason, He never answered me at the time.

The following Tuesday, four days later, I received it back in the mail. On the first page were many stains from a coffee cup. In an attached note, the pastor's secretary had written that the pastor told her to mail it back to me. She said he stated that he was too busy at the time to read it. She added a further explanation. He and the other two associate pastors had left that morning on a three-day trip to attend a church conference. I had no problem with that. Nevertheless, I wondered why he had not considered holding on to it to read later when he was not so busy.

Unknown to me, or the rest of our church body, the church leaders had already made plans for significant changes. These changes would prove to have a disastrous effect on our church and its future.

† † †

Following the next Sunday service, the senior pastor spoke to the congregation. He explained about the conference the pastors had attended at Willow Creek Community Church. He went on to elaborate in detail how "sold" the three of them were on the methods used at Willow Creek. Their efforts focused on reaching a wider audience by adopting a "seeker-friendly" and "non-threatening" format.

The senior pastor went on to assure the body that this was not a sudden decision. He stated that the pastors and elders had prayed at length about it. They felt led to adopt this format as the future direction for our church. He claimed this move was a method proven to reach more of the lost in a targeted area. He finished by saying, "We need to prepare this body for the abundant increase that will soon be upon us. God spoke to this body almost three months ago about this, and He did so in a lengthy prophetic message which most of you heard."

It was evident that most of those in the congregation knew which message he was citing—the one the Spirit had chosen to bring through me. That message had now become his primary justification for the changes they were implementing.

The senior pastor then went on to announce that we would start using a format like Willow Creek, beginning the following week. "Going forward," he explained, "the Sunday services will have one focus only. Our emphasis will be on reaching new attendees with a simplified Gospel. We will present this through non-threatening messages and dramatic presentations."

Their joint decision also restricted the movements of the Holy Spirit to Wednesday evenings. The pastor explained, "We'll still have prophetic words, prayer for healing, and such. However, we do not want to do anything on Sunday mornings that would discourage visitors. Much of the supernatural stuff that most of you now take for granted could scare them away, and then we would miss the chance to share the Gospel with them and win them to the Lord."

On exiting the church, several individuals snapped off rash comments within my hearing. Others stared at me with anger visible on their faces. I knew in my spirit that my obedience to the Holy Spirit's leading was not the cause of what was now occurring. In the same way, I also understood that the pastoral staff had taken what the Spirit said that day entirely out of context. That message became the leadership's justification for exclusively focusing on increasing attendance and membership, disregarding the ongoing spiritual growth of the present body. To accomplish their aim, they were willing to restrict the movement of the Holy Spirit.

That afternoon I found a quiet place where I could be alone and hear from the Spirit. When the Lord finally spoke, it was to assure me of one thing.

"They had already made up their minds and were unwilling to hear Me," the Holy Spirit said. *"Now they will walk for a season down the path they have chosen. This body has grown to be like a close-knit family. The leadership's choice will bring tremendous pain and heartache to many. That which is about to occur was avoidable if your pastor had read and considered the study on 'Division' that I had you send to him."*

That last part puzzled me. I did not understand how that study could have altered or stopped what occurred that morning, so I asked the Lord to explain it to me.

*"Son, Division finds an entrance in a multitude of ways. Sometimes it is the words of one individual or group negatively influencing many others. It can also be the actions of one person or group, blocking or hindering the move of My Spirit while promoting their own agenda. In doing so, they blaze a path for Division and Discord to travel. I have spent many hours teaching you about this. Two things **always** occur when My Spirit initiates, directs, and anoints any word or action. **It brings forth new life in the body, and does so in harmony with My Word and the movement of My Spirit.**"*

"Many a person or group of individuals starts down a path believing that they are following My leading. Too late, they realize that their thinking and ideas misled them.

Once they start in the wrong direction, the Deceiver encourages them further in the pursuit of the deception."

"Always remember, son! Even as Satan is capable of deceiving humanity by appearing as an angel of light, so also can he mislead the 'sincerest' of my people when that claimed sincerity is born of and undergirded by a desire for self-determination. Such a desire is most destructive when it restricts and supplants the movement of My Spirit."

"For now, I want you and your wife to lift your hearts and voices in intercession. Pray for all who this decision will harm. I still have plans for this church and body. My Spirit has already put into motion what is necessary to one day bring them back on the path of My choosing."

My family and I continued attending that church for six more painful months. The Holy Spirit then released us to leave. During those six months, we watched in agony as things changed. All mention of the Holy Spirit disappeared from the Sunday morning service. The exuberant joy of the Lord that was our church's hallmark began to fade. For many, it became unbearable and they departed. Within four months, over sixty percent of the original body moved on to other churches. Giving decreased, and the board struggled to meet the monthly financial obligations.

When we finally left that church, it was with heavy hearts. We had witnessed the senseless destruction of one of the area's most Spirit-led churches.

The new church that the Lord led us to was thirty minutes from our home. There we discovered, and joyfully reunited with, many of the former members of the church we left.

Learning to War

We may have been the most unlikely threesome that the Living God could ever have sent to represent Him. Two of us had struggled to relate to our heavenly Father. Our struggles were due to our own non-existent or weak father-son relationships. Each of us battled in many ways throughout our lives with feelings of insecurity and inadequacy. Much of this resulted from repeated hurt or abuse from others.

The eldest of our group had reacted by withdrawing into silence most of his days. He associated with other Christian men he admired. Still, he never allowed God to move him to the forefront in any situation. The second man had taught himself to laugh off the hurt and pain, which he did until he was alone. It was then that his past too often would arise to overwhelm him. Then there was me, the youngest of our trio. I had *trained* myself to act with confidence and boldness as my attempt to disguise insecurities and an overshadowing sense of inferiority. Both hounded me day and night. I struggled to present to the world a false front of calm assurance. However, deep inside, where it mattered most, memories and feelings that I could not seem to shake plagued me. Despite this, it was to me that the Holy Spirit had spoken, several months earlier, about His desire. That conversation began with His questioning my actions and the intentions of my heart.

"Son, why are you so willing to encourage and fund your children to follow My calling upon their lives, while ignoring My calling on your own life?"

The question nagged at me for weeks, morning and night, at work, and rest. Finally, in a moment of desperation, I had fallen to my knees at the side of my bed and called out to God.

"Lord, thank You for all the times You have been willing to use me in the past. Even so, I'm begging You, Holy Spirit. Please help me to change. Free me from the clutches of whatever it is that always holds me back from giving myself over wholly to You."

That day the accumulated tension in me broke. A dam of emotions released when I heard the tender response of the Holy Spirit.

"Though it may not appear to be so, I am still directing your path and ordering your steps. Do not lose hope, My son. Help is coming. I have opened your spiritual ears and eyes to begin hearing and seeing that which you could not until now. I am working things out, moving you into position. Meanwhile, the Father would ask something of

you. I have moved upon the hearts of two other men who will join you on a journey. Welcome them and do not question My choices. There is a divine purpose that I will reveal to the three of you later."

All three of us had received the baptism in the Holy Spirit. We knew how to petition heaven from a sincere heart, but we were not what most would consider as intercessors. Neither did the Lord give us any divine strategy to follow. The Spirit only gave me a few simple instructions. Each of the other two men confirmed these when they stated their desire to join me.

We boarded the plane, unaware of the depth of the situation into which we were heading. We knew only two facts. Turmoil existed at the international and national levels of Full Gospel Business Men's Fellowship and the resulting chaos had worked its way down into the local chapters, including our own. In disgust with everything that was occurring, tens of thousands of men were canceling their memberships nationwide.

The battleground to which the Holy Spirit had called us was a hotel in Anaheim, California. The front line was the Full Gospel Business Men's annual World Convention. It was to occur at the Anaheim Convention Center situated adjacent to our hotel. This Spirit-ordained and Spirit-blessed organization had been instrumental in encouraging and activating men throughout the world. Through the actions of those men in the Fellowship, millions of souls had become part of the kingdom of God. Now, this organization had come under massive attack. Our beloved founder, Demos Shakarian, had died. A confrontation over the transition of leadership and authority followed and proved to be the perfect opportunity for Satan to unleash a tremendous assault. It appeared that he aimed to slow or completely stop the organization's efforts.

Before the three of us had arrived and checked into our shared room, the Holy Spirit had moved on us. He unified our hearts, minds, and spirits in a common focus. Later, He spoke specifics to me.

"Son, do you recall what I revealed to you five years ago about the spiritual realm? I showed you then that the battle is, and always will be, between heaven and hell. Men believe they are controlling events and circumstances to bring about their desired conclusions. In truth, they follow the leading of one or the other in the spiritual realm – the Father or their enemy, **but not both**. For this reason, it is vital that My people hear My voice, and can confidently distinguish it from the voices of their enemy, which are many and continue without ceasing."

The Spirit then showed me how Satan had dispatched a mighty army of demon spirits. Each understood its part in influencing the hearts and minds of hundreds of key leaders in the organization. Next, the Lord directed me to write down a list of the evil spirits we were to come against in prayer. When I finished, I looked in amazement at what I had written.

Listed there was Accusation, Anger, Bitterness, and Condemnation. Others were Contempt, Contention, Control, Criticism, and Deceit. Next, there was Distrust, Division, Domination, Doubt, Frustration, Impatience, and Insincerity. Another group included Intimidation, Intolerance, Jealousy, Manipulation, Pride, Quarreling, Rebellion, and Rejection. Last, He spoke of Resentment, Retaliation, Self-Deception, Self-Justification, Self-Righteousness, Self-Will Slander, Strife, and Suspicion. Additionally, the Holy Spirit said we would always encounter, in any situation like this, strongholds of Discord and Religion.

He explained to me further the combined impact these demonic forces could have, with their most significant efforts being against the highest levels of leadership.

"Some of the leaders have knowingly, and others unknowingly, aligned themselves with these demonic forces. They have stepped out from under the covering of My blood. They now attack one another with accusations and counter-accusations. They bring lawsuits and countersuits. They tear down their brethren by publishing and distributing slanderous articles, emails, and letters."

Indeed, the Fellowship had begun to fracture into two separate groups. Dissenting national and international leaders were persistent in encouraging local leaders to support them. Some of the most influential national players had already established a new organization. They said it would operate under the same concepts and principles as the original. They spoke of redirecting efforts into this new organization. Their **claim**—that this "redirecting of efforts" would occur ONLY if the dividing issues in the Fellowship remained unresolved—was a camouflage. Meanwhile, the dissenting parties were investing thousands of their own money in this alternative. It went toward "informing" chapters throughout the nation of the "problem." The packages they sent by mail described the shortcomings and faults of the current leadership. Their whole approach promoted the differences between the two groups as being beyond resolution. The plans that Satan set into motion seemed to be having the effect he had intended.

The three of us that the Spirit had sent into the middle of this chaos had no particular influence with current leaders at the national or international level. The only weapon the Spirit said to bring to the upcoming battle was His love, without which nothing would change. He also knew how much we each cherished the Christian Business Mens' organization and all that it had come to mean to us over the years. The Lord then encouraged me further.

"Be faithful to do all I may ask you to do. Only interceding with a surrendered heart will make it possible for My love to move through you, affecting and changing the hearts of those who I desire to reach."

The first six days of the convention passed quickly, and then it was time for the scheduled annual Fellowship business meeting and elections. Bylaws restricted attendance and participation in the business meeting to national and international officers, as well as certified chapter delegates. I attended as the recently elected president of our local chapter. The other two men continued praying in the hotel hallway surrounding the massive hall where the meeting was being held.

Upon entering the ballroom, I saw that there was close to a capacity crowd. My spirit began grieving over what I observed and heard there. I expected to see humble servants of God seeking to serve their brothers in Christ. Instead, I found multiple groupings of angry, prideful men. Many were men I had known for years and come to respect. Behind closed doors—where the general membership could not now observe them—their character changed. A group on one side of the room was shouting accusations. Jumping to their feet, groups in other parts of the room responded. Another string of allegations and condemnation arose from a third group, which a fourth group countered. Such disorderly behavior continued for over one hour before the scheduled starting time of the meeting. The noise level and chaos in the room was out of control.

Pounding a gavel furiously on the table in front of him, the one chairing the meeting brought the hall to order. Still, an undercurrent of mumbling was evident throughout the room. In short order, the chair addressed the few general business items on the agenda. It then was time for the elections.

"Before we nominate and elect officers for the upcoming year," the chairman stated, "we have time for about a dozen brief comments. However, I want this done in an orderly fashion. Those selected will come forward to the microphone so everyone may hear what you have to say. You will each have three minutes and only three minutes. The rest of you, please show a little respect for your brothers in Christ. Do not talk or interrupt them while they are speaking. Now, would anyone like to comment, in an orderly way? If so, raise your hand, and I'll select twelve."

Pandemonium erupted. Voices called out for recognition, as hands shot up everywhere. Some of the men stood, waving their arms, attempting to gain his attention. It was then that the Holy Spirit spoke to me.

"Raise your hand."

I knew it was His Voice, but I held back, not eager to stand before this angry group. I watched as the chairman started selecting men from various parts of the room.

Suddenly, there was another voice speaking to my mind. *"Why would you want to go forward in front of this hostile crowd? If you did, what could you possibly say to make a difference?"*

Nonetheless, the quiet voice of the Holy Spirit prompted me again, more firmly this time. *"Trust Me, son. Raise your hand."*

From where I sat, I watched the continuing chaos. Although I was still uncertain, I obeyed. Just at that moment, the chairman said, "That's eleven. We'll take one more." Hundreds around the room began shouting, waving, and whistling to gain his attention. Several of the men started down the aisles, trying to force him to choose them. Instead, he turned away from them and, facing in the direction where I was sitting, selected me as the twelfth. Surprised that he saw me on the far side of the room, much less selected me, I went forward and stood at the end of the line. One of the other men at the head table began pounding the gavel to get the crowd quieted down and back in their seats.

The chairman moved to the first man in line, maintaining control of the microphone. He reminded the one about to speak of his three-minute time limit before allowing him to begin. When each person's time was up, the chairman pulled the microphone away. Thanking the one who spoke, he then moved to the next man in line. Most of the comments expressed were angry, accusatory, demanding, and some even threatening. Loud responses, for and against the views expressed, rang out from the crowd.

I listened to each speaker and watched the crowd's reactions. The line in front of me grew shorter. I could feel Fear attempting to grab hold of my bowels. I had no idea what I was going to say. Next, the Voice that had guided me in prayer all week spoke to me.

"Be at peace, son. When it is your turn, take a breath, be still for a moment until the crowd quiets, and then open your mouth. Trust Me to fill it, just as I did at your church when I used you to present the vision and its meaning."

A calming Presence settled over me, driving away all fear and worry. I closed my eyes and began praying in my spirit language, and the peace intensified.

When it was my turn, I did as the Spirit directed and waited for quiet. I stared down at the floor to keep from having to look at the thousands of faces now staring at me. The Lord urged me to open my mouth, and words I did not have to think about flowed forth.

"'You did not come here today to argue among yourselves, or to accuse one another. Neither are you here to pressure one group of men to conform to the opinions or desires of another group. Those on the platform are currently serving as your elected leaders—whether you agree with them or not. They freely gave of themselves. They dedicated time away from their businesses or places of employment to work for you. Sometimes, they used vacation days to do so. Like each of you, they received no compensation. They could have spent this time with their families. Why did they do this instead? They offered their services as though they were doing everything directly for the Lord Himself. They acted as willing vessels through which My Spirit has been able to carry forward the vision that He gave to your deceased brother, Demos. They deserve to be honored, not treated with dishonor. Each of you would do well to remember that you are here to express more than your desire. You are here

representing hundreds of thousands of others who could not attend. Even so, many here mistakenly believe that their votes set men into positions of authority, or remove them. If you are truly the Lord's vessel, then you should be representing His heart, because it is to Him that you will give an accounting. Do you so soon forget that the Word of God says, '*...there is no authority except that which God has established'?*"[1]

"'You are all a part of the Body of Christ. If you attack this part of the body, tearing it asunder to conform it to your present desires, how then can you possibly expect the Father in heaven to bless it?'"

Before I had used my allotted three minutes, many throughout the room began jumping to their feet. They yelled out, forcing the crowd to hear what they had to say. Soon, half of the men in the assembly were also standing—talking, yelling, and arguing.

I walked away from the microphone and hurried back to my chair. Sitting down, I stared at the floor and questioned the Lord.

"What was the point, Holy Spirit? No one even listened."

The chairman returned to the head table while another officer pounded the gavel until the crowd quieted. Accepting and seconding of nominations proceeded. The Chairman declared majority winners for each office, after show-of-hands voting. The secretary made a record of the proceedings, and the business meeting ended. Attendees poured out of the ballroom with anger and frustration showing on the faces of many. Others responded by spewing forth their bitter thoughts in the hallways.

I was one of the first to exit the side door. I flagged down my two companions, and together, we headed to the elevator to return to our room. Once there, I related all that occurred. Having watched and listened through the crack where the double entry doors met, one of the two men confirmed what I'd said. He said it horrified him to see how angry and uncooperative most of the men were. Not knowing what else to do, we prayed for the elected officers. We asked the Lord to bring peace to our troubled spirits. I concluded by asking the other two men if they would mind if we could refrain from discussing it any further that night. In my opinion, it was over and finished, and we were flying home in the morning. I wanted to be sure that I could greet my wife and children with a genuine joy reigning in my heart.

While lying in bed that night, my spirit was in utter turmoil, and I could not get to sleep. When I looked at the clock for the tenth time, I saw that it was almost three in the morning. As the other two men slept, I poured out my heart to my Heavenly Father, speaking in a whisper.

"Lord, why did you make me come here. This trip was an absolute waste. Too many of those in that meeting were angry and hostile. No one listened to a word of what You had me say! I've invested many years of my life into this Fellowship, and it's been a real blessing. That's why it hurts so much to see this destruction occurring. How do I explain this to our remaining chapter membership? How do I do so without inducing hopelessness? Why did I have to go through this, Lord?"

I waited in the dark for His answer. Fifteen minutes later, the Spirit of God finally spoke.

"I brought you here to intercede on My behalf, son. I brought you here to learn how to war in the spirit, through My Spirit, and to see firsthand how your enemy operates. A man can learn only so much about how to battle in the physical realm by training, reading, or listening to others who have themselves battled. There comes a time when he must observe with his own eyes and begin to apply what he has learned. To do so, he must go to where the fighting is occurring."

"It's the same in the spirit realm, son. It's when the heat of the battle is at your doorstep, and your enemy is breathing in your face that your character becomes most evident, and your resolve thoroughly tried. Will you fight anger with anger, hostility with hostility, aggression with aggression?"

"Instead, will you consent to My truth girding you about and My peace guiding your feet? Will you allow My mighty right hand to uphold you? Will you allow Me to be your Strong Defense, your Confidence, your Strength, and your Shield? Will you permit Me to prove—through you and to you—how My love never fails?"

"Or would you resort to speaking My words in vain, with no real belief or understanding in the truth behind them or explosive power inherent in them?"

"When everything your eyes behold tells you that your enemy has won, what will you do? Will you still be able to declare with unshakable conviction and assurance: 'My God reigns!'?"

"Yesterday, you saw the devastation which can occur when evil reigns through men. Do not ever forget this, son. Learn from it and, most of all, know that I brought you here as My ambassador, My envoy, My voice in the storm. You did what I sent you to do. Dwell on it no longer. The outcome is now in My hands."

With those final words, the burden I had felt for hours disappeared. A deep comforting peace settled over me in its place as I drifted into a welcome slumber.

*"Neither the cultivation of a
rebellious nature nor giving in
to the longing for idols
will instantly transform your soul.
Consider well that good and evil are
GROWTH processes…you GROW
into the image of the Risen One,
or the fallen one.
The resultant character is neither
instantly attained nor instantly lost.
For this reason, I was most careful
to say through Isaiah,
'the hearts of this people
have GROWN dull.'
Always remember!
The vine that strangles
one's ability to hear My Spirit
roots itself deep in the soil
of a disobedient heart."*

Drawn Aside

In the year following that Full Gospel World Convention, our local chapter membership kept declining. At its peak, there were fifteen hundred members. Of those, three to four hundred participated on a somewhat regular basis. Now we had just two hundred members, of which only thirty or so were active participants. At the annual local elections held that next November, none of the members who were not currently officers opted to run for the leadership positions for the following year. Those in attendance that day instead asked the current officers to carry on for another year. Unsure about what else to do, the other officers agreed to continue if I would retain my position as president of the chapter.

One month later, the International Office announced plans for the next World Convention. It would be in early July, in Dallas, Texas. Our chapter officers discussed it at length, and no one was eager to attend. We had attempted to provide the same Spirit-led environment and agenda at our local chapter gatherings. Despite this, men continued to cancel their memberships. Many stated, in doing so, that they wanted nothing more to do with the chaos in the organization. Others switched their allegiance to the new organization that had recently established a chapter in our area. Both actions were quite disheartening to those who had remained faithful.

I prayed and prayed about our chapter's World Convention representation. One day, I heard the Holy Spirit tell me to offer to attend the convention as our chapter delegate. I was willing, but only under one condition. Upon my return, there had to be focused prayer and serious discussion about the future of our chapter. By this time, the number of those attending the monthly functions had dropped to less than twenty.

When I left for Dallas, I believed I was going for the singular purpose of representing our chapter. As I found out later, the Lord had something far different in mind.

I arrived a day early with plans to spend those extra hours in prayer with the Lord. I intended to relax and enjoy the scheduled featured speakers. On the morning of the last day, I would attend the business meeting, observe, and vote. In doing so, I would be able to report the state of the Fellowship to those in my home chapter.

Checking into the same hotel where the functions were going to take place, I located my room on the tenth floor. After unpacking, I prostrated myself before the Lord on the carpeted floor. Soon, the tangible Presence of the Spirit saturated the room. My spirit entered into the perfect peace of the Lord, and then a voice spoke to me.

"*Get up and go downstairs, son. There's a book I want you to buy and read.*"

My initial thought was that this sounded a bit strange, causing me to wonder if it was God who was speaking. A minute later, the undeniable Voice of the Holy Spirit repeated His request.

Making my way to the lobby, I spotted the hotel gift shop and walked toward it, but it was not open for business. I stood there a moment, puzzled, thinking to myself, "*Was I mistaken?*"

Returning to my room, I prostrated myself on the floor once more. No more than five minutes later, the Voice again spoke.

"*Get up and go downstairs, son. There's a book I want you to buy and read.*"

This time I hesitated even longer. I said aloud to the Lord, "I went downstairs when You asked the first time, but the bookstore wasn't open."

I waited and waited, but there was no response. Arising once more, I returned to the lobby. This time the gift shop was open, and I went in, feeling somewhat guilty about having doubted the Lord. Looking at the selection of books for sale, I whispered to the Lord. "Which book should I buy, Holy Spirit?" The response was immediate.

"*None.*"

Confused, I again wondered if it was some spirit other than the Holy Spirit messing with my mind. Without saying a word, I left the gift shop and retraced my steps back to my room. There I paced the floor, talking aloud to the Lord. Irritated and uncertain, I plopped onto the edge of the bed. For a third time, I heard the same clear voice speaking to me.

"*Please go downstairs, son. There's a book I want you to buy and read.*"

For quite a while, I did not respond. Unsure of myself now, I waited for the Voice to elaborate. Finally, I heard His further instruction.

"*Ask at the front desk, son.*"

Returning to the lobby for the third time, I headed to the front desk and inquired. "Other than the gift shop, is there any other bookstore in the hotel?"

"If you're with Full Gospel, go down that hall," the woman said. She pointed to the hallway past the elevators. "Second set of double doors on the right. Your group reserved two large, adjoining conference rooms to display books for sale."

Relieved, I smiled and thanked her, then headed in the indicated direction. On the double doors that stood open, there was a small poster board with a single word: BOOKSTORE. Inside, men were unpacking and displaying thousands of books. There were stacks of books on every subject imaginable on dozens of long tables. Most related to the Bible or some facet of Christianity. For more than an hour, I wandered from table to table, reading the backs of hundreds of paperbacks. I wondered in my mind what I should buy. *How much extra money did I have? How many books could I fit in my luggage?* Even so, each time I held onto a book, thinking about purchasing it, the Spirit spoke.

"*No.*"

After hearing this same thing for more than ninety minutes, I began to grow frustrated.

"Why am I here? How am I supposed to know which book? There are thousands of books here!"

The response came immediately.

"*Ask me, son, and I'll tell you.*"

Feeling foolish for not considering it sooner, I wasted no further time. "What book should I buy, Holy Spirit?"

I sensed a prompting within to turn and look to my right. Like a compass needle locking in on true north, I felt my eyes drawn to a table near the center of the room, about thirty feet away. Making my way to that table, I scanned the titles exhibited there. Midway down the table, I felt compelled to pause.

"*Buy that one, son. Go back to your room and start reading it. I'll speak to you there.*"

The book was "*Battling the Hosts of Hell: Diary of an Exorcist.*" The author was a Baptist pastor named Win Worley. Upon seeing the book and hearing the Spirit's directive, my heart seemed to skip a beat. Hesitating, I thought about my wife's reaction the last time the Holy Spirit led me down this path. Finally, at the Spirit's repeated urging, I bought the book and headed for the elevator.

It was getting to be near dinner, but my curiosity about the book was far greater than any hunger I was feeling. Turning on the desk lamp, I sat there and began reading one chapter after another. I finished the book in thirty minutes. While pondering what I had read, the Holy Spirit surprised me when He urged me to reread it. The second time through, emotions and feelings that had troubled the depths of my soul for years began to stir. The Spirit of God started speaking to me about what I was reading, as well as my reaction to it.

Late into the night, I continued to absorb the content of that book. I listened as the Spirit led me to Scriptures speaking on the same subjects, recognizing many that He brought to my attention in the past. I filled several pages of my journal with notes. When four hours had passed, I felt the beginning of an upset stomach and instinctively knew it was not because I was hungry. Pausing for a few minutes, I stood at the window, looking at my reflection in the darkened glass. As I waited for the turmoil within to subside, I talked aloud to the weighty Presence of the Lord in the room.

"Jesus, You blessed me in a way I'll never forget when I received the baptism in the Holy Spirit," I said. "Since then, You've moved in and through me from time to time."

I paused once more, waiting without speaking for several minutes. I was not quite sure what I expected to hear, but I thought sure the Holy Spirit would respond in some way. Instead, a spirit of Doubt began to invade my thoughts, speaking to my mind.

"Are you sure you are his? If you were, he would respond. Right? You know what the Bible says, that '...the gifts are given without repentance.' Don't forget! Speaking in tongues and giving a prophetic word is not a sign that you are his. He also said, 'many will say in the end, Lord, Lord, I have prophesied for you.' How did he promise to respond? 'Depart from me... I don't know you.' You know the Bible. Isn't that what it says?"

Confused and shaken, I fell to my knees, crying out, "Help me, Jesus!"

At once, the peace I had experienced earlier that day swept over me. The sweet voice of the Holy Spirit then addressed my spirit.

"Son, an evil spirit tempted you, even as Satan tempted the Son of God in the wilderness. We have talked about this in the past. My Word says **'Always be ready to give a defense to anyone who asks you for a reason for the hope that is in you.'**[1]

Realize, though, that 'anyone' includes demon spirits. This 'command to respond,' however, is NOT a license to speak to or argue with demonic hosts. The DEFENSE that you are to give is the Word of God, and **only** My Word, as Jesus did. I will quicken the Word to your mind, as I did for Jesus when Satan tempted Him. In situations like what you experienced, the Word alone has the power to silence your enemy."

"Never forget what My Word states. **'He anointed us, set his seal of ownership on us, and put his Spirit in our hearts as a deposit, guaranteeing what is to come.'**[2]

"But remember what else My Word declares. **'Everyone who confesses the name of the Lord must turn away from wickedness.'**[3]

"My Word has a further instruction that also applies. **'Flee the evil desires of youth and pursue righteousness, faith, love, and peace, along with those who call on the Lord out of a pure heart.'**[4]

"I encourage you to rest in the knowledge that you are Mine, son. Your spirit has been '...**sealed unto the day of redemption.**'[5] My Spirit dwells within you."

"Recall how Satan harassed My servant Paul to the extent that he proclaimed, *'I do not understand what I do. For what I want to do, I do not do, but what I hate I do. And if I do what I do not want to do, I agree that the law is good. As it is, it is no longer I myself who do it, but it is sin living in me. I know that good itself does not dwell in me, that is, in my sinful nature. For I have the desire to do what is good, but I cannot carry it out. For I do not do the good I want to do, but the evil I do not want to do—this I keep on doing. Now if I do what I do not want to do, it is no longer I who do it, but it is sin living in me that does it.'* "[6]

"*'So I find this law at work: Although I want to do good, evil is right there with me. For in my inner being, I delight in God's law; but I see another law at work in me, waging war against the law of my mind and making me a prisoner of the law of sin at work within me. What a wretched man I am! Who will rescue me from this body of death? Thanks be to God, who delivers me through Jesus Christ our Lord!'* "[7]

"Understand by this, son, that evil spirits have tormented your body and soul for many decades. They influence and control you in any way they can. As Paul came to realize, their attempts will not end until the day you stand before Me in eternity. Many of the spirits that currently harass you prey on some abuse, accident, or prolonged illness. They latch onto you when your ability to resist is minimal or nonexistent. Some demons believe they have the right to harass you because they did so to both your parents and grandparents without resistance. Now they are attempting to press their claim to further generations. However, most gained hold as you yielded to their temptations, from your youth to the time you became Mine. The blood of the Lamb covered these sins and set you free, canceling their rights over you. Now you must learn what I expect of you as My son and then walk it out daily, even hourly, as a child of the Light. My Spirit said this through Paul when he wrote, **'For you were once darkness, but now you are light in the Lord. Walk as children of light (for the fruit of the Spirit is in all goodness, righteousness, and truth), finding out what is acceptable to the Lord. And have no fellowship with the unfruitful works of darkness.'**[8] *I further remind you that Paul also asked,* **'Who will rescue me from this body of death?'**[9] *This was a rhetorical question, son. He clearly understood that there was only ONE answer, which is why he declared with his next breath,* **'Thanks be to God, who delivers me through Jesus Christ our Lord!'**[10]

It would be wise for you to remember the following. There is a far greater depth to what Paul states in that one sentence than you, or most, realize. Yes, he was referring to the day he would be free from his body at the time of his death, and be in union with Christ in eternity. But Paul was also talking about the here and now, before physical death. Similarly, Paul spoke of Christ extending His hand to deliver him from the enemy's hold. He did that for Paul. He is as willing to do so for you. Ultimately still, what Paul described and declared was the need for **surrender**. This surrender is three-fold. **First, there must be a surrender of one's mind to the Mind of Christ.** No longer must you rely on your intelligence, understanding, thoughts, plans, and strategies. **Next, there must be a surrender of one's will to the will of the Father.** Such a surrender involves the relinquishing of your pride, arrogance, self-assertiveness, self-confidence, and self-determination. **And last, there must be a surrender of one's emotions to the control of the Spirit of Christ,** which involves the releasing of all anger, bitterness, fear, jealousy, lust, resentment, and such. Remember! Christ will only freely and fully reign in and through you when you have fully surrendered **ALL** to His Lordship."

"Understand this also! Two things will give your enemy the means to draw you out from under the covering of Jesus' blood. The first is your **rebellion** expressed by your willful and repeated disobedience of My commands. The second is embracing **idolatry**. The enemy of your soul knows this. He works to find the right enticement to lure you away, thereby ensnaring your soul. In this way were many men and women drawn away. All the caution signs were there, as were My Spirit's repeated warnings. They chose to accept and follow the enticing words of their enemy, ignoring Mine."

Consider the time when I spoke through Isaiah, and again when I spoke through Matthew. In both instances, I was speaking of all who choose to leave Me when I declared '*...the hearts of this people have grown dull. Their ears are hard of hearing [My repeated warnings], and their eyes they have closed [to the truth of My Word], lest they should see with their eyes, and hear with their ears, lest they should understand with their hearts and turn, so that I should heal them.*'"[11]

"Be warned again, My son! **Neither the cultivation of a rebellious nature nor giving in to the longing for idols will instantly transform your soul. Consider well that good and evil are GROWTH processes.** Some choose to 'grow' in righteousness, godliness, purity, faithfulness, and obedience. These grow to be like Jesus, the Son of God, who is the Risen One. Others choose instead to 'grow' in unrighteousness, ungodliness, impurity, unfaithfulness, and disobedience. They grow to be like Satan, the son of Perdition, who is the fallen one. Be not deceived! **Both paths are intentional.** Those who are the sons of God have intentionally chosen to accept Jesus as their Savior, and now they follow Him. **Of those who remain, some knowingly decide to follow the evil one. However, many others do so unknowingly by NOT choosing to follow Christ. In either case, they GROW into the image of the One, or the other. The resultant character is neither instantly attained nor instantly lost.** With this in mind, notice how I chose My words with great care when I spoke through Isaiah, saying

'*...the hearts of this people have GROWN dull.*'[12]

"Always remember, son! The vine that strangles one's ability to hear My Spirit roots itself deep in the soil of a disobedient heart."

"This, My son, is the reason why I urge My children to adhere to what the Spirit said through Paul:

'*...whatever things are true, whatever things are noble, whatever things are just, whatever things are pure, whatever things are lovely, whatever things are of good report, if there is any virtue and if there is anything praiseworthy—meditate on these* *things. The things which you learned and received and heard and saw in me, these do.'"*[13]

"Realize also that demonic forces often stand their ground for the simple reason that you don't. Even so, You must **NOT** trust in SELF, but trust in the Solid Rock, which is the Living Word of God. Much of what occurs is due to your lack of understanding of My character and nature. Have I not repeatedly emphasized to you through the years to *'take My yoke upon you and learn from Me'*[14]? With these words, I refer to your becoming My vessel, including gaining My knowledge AND understanding that you might be wise in the ways of the Lord. This understanding increases as you are faithful to spend intimate time with Me. For this reason, I have also repeatedly encouraged you to *'Be still, and know that I am God.'"*[15]

"Once you stand, having found your footing upon the Solid Rock, you must learn how to **withstand** your enemy's relentless assaults. You do so by applying what you have learned from Me. Such "withstanding" does not occur by sitting passively by, tolerating your enemy's attacks. Neither will you ever convince your enemy to leave by the use of your own words or wisdom. You must use My Word as your weapon. It alone will *'demolish arguments and every pretension that sets itself up against the knowledge of God.'"*[16]

"Next, *'take captive every thought to make it obedient to Christ.'*[17] In like manner, your acting to "take captive" must not be through your strength or knowledge. Neither will it occur by quoting memorized Scriptures, especially if your heart does not believe what your mouth is speaking. Never forget! My Spirit operates best in your weakness, humility, brokenness, and absolute surrender. You then make it possible for Me, the Lord your God, to show Myself strong on your behalf."

"Hear what I am about to say to you, son! I am aware that, to most, what I tell you now will sound quite illogical. Nonetheless, I challenge you to trust the LORD to watch over you with jealousy that knows no bounds. Do you, in all honesty, know what that means? Let me elaborate. Do you recall how jealous the LORD was for David, Our precious one? He testified: **'When the waves of death surrounded me, the floods of ungodliness made me afraid. The sorrows of Sheol surrounded me; the snares of death confronted me. In my distress, I called upon the Lord, and cried out to my God; He heard my voice from His temple, and my cry entered His ears. Then the earth shook and trembled; the foundations of heaven quaked and were shaken because He was angry. Smoke went up from His nostrils, and devouring fire from His mouth; coals were kindled by it. He bowed the heavens also and came down with darkness under His feet. He rode upon a cherub and flew, and He was seen upon the wings of the wind. He made darkness canopies around Him, dark waters, and thick clouds of the skies. From the brightness before Him, coals of fire were kindled. The Lord thundered from heaven, and the Most High uttered His voice. He sent out arrows** *and scattered them; lightning bolts, and He vanquished them. Then the channels of the sea were seen, the foundations of the world were uncovered, at the rebuke of the Lord, at the blast of the breath of His nostrils. He sent from above, He took me, He drew me out of many waters. He delivered me from my strong enemy, from those who hated me; for they were too strong for me. They confronted me in the day of my calamity, but the Lord was my support. He also brought me out into a broad place; He delivered me because He delighted in me.'* "[18]

"Yes, the Spirit did this for David because he was a man after My own heart. When the Spirit describes him as such, it does not mean that David was simply one who chased after the LORD with passion. No, it means so much more than that. His heart had become conformed to the express image of Mine. It had become humbled, broken, surrendered, and obedient. He had a passion for loving, like the Father-heart of God. In other words, I could look into the very depths of David's heart and soul AND SEE MYSELF. When necessary, I came to his rescue with a fury. That was not because I had a deeper love for him than I have for others. The Father loves all of His children in the same manner. If you recall, David was still under the Law. As such, it was because of his righteousness and the cleanness of his hands. What also mattered was that he kept the ways of the LORD and did not wander away from them. My statutes were ever before him; he did not violate them. He remained blameless before God and kept himself from iniquity. So, I rewarded him according to his righteousness, according to his cleanness in My eyes."

"Don't forget what My word also says. **'For if, by the trespass of the one man, death reigned through that one man, how much more will those who receive God's abundant provision of grace and of the gift of righteousness reign in life through the one man, Jesus Christ!'**"[19]

"No longer must you earn a place in the Father's heart, satisfying a holy God with your righteousness. Made worthy through **MY** righteousness, you enter in by **MY** grace because **My** blood poured out in your behalf."

"Knowing this, consider well what I am about to say to you, son. When your enemy is assaulting you relentlessly, **cry out to Me**. Do so from a sincere heart. Implore Me to be your Rock, your Fortress, your Deliverer, and the God of your strength in whom you trust. When turmoil surrounds you, **boldly remind Me of My promises** to be your Shield, the Horn of your salvation, your Stronghold, and your Refuge. Moreover, **with unshakable confidence, acknowledge aloud who I am to you**. I am your Savior and Lord. Trust that you may call on Me, with absolute confidence that I will save you from your enemies. Declare this with assurance, as David did, from a pure heart in right standing with Me. I will similarly respond to you, arising in My fury to defend and deliver you, My beloved son. You are THAT precious to Me!"

For a considerable time, the Spirit spoke no more. Meanwhile, I was on my face sobbing from a shattered heart as the Lord embraced me like a well-loved son. I no longer resisted, melting into the waiting arms of He who loved me most.

Ninety minutes passed before I arose from the floor and sat on the bed. I was unwilling to do anything that might interfere with the moving of the Spirit. An overwhelming peace continued radiating within me. The Holy Spirit's unity with my spirit saturated my soul in waves of glory.

After a while, the Spirit spoke, explaining why He—and not I—had arranged for me to be alone in Dallas at that specific time, in that very room.

"Son, do you recall, one year ago, when I urged you not to lose hope and told you that help was on the way? I brought you here to fulfill My promise to you. I have a plan and a future for you, and I have much to teach you. First, I must address the turmoil within your soul, which will then allow Me to set you back on a path of holiness, that healing might occur."

*"For now, begin rereading the book, but much slower this time. Stop noting that which **you** find 'interesting.' Allow Me to speak to you about what you are reading and listen to what I desire to say. I want to begin to show you the hidden part of you."*

"As you read, know that I have not ignored you. I heard you ask, many times, 'Why haven't all things become new, as Your Word promised?'"

*"I know that My Word says, **'Therefore if any man be in Christ, he is a new creature: old things are passed away; behold, all things are become new.'**"*[20]

*"What you fail to understand is that while I am, indeed, **IN** you, you have not yet, in many ways, chosen to be **IN** Christ. You **must** surrender, willingly and unreservedly, to My transforming power. You **must** die, that Christ may live through you. I could set you free of all that your enemy has brought against you, but I need you to see what I see when I observe you. It is about time that you understand where you have allowed your enemy's strongholds to exist. I want you to comprehend how those strongholds came to be. I also desire to teach you why, despite your best efforts, they have persisted in returning. It will not be easy or pleasant, but I will reveal the truth to you, son. Only **My** truth will allow you to **remain** free from all that hinders you from drawing any closer to Me."*

*"If you allow Me to move freely within you, I will lead you to 'SELF' death, **bringing you alive IN Christ**. Such a result is what Jesus meant when He declared, **'If the Son, therefore, shall make you free, ye shall be free indeed.'**"*[21]

Darkness descended upon the city outside my hotel room window as I resumed reading. While I did, a turmoil increasingly built within my stomach. A few hours before dawn, I collapsed onto the bed, exhausted, and fell into a restless sleep.

Awakening to daylight shining through the window, I lay still for a while. I thought about all that the Spirit had revealed to me during the night, and then I began to hear the voices. They were not sweet or peaceful. They came with intensity and unrelenting fury, accusing, threatening, and cursing. They bombarded my mind with clear images of all the evil in which I had willingly participated throughout the years. I recalled vivid pornographic images, many that I remembered having seen before reaching the age of nine. Then a loud, taunting voice spoke to me.

"*Don't think you'll get free of our hold. We've directed your thoughts and actions for too long. You may convince yourself while isolated in this room that it's possible to stay free. But, in a few days, you'll be back in the real world, and we won't let you rest.*"

Fear grabbed hold of my heart and mind; my stomach became sour, and bile rose up in my throat. Jumping out of bed, I paced back and forth, proclaiming aloud the first and only Scripture that came to my mind.

"**For God did not give me a spirit of fear, but of power, and of love, and of a sound mind.**"[22]

I declared it aloud several times and then switched to praying in my prayer language. The voices faded, but I could not deny their effect on my soul. I fell to my knees and thanked my Heavenly Father for the Presence of the Holy Spirit that had swept over me. Once more, the Lord spoke to my spirit.

"*Son, your enemy accuses you with a lie. He attempts to get you to accept responsibility for what I already pardoned. Be at peace and know that I am here with you. I promised you '**I will never leave you nor forsake you.**'*[23] *I have not, and I will not. Those whom the Father has given me, I will not lose.*"

Without warning, I found my conscious mind recalling a story I had heard many years earlier. The one who told this story was one of a group of seven men that the media had come to label as the Kansas City Prophets. God brought each of these seven men together in a particular place with a similar divine purpose and anointing. Although none of them spoke of themselves as such, each walked in the Biblical office of the Prophet, and what they prophesied occurred with incredible accuracy.

The Spirit enabled me to recall a specific incident in that story that I had heard many years earlier. One of these seven men had been teaching a group at their church. Led by the Holy Spirit, that man had spoken forth a prophetic word to the group. This man of God then went beyond the instruction of the Lord by adding his thoughts. In doing so, he had, without even realizing it, exposed those listening to error. The next day, one person had confronted him about what he had done. The prophet's spirit grieved about the situation. He had quickly repented before God and the church, telling them what he had done, and asked them to forgive him, which they had. Still, he had been unable to shake the lingering feeling of guilt that plagued him night and day. This guilty feeling had continued for some time, with him pulling away from others in the Body for a while. He had a concern about the possibility of his repeating this type of error and causing even more significant harm. Wanting to end this situation, the Spirit of God had spoken to him one night through a vivid dream.

In that dream, the prophet had seen Jesus as a middle-aged man who was holding his hand, leading him down a hallway. He also had seen himself as a toddler in a diaper. The diaper had been doing a poor job of containing the mess in it as the two of them walked along. At the end of the hall, Jesus had opened a swinging door and led him down the aisle of a courtroom, halting before the Judge's bench. High above where the Judge sat, the toddler (this prophet) had observed a brilliant light and heard a deep voice speak to Jesus.

"*What do we have here, Counselor?*"

The Son had smiled down at the one holding His hand, looked to the Father, and replied.

"*It seems he's made a pretty big mess of things, and he can't seem to get over it.*"

The Father had leaned forward then and looked at the mess that had begun to run down the legs of the toddler (this prophet). Sitting back in His chair, the Father had returned his attention to the Advocate—His dearly beloved Son—once more.

"*Doesn't he know he has an insurance policy with no termination clause? It's the Blood of the Lamb, which is more than sufficient to cover any messes he may make. Now, clean him up and send him on his way. We have work for him to do.*"

When the Father had uttered those words, the "mess" had disappeared. The prophet had then awakened from the dream, rejoicing with hope and joy radiating from his spirit and flooding his soul.

† † †

When this recalled memory had ended, the Spirit spoke to me in a voice filled with love.

"*I remind you again, son. It most definitely is true that I will never lose those whom the Father has given to me. Still, some choose to forsake Me, walking away from Me, willfully moving out from under the covering of My Blood by their continued actions.*"

"*You have also forsaken Me and ignored My Word at times through the years. The accumulative effect has been devastating to your soul and body. Your enemy has used these times to create confusion in your mind and heart. However, recall how many times Israel turned away from Me. Nonetheless, those who genuinely repented of their wickedness and turned back to Me, I forgave and received back with open arms.*"

"*Consider also My servant David. I declared him 'a man after **My own heart, who will do all My will.**'*[24] *Even so, he committed evil in My sight. When this occurred, he became aware of how it opened up his soul to devastation from the wicked one. **I heard***

David when he cried out with sincere repentance for Me to restore his soul. He fully understood that for him to be 'WHOLE' again, I needed to free that part of his soul over which the enemy had attained influence. Wasn't I faithful to do this for him?"

"In a similar way, you have, at times, walked the path of *your* choosing, rather than allowing Me to direct your steps. You have lusted and sought after the things and ways of the world. Still, the Father's heart never stopped longing for you. When you go astray, My Spirit and My Heavenly host will always make every effort to guide you back to Me."

"When you return with a humble heart, confessing your sins to Me, I will always be faithful to forgive you. My mercies and compassion, which truly are **'new every morning,'**[25] will enfold you. My blood will wash over and through you. And My grace will restore you, making you whole, even as the prodigal son's father restored him upon his return."

"But, **woe unto those who refuse to turn from their wicked ways, and then die in their sin! It would be better for them if they had never been born.**"

For more than a week, I stayed in that hotel room, reading, and writing. For hours at a time, I was on my face before the Lord, soaking the carpet with my tears. I listened as the Lord recounted recent times when I had allowed evil spirits to influence and, at times, rule over my soul.

Early on Saturday morning, the Spirit woke me. He directed me to pray in the spirit for those planning to attend the business meeting. When the Spirit prompted me, I honored my commitment to my local chapter by attending. The meeting was not as chaotic as the year before. Still, bitterness and resentment were evident, and I did not feel much of the Presence of the Lord there. When the business meeting and voting ended, I returned to my room. I felt driven by an intense desire to spend every remaining minute with the Holy Spirit.

My flight home was set for ten o'clock the following morning. That evening I went to bed early, hoping to get a full night of peaceful sleep. However, as I soon discovered, the Holy Spirit had a different agenda in mind.

Facing the Truth

After lying there for several minutes, a feeling of unease began building in me. The Holy Spirit then spoke, gaining my attention.

"*Son, tonight I want to begin freeing you and restoring your soul. You must learn to walk on a more consistent basis in the freedom I purchased for you through My shed blood. However, you must never forget one important thing!* **It's the truth that sets you free, and I cannot free you if you refuse to accept what I say to be the truth.**"

As I contemplated what He had said, a powerful fear began to grab hold of me. Fear of what, I wasn't sure, but I could feel another presence in the room.

I spoke of this aloud to the Holy Spirit, for no reason other than to hear my voice. I didn't want to wonder later if I had only imagined this to be happening. "I'm frightened, and I don't know why, but whatever You want, I'm willing."

With the release of that verbal commitment, all hell seemed to break loose within me. My stomach started churning. My head began aching, and many of the voices, which had harassed me for years, returned with a fury. The unexplainable terror I felt increased as I started shaking like a leaf in the wind. Struggling to regain control of my mind and thoughts, I called out, "JESUS!" Instantly, the fear and tremors subsided, my bowels began to calm, and then the Lord addressed me.

"*Son, the fear you were experiencing right now was **not** your own. Recall what you finished reading a few minutes earlier. What you felt gripping your soul was the cumulative reaction of many spirits of Fear. They have plagued you for too many years. Now, they are rebelling against the threat of finally losing their influence over you. You allowed them to constrain you when you chose not to resist their lies by considering in your heart if what they were saying **might** be so. In some instances, you accepted those lies as truth. I call the enemy of your soul the Deceiver for a reason, son.*"

While the Lord spoke to me, memories flashed through my mind of recent times when this had occurred. Next, irrational compulsion to put forth a defense against what the Lord had said strongly surfaced in my mind.

"Holy Spirit, I've read the Bible and listened to it on cassettes until I wore out two sets. I've studied Your Word, and You've talked to me through it. I pray daily in my spirit language. Why then am I still so tormented and harassed by evil spirits and impure thoughts? Why, at times, do I feel almost powerless to resist? Will I ever be free of their harassment and influence over me?"

Several minutes dragged by in absolute silence. Meanwhile, Insecurity and Uncertainty sowed their seeds in my mind.

"*Why is he not answering? You must have said or done something wrong,*" a voice taunted. "*If not, why has he grown quiet?*"

Abruptly, the Voice of the Lord spoke, silencing the demon voices.

"*Why are you so quick to doubt Me and My Word, son? My promises are faithful and sure. I promised you that My Word would not return void. You chose to study and listen to My Word because I birthed that desire in you. I knew this very day would come. Yes, you have been consuming My Word, **but it must become far more than knowledge**. Such an aim only fulfills your curiosity and puffs you up with religious pride, and that then provides the opening for a spirit of Intellectualism to mislead you. <u>My Word must come alive **TO** you and **IN** you before it can be alive **THROUGH** you</u>, and it is My Spirit who brings that Word to pass when you act on it in faith or speak it forth.*"

"*Did I not say that I knew you before I formed you in your mother's womb? I know the plans I have declared for you, and I have assigned My angels to watch over you all the days of your life. I alone know the agony you have been through since childhood. I was there to witness each deep hurt you endured. I saw Fear stretch its tentacles further and further into your mind and bowels. That allowed Shame to overwhelm your heart. I watched as Anger, Bitterness, and Resentment encouraged the direction of your thoughts. You took the baton they passed you, and have been running for all you were worth ever since. I observed at times as you glimpsed freedom, tasted of it, but let your enemy draw you back. Your heritage is religious, and you had not yet come to know Jesus as your Savior. Your efforts became futile as you operated without the benefit of My wisdom. Likewise, your knowledge of the spiritual realms—Mine and that of the fallen one—was minimal. You had little understanding of My authority and power or the ways of your adversary. Doubt and Anxiety began enveloping and hardening your heart. With no foundation of trust or relational experience in God as a youth, you grew more distrustful of every one year after year. You acted on your enemy's prompting when he said that the only one you could count on was yourself. With false bravado, you then went through life acting confident, bold, and sure of yourself. In your heart, where it matters most, self-doubt, insecurities, worries, and fears reigned. When you were alone, you let down your defenses, and the same injured, scared, and hurting little boy was still there. The enemy of your soul drew your thoughts back repeatedly to those painful times. As a result, the wounds never fully healed.*"

By now, my tears were flowing freely as my heart reacted to what He was asking me to recall. In agony, I cried out, "Lord, why are you making me remember all of this now? I don't want to think about it because it hurts too much!"

"*Believe Me when I tell you that I heard your every cry, son. I was a witness to your enemy's attacks. You did nothing to deserve the torment and humiliation thrust* upon you. You are in no way guilty. However, your enemy has hounded you night and day since those times to make you believe you are. Isn't this so?"

Overcome with emotions, I nodded my head in confirmation, and the Spirit continued.

"My child, if a deep wound occurs and it is not **'permitted'** to heal, then that wound will wreak havoc on the soul and body. This scenario is what has been occurring in you. If you will not **'permit'** me to correct this situation, it will destroy you. Cracks are already beginning to develop in various areas of your life. These could be deadly to both you and those you love."

"Was it so long ago when you felt overwhelmed by Despair, Guilt, Fear, Shame, and Desperation? All the while, you struggled to make those around you think everything was fine. Do you remember? You stood on that hotel balcony, staring down sixteen stories, and seriously considering jumping. Where is the little boy that I created with boundless joy flowing from his heart? What happened to your contagious passion for life and fearless, adventuresome spirit? Are you certain that you want to keep these many things buried within you for the rest of your days? There they will rot and spread their poison into other areas of your soul and body."

Through brokenness and tears, my response came forth as a near-whisper. "No."

"You need to understand, My son, who your enemies truly are. Next, you must renounce any covenants, ties, and associations you have allowed. My forgiveness will then be free to wash over you. My Blood Covenant will purge those freed areas of your soul, allowing healing to come."

"What I'm saying is you must **choose to receive** My love. Understand that only in those areas in which you **permit** Me to be your Deliverer, will I become so. I am a patient and loving Father who wants to see His son made whole, but I cannot help you if you refuse to trust Me. I am aware that this area of placing confidence in others has been one of the fallen one's greatest strongholds over you. In the past, many men that you had trusted either hurt, offended, intimidated, or humiliated you. Even so, let us start anew tonight. No matter what occurs in the remaining hours here, know that I am with you. Resist the urge to give in to the fears that will attempt to overwhelm your heart and mind, including Fear-of-the-Demonic. This spirit gained influence over you in your youth. It preyed upon your insatiable curiosity about and interaction with an Occult spirit. Know that I will deal with all of these in time. For now, relax and allow My Spirit to lead, as I begin to expose your enemy and set you free. Rest in the hands of My Spirit and determine to learn from Him as He guides you through what the Father wants to address first. All I ask of you is your obedience. Trust that I only want what is best for you, My son. I, the Lord your God, am a loving Father who would never hurt His son. Believe that, and believe in Me."

I shook my head and said, "Yes, Lord. I will."

"Son, I want to show you some of what has been impacting and influencing you for most of your life, and why. I drove out these spirits once, but your later actions have made it possible for them to return. Now they have gained an even stronger hold. Keep this in mind. They have no authority other than that which you have relinquished to them. Rest your body on the bed and, in the name of Jesus Christ, command any evil spirit influencing you to manifest and name itself."

Immediately my mind reacted, and I replied, "Isn't it wrong, and even sinful, to talk with evil spirits?"

The same loving Voice explained, *"I did not ask you to speak with evil spirits. I said to COMMAND them, in the name of Jesus Christ, and they WILL respond. They will not do so because of your words, but because of your faith in He Who is Savior, Healer, and Deliverer. They know the power and authority inherent in His Name. Now, relax. Be at peace, and command, son."*

Lying back and relaxing, I commanded, as the Spirit had directed, yet nothing happened. I repeated the command a second time with more intensity in my voice. Another minute passed, and still, nothing occurred. For a third time, I spoke as He'd instructed, even louder and more forceful. When I had finished speaking this last time, the Holy Spirit interrupted me with a question.

"What are you doing, son?"

Perplexed, I answered, "Exactly what You told me to do, but nothing's happening."

The Spirit then replied, *"You are not commanding. You are demanding. It is not about you, or the firmness of your voice, or even about your insistence that they obey. It is about your genuine faith in My power and authority. That power and authority is resident in the name of Jesus Christ, the One who triumphed over the enemy. So, speak again, son, only once, with a genuine expectation in your heart that there will be results. After that, focus on Me, and do not doubt."*

I paused a moment to bring my heart and mind into oneness with the peace of the Lord. Then I spoke—once—and waited with my eyes closed. In my thoughts, I declared God's greatness and absolute authority. I thanked Him in my heart for being my Deliverer.

After what seemed an eternity, my stomach started churning and vibrating. Thoughts bombarded my mind. Vivid scenes surfaced of the many times in my youth when I had stolen what I had wanted and could not afford. At other times, I had done so for no reason other than the challenge of doing it without anyone catching me in the act. Next, I recalled my teenage years, a time when I ran with a gang of twenty or more boys and girls. Invading department stores and grocery stores as a group, we stole as much as possible. Later, we met up to split our take. In my mind, I then saw memories of lumber, hardware, and tools we had stolen from construction sites in the area. We used these to build a giant treehouse in a large elm growing in a nearby graveyard.

Moments later, my thoughts shifted once more. Now I recalled the many times I had participated with a small group of boys from our church. We were all eager to serve the priest in the early Sunday Mass, but not because we were good Catholic boys. Instead, we used the occasions to steal from the collection baskets.

Incident after incident flashed through my mind in rapid sequence. Each time, my body would tense up and then relax. After several minutes of this, it built to a climax. Something was working its way to the surface, filling my conscious mind. I felt an incredible urge to shout the word *STEALING*. When I could hold back no longer, my mouth opened and a roar poured forth from me as a singular voice. Obedient to the command given in the name of Jesus Christ, the spirit identified itself. However, it did not say "*Stealing*." Instead, I heard "*Kleptomania*." Several minutes of spasmodic coughing occurred, followed by a peace settling over me. I rested there, sweat from my forehead and tears now mixing as they both ran down my cheeks. I thought about what had just happened and asked the Lord a question.

"While the thoughts were flooding my mind, everything within me was focusing on the word *Stealing*. Lord, I know *Kleptomania* is compulsive stealing, but I've stolen nothing since I accepted You as Savior, and that was decades ago."

The Spirit of God responded immediately by showing me an image of my desk at home. Next, He showed me the trunk of my car, the inside of my briefcase, and even several storage shelves in my garage. What I saw was all of the materials supplied by my employer that I used every day as part of my job.

"But, Lord," I protested, in an attempt to justify myself, "I use all those supplies every day. How is that stealing, or worse yet, *Kleptomania*?"

The Spirit of God did not hesitate before responding.

"What I have revealed to you is the truth. You take whatever you want, whenever you want it, and never hold yourself accountable for it. What would your employer think if they knew about all that you have helped yourself to over the years? Most times, you take it without asking. You seldom account for it to those who are responsible for its distribution. Do you have any idea how much of what you used was not work-related, or how much you allowed your children to use over the years? Do you now understand? The spirit, which had such a hold on you, was, in fact, Kleptomania, and not Stealing. This compulsion, given into as a youth, transitioned into a stronghold for your enemy. That enemy encouraged your thoughts and ways. You began to steal without even thinking about the act and often did not need the items you were stealing. Do you understand how that spirit has affected your character for more than thirty years? That which was a compulsion, from which I had once set you free, returned. It continues to influence you to this very day, albeit to a lesser degree. As I allowed those thoughts to flood your mind a few minutes ago, your enemy was also working. He was trying to deceive you into believing that you were confronting 'Stealing.' He aimed to prevent

the truth from setting you free in this area. The fact is that the stronghold was far greater than you imagined. It had become an accepted habit for you, affecting and shaping your character. Even worse, your actions began to impact your family and others with whom you associated."

"Once again, I remind you that when you asked Me to forgive you, son, I covered your sins with My blood. Even so, you failed to resist future temptation, and instead, reverted to your old habits. You gave your enemy means to reclaim his hold on you. Yes, you accepted Me as Savior. Still, your hesitation in allowing Me also to be your Deliverer and the Lord of your life made it possible for this to occur. The Father desires that His Word would complete its perfect work in you—beginning today."

"This day, I, the Lord Jesus Christ, have broken the hold Kleptomania had over you. Remember what My Word states: *'...you were once darkness, but now you are light in the Lord. Walk as children of light (for the fruit of the Spirit is in all goodness, righteousness, and truth), finding out what is acceptable to the Lord. And have no fellowship with the unfruitful works of darkness, but rather expose them.'*"[1]

"It's not enough to have My Word in you, son. When you walk it out daily, it activates, coming alive in you. Keep the following in mind! **'I HAVE given you authority to trample on snakes and scorpions and to overcome ALL the power of the enemy.'**[2] However, <u>having the authority and acting on it are two entirely different things</u>. It is not enough that you guard your heart and mind against the attacks of your enemy. You must daily put on the full armor of God and take a STAND. Be mindful that My words, **'having done all, stand,'** also involves substituting new habits for old, which will reshape your character. In doing so, you prevent the enemy of your soul from enticing you back into previous ways. Remember what My word also says. **'Let him that stole steal no longer: but rather let him labor, working with his hands what is good, that he may have something to give him who has need.'**"[3]

"When you reach your home, gather up all that is not yours and return it to your company Monday morning. Only keep what you need to complete the job at hand. Ask me, and I will guide you about the restitution you are to make to your employer. I will also direct you on making restitution to others from whom you have stolen. Yes, I forgave those sins. Even so, the act of making restitution will accelerate the remolding of your character. It will also prevent your enemy from reclaiming influence over your heart and mind in these areas. Likewise, I will bring before you those in need that you may begin to give, replacing the old nature with the new. Start with your employer, son. In the future, hold yourself accountable to my commands. In this way, Satan's host will not tempt you away."

Agreeing with what the Spirit directed, I thanked Him, then closed my eyes and rested for a while. Twenty minutes later, the Spirit of the Lord began speaking again to my spirit.

"You've experienced first-hand how real your enemy is. You also now understand that he has no choice but to obey when commanded, in faith, in the name of Jesus Christ. Permit me to show you other spirits that once intentionally led your soul down ungodly paths, spirits that have now returned. You are not even aware of their existence or current influence. Lately, though, you have ventured back to these old paths. Now, those demonic spirits lead you to follow what you believe to be 'your' habits and desires. Lie back, rest, and repeat the same command as before. Do not imagine which spirit might respond. Allow Me to move on your behalf."

Closing my eyes and relaxing, I obeyed. This time a similar reaction came after a minute or so. Two distinctly different voices boasted aloud, declaring their identities.

"Melancholy," said one. *"Malaise,"* blurted the other, *"and we both have a right to be here,"* the second voice declared.

My mind was in turmoil, and my pulse accelerated. Sitting up, I interrupted what was occurring. I begged the Holy Spirit to explain what the evil spirit meant when it said, *"...we both have a right to be here."*

I thought I understood what *Melancholy* and *Malaise* were. I asked the Lord, "Aren't they both similar—sort of a laid-back, day-dreamy, moody attitude?' The Lord answered, explicitly defining their natures. He also explained my participation with them.

"*Melancholy works in unity with Depression and a plethora of other evil spirits. These include Despondence, Downheartedness, Joylessness, Oppression, Sorrowfulness, Unhappiness, and others. Malaise is a feeling of mental or moral unease, with additional influence coming from Fatigue and Headache. Combined, these describe how you have felt during too much of your adult life. Am I correct? During this same period, you struggled to present a cheerful and positive disposition.*"

"*These two dominant spirits also latched onto you when you were a youth, immediately after your enemy deeply wounded you. That incident caused you to become withdrawn and quiet for extended periods. I banished both of them when you became mine. Now, they have returned to goad your thoughts. They present to your mind reasons to justify your general distrust of others. They remind you of your past and urge you to keep it secret. They attack your mind, suggesting what people will think of you if they knew about your history. When they torment you like this, a very palpable fear seizes you, reopening a wound that had begun to heal. As a spirit of Fear increases its hold on you, Paranoia and Shame find you easy prey. Together, Melancholy and Malaise have a significant effect on the path you take. They affect the choices you make and cause you to suffer from periodic bouts of depression. These continue to impact your marriage and your relationship with your children. Most of all, it interferes with your having a closer relationship with Me.*

Once again broken and crying, I buried my face in the pillow until the gentle voice of the Spirit drew me out.

"Son, I know it's not pleasant to have things like this revealed. Now that you're aware of them, please allow Me to set you free."

When I had calmed, I renounced my participation with these spirits, at the Holy Spirit's prompting. I then commanded them in Jesus Christ's name to release their hold on me. Lying very still, I once again began focusing my mind and heart on proclaiming Jesus as my Deliverer. Almost immediately, I felt a righteous indignation rise in my spirit. It was toward those evil presences that had ruined so much of my life. I started gagging and coughing for a lengthy period, as the hold on me loosened, and Jesus evicted them. That confrontation ended, leaving me feeling exhausted. My stomach felt as though someone's fists had pummeled it. I lay there, basking in the peace of God that rushed in to take their place, as the Lord stirred up new hope in my spirit.

I'm finally getting free of these, I thought to myself. The Holy Spirit responded to my thoughts with evident joy in His voice.

"Yes, My son. You most definitely are."

Exhausted but unable to sleep, I looked at the clock and was amazed that six hours had passed as though it were but minutes. Even so, those were to be the last of the spirits cast out that night. The Holy Spirit instead directed me to get my journal and pen. For the remaining hours until dawn, I wrote down all that the Spirit spoke to me.

"Son, many spirits have returned in the hope that they might once again direct your life. They affect your actions, reactions, thoughts, and even the intentions of your heart. Day after day, this occurs, all because you have consistently failed to resist their temptation. The demonic stronghold over you is Lust. This influencing force began through no fault of your own when you were a young boy. Soon after that physical attack, the voices began. They repeatedly encouraged you to throw off restraint. They promised you that, in doing so, the other boys in the neighborhood gang would accept you. In your weakened state, you followed their direction, allowing these spirits to gain more influence over you as you joined with other youth of like spirit. The older boys in the group introduced you to every wicked and sinful thing which man could conceive. Your heart and mind filled with pornographic images and movie scenes. Various spirits of lust gained an even stronger hold on you during your youth and early adult years."

"This all occurred during a time when you did not yet know Me. I freed you from your enemy's grasp when you accepted Me as your Savior. However, at times, your later thoughts have opened the door for some of these demons to reestablish these wicked strongholds, once again directicting your mind and imagination. For too many years, they kept you from understanding and appreciating genuine love—your wife's *love, when I brought her to you, and Mine, despite My countless attempts to fully heal you."*

The Spirit continued His explanation, showing me the various regained strongholds. He pinpointed the moment when each evil spirit gained access, influence, or control. After urging me to make a note of these, He then instructed me to bind them, one by one, in the name of Jesus Christ.

*"This will prohibit them from creating further damage in your life. Then, soon, I will set you free from them and their influence. However, I am not simply freeing you, son. This week has also been an intentional period of isolation dedicated to training you. Additional lengthy periods of training will follow. The purpose of all this is so that—once you are free—your gained knowledge and understanding might help others attain their freedom too. To do this, you must diligently study your enemy and their tactics as I teach you. You will then be able to confidently work **with** Me to set other captives free, and teach those individuals how to stay free."*

"When you leave this room to return to your family in a few minutes, don't forget what I've shown you here. The battle for the restoration of your soul has begun. Your enemy will be relentless in attempting to drag you down and talk you out of believing that there is hope. Despair not! The victory is already Mine, and I am with you always. Call upon Me in those times, and I will strengthen you that you might resist."

With those promises reverberating in my heart and mind, I departed for home.

*"It is not enough to
have My Word in you, son.
When you walk it out daily,
it activates, coming alive in you.
I <u>have</u> given you authority.
However, having the authority
and 'acting on that authority' are
two completely different things.
It is not sufficient that you
guard your heart and be alert
to the attacks of your enemy.
You must…take steps in
the opposite direction,
reshaping your character by
creating new habits
to prevent you from reverting
to your previous ways."*

Observing the Battle

The following Thursday morning, I was back at my desk, completing some paperwork. Unexpectedly, I heard what I thought I recognized as being the same Voice that spoke to me in Dallas.

"Call the pastor's church."

It sounded so loud and clear. However, none of the others sitting near me showed any sign that something unusual had occurred. Concerned about deception from Satan, I looked down at the desk, closed my eyes, and whispered, "Is that You, Holy Spirit?" The response came immediately.

"Yes. Call the pastor's church."

I knew without asking to whom He was referring—the man who had authored *"Battling the Hosts of Hell: Diary of an Exorcist."* I had brought the book with me to review once more over my lunch hour. Still, His command puzzled me, and I thought about it. *I don't know the church's phone number or location.*

Again, knowing my thoughts, the Spirit spoke without hesitation.

"Look on the last page of the book."

At the end of the book were five blank pages where the reader could add notes. Although I had read the book numerous times, I had always closed it when I got through reading the last printed page. For that reason, I had never seen the contact information. In small print at the bottom of the final physical page, I found the name, address, and phone number of the church. Obeying the Spirit, I went into the conference room and closed the door before placing the call.

Greeted by a cheerful voice on the other end of the line, I explained my purpose for calling, "I picked up a copy of your pastor's book recently and read it several times. Does your church ever conduct seminars that are open to those who aren't part of your church?"

"Absolutely," she replied. "In fact, we're holding one right now. Why don't you come and join us?"

Caught off guard at this turn of events, I felt my stomach react. By now, I understood this to be the spiritual realm responding to a new potential threat. The woman, on the other end of the phone, sensed my hesitation and encouraged me further.

"We started this morning, and it lasts all weekend. The cost is only twenty dollars. If you can't afford it, we won't let that stop you from participating. I'm guessing the Holy Spirit is strongly encouraging you, or you wouldn't have called, right?"

"I'm not sure I can get off work on such short notice," I claimed. My more valid concern lay with what to expect if I was actually to go there. It was one thing to deal with things in a room where no one other than the Lord and me were present.

"Folks come here from all over the world," the woman said. "The Holy Spirit gives discernment, showing us exactly how to help each person. Why don't you come and decide for yourself once you've witnessed His loving presence and power?"

Considering what she'd said, I wrote down the directions, telling her I would think about it, and then hung up. Several minutes passed as I hesitated before making the next call. I was uncertain about how my wife would react to the idea of my going away for another extended period. I was positive the subject of this considered trip was one she would find to be frightening and repulsive. To my surprise, when I finally called her, she encouraged me to go. With this hurdle out of the way, I arranged with my employer to have the following afternoon off.

That night I awoke several times in a sweating panic, thankful that my wife had not stirred. Intense pornographic scenes and seductive voices had flooded my dreams. It had been decades since this last occurred. With my heart racing and my body sweating after each incident, I had prayed until peace had come.

In the morning, I threw some clothes into a bag with my gym shoes and kissed my wife goodbye. My thoughts remained unsettled throughout the forty-five-minute ride to the office. I was most worried about what had occurred during the night. Even worse, what troubled me the most was how much it had aroused me.

Those morning hours passed rapidly, and soon, it was time to leave. Several of my peers, noticing that I was taking off early, asked where I was going this time. Uncertain of what to say, I offered as brief a response as possible. "To a church conference," I replied, as I hastened to exit the building to prevent any more questions.

†††

Many hours later, I saw the exit ramp off the Interstate about a mile west of the church. Picking up some dinner at a fast-food restaurant, I checked into the hotel room I had reserved. I was sure that no one would be at church on a Friday night.

When they opened the church doors at seven o'clock the next morning, I was waiting to enter. I heard vacuum cleaners running down several hallways. Men were mopping floors and emptying trash. Two women were setting out trays of donuts and pouring juice into cups in a room off the main hall.

"Are you expecting many people today?" I asked the woman who was setting up the reception table.

"Definitely," she replied. "Saturday crowds are always the biggest. And the Saturday evening service—in which we minister to everyone—always lasts far longer than the Friday night service."

Surprised that there had indeed been a Friday night service, I replied, "This is my first visit. How long was your service last night?"

"We left here at about one o'clock, which is typical for these conferences. That's why we wait and clean up in the morning," the woman said with a laugh.

Amazed, I thought about what she had said. *What in the world could have been happening last night? Why would people want to stay at the church on a Friday night until one in the morning?*

"Have some juice and a donut," she offered. "We'll open the doors to everyone about seven-thirty. The teaching sessions run all day, from eight until five. And then the climax—the Saturday evening service—starts at seven and ends when it ends."

By eight o'clock, hundreds of participants had arrived. They filled every classroom, conference room, and part of the main sanctuary. One-hour class sessions were available through live and video presentations. The instructors covered up to ten different subjects during any given hour. That day's schedule offered thirty different teaching sessions. The pastor encouraged all attendees to move freely from room to room. "You're welcome to sit in on whatever sessions pique your interest. But focus on those subjects that address issues relevant to that with which you now struggle."

At five o'clock, the attendees went to eat dinner. The staff, however, remained at the church. After a quick sandwich, they prepared for the evening service, set to begin two hours later.

† † †

I ate a quick dinner alone, then sat in my car in the church parking lot until the service was about to begin. Upon entering the church, I found every pew tightly filled, as well as the many additional folding chairs set up in the center aisle. Inching my way along the back wall, I found a place to stand in the back corner. Many others, who had likewise arrived too late to get a seat, now leaned elbow-to-elbow against the side and rear walls. The atmosphere in the sanctuary reeked of nervous anticipation.

The service opened with a short prayer. Following an abbreviated period of praise and worship, everyone with a place to sit did so. The pastor made his way to the podium and introduced himself for the sake of all who might not know him. He then invited folks to call out where they lived. As they responded, everyone got an idea of how universal the need was for the help this church staff was offering. Standing in the back corner, I listened with amazement. Dozens of individuals had come from four continents outside of North America. Some traveled as much as twenty-six hours one-way to attend a four-day conference.

Next, the pastor made a statement to help everyone understand how the church operated. "Over the years of this church's ministry, we've documented every deliverance session. We did so at the Holy Spirit's direction, using both audio and video recording. Within days after each service, a group of intercessors and I meet to review the recordings. We look for things not previously seen or experienced. As we do, we remain open to insight and instruction from the Lord. The Holy Spirit identifies the particular demon or demons involved in each situation. He then indicates which part of the Word of God will be most effective against it in the future. What we learned, we have applied, and God has blessed our obedience. He has allowed us, for more than twenty-five years, to be a blessing to tens of thousands of men, women, and children desperate for His help. This church body has been involved in more hours of deliverance ministry than we ever imagined possible. Over that period, we've confronted thousands of demon spirits and kept a list of their names. Once again, this was at the direction of the Holy Spirit. These we then broke down into demonic groups. Examples of these groups are: Religions, Lusts, Illnesses and Infirmities, and so on."

"Over the first hour or so of this service, I will lift my heart and voice to the Lord on your behalf. I'll do so as a continuous petition to Father God to reveal to each of you those spirits that may be troubling you. Your part in this is to be genuinely open to the prompting of the Holy Spirit. Be alert to any stirring, reaction, or pricking of your heart or mind by any spirit I name. If this occurs, I encourage you to ask the Holy Spirit about it immediately. When you do, be willing to hear the truth, and He will answer you. Ask Him to forgive you, and renounce any ungodly ties you may have allowed to form with that spirit. Hang loose then until I finish with this first part, and then we'll begin evicting those demon spirits. Okay?" Some of the crowd responded with a subdued, "Yes." Others said nothing.

With that out of the way, the pastor began praying his way through the lists of spirits. The crowd grew more and more restless. When he had finished, he paused for several minutes to drink some water. At his signal, the illumination from the overhead lighting increased, eliminating all shadows. The technicians controlling the sound system turned up the volume. Afterward, the pastor moved back to the microphone.

"How many of you know what's next?" he asked with a smile. A mixed response came from various parts of the church. Some smiled, but others seemed ready to flee. "What I'm going to do now is read back through the same list, but this time, I'll command each spirit noted on the list to manifest if they are present in this sanctuary. If you're truly open to God's help, I promise you that they will respond."

"There are eighty loving, well-trained members of this body spread out among you. So, relax. Focus your heart and mind on the Lord. He is the Deliverer. We are here at the Lord's direction to help you, and we'll do so if you'll let us. If we see signs of your reacting to any of the spirits I've named, someone will quickly assist."

The pastor began commanding the demonic realm in the name of Jesus Christ—and all hell broke loose. Demon spirits in some people started screaming. Other individuals stood, rigid, covering their ears in an attempt to block out the pastor's voice. Many bent over or fell to their knees, holding their abdomens, dry heaving, or coughing up phlegm. One by one, the spirits they had been harboring or fellowshipping with fled, and peace came. Several individuals bolted for the doors, hoping to escape. Ministry team members calmly stopped them, sat them down in a pew or on the floor, and proceeded to help them. A few individuals grew angry. The spirits in them responded by urging the person to curse everyone and everything. On one side of the church, spirits of Rage manifested in two men sitting near each other. Within minutes, a fight broke out.

In all cases, those doing the ministering remained peaceful and loving. They worked with more and more attendees, seemingly unfazed by what was going on around them.

In the back corner, I stood very still, staring wide-eyed at a scene that was unlike anything I had ever seen or could have imagined. At the same time, I struggled to present a calm demeanor until a voice spoke to me—a voice that did not come from any person near me.

"Stay very still, and no one will ever suspect anything."

Overwhelmed by what was occurring around me, and now to me, I reacted. A spirit of Fear urged me to make my way slowly toward the rear doors. When I saw an opening, I slipped outside before anyone could stop me.

Returning to my hotel room, I sat there on the bed through most of the night, thinking about what I had seen. I was unwilling to turn out the lights. Too distracted to read my Bible, my mind never even considered praying. Sometime early Sunday morning, I gave in to exhaustion but awoke a few hours later with a pounding headache.

In the clarity of daylight, I thought about the night before and knew I had overreacted. After checking out of my hotel room, I drove back to the church. I had decided to attend the Sunday morning service before driving home. *Folks will dress in their Sunday clothes and all,* I thought to myself on the way to the church. *It is bound to be less crowded and more reserved than last night.*

Are You SURE God's Not Talking? (Or Are You Just NOT Listening?)

Forty minutes after the service started, the pastor finished his abbreviated sermon to the standing-room-only crowd. He then solicited testimony from those helped through the conference. For more than an hour, one individual after another stood and spoke. The emotion-filled statements moved the hearts of those hearing and identifying with them. Meanwhile, an undercurrent of mumbling and restlessness grew in the room. When the testifying ended, the pastor made an announcement.

"We're going to conclude the service the way we always do for these conferences. We are going to play a video of our former pastor, who has gone on to be with the Lord. He is the one to whom the Lord spoke, setting this church body on the path it has maintained ever since. His wife made the recording a few months before he passed. It is nothing more than a video of him playing and singing love songs to Jesus. I pray that his passion for his Savior, Healer, Deliverer, and Lord will leave a lasting impact on your heart."

On a big-screen television elevated on the platform, the video began. The first segment showed Pastor Worley singing. Tears flowed unashamedly down his face. A man seated nearer to the front of the sanctuary sprang to his feet as a spirit in him began cursing the pastor's image. A moment later, he threw his Bible toward the television, followed by everything else he could grab, including other people's Bibles, songbooks, and finally, his shoes. Throughout this sequence of events, the demon spirit in him continued to scream and curse.

Several men finally encircled him as others vacated the pew to allow access to the man. Gently restraining him, they moved the man into the nearest aisle, where they helped him to the floor so he would not hurt himself or others and began ministering to him. Meanwhile, spirits began manifesting in many other individuals throughout the sanctuary. More deliverance team members stepped forward to help them.

Troubled by what was happening around me, I closed my eyes, trying to fix my mind on the Lord. A few minutes later, a petite woman seated next to me tapped my shoulder. I opened my eyes and turned my head to look at her.

"I've wanted to come here for twelve years," she stated. "I've been getting their monthly cassette tapes by mail, and they helped. But, it's nothing like being here in person, is it?"

I shook my head in agreement, not quite knowing what else to say. Facing forward again, I closed my eyes and refocused on the Lord. Several minutes later, the same woman interrupted me again.

"I love Jesus so much, and I have to tell somebody! I hope you don't mind."

This time I gave her a slight grin, and said nothing. I then turned away once more. In my thoughts, though, I knew irritation had arisen, causing me to hesitate to pray. Unexpectedly, anger toward her surfaced, goaded on by a demon spirit's voice.

"The lady is a real pain in the ass, isn't she?"

What I was experiencing baffled me. I found myself wanting to agree with the voice, even though I knew it was not of God. Moments later, the woman tapped my shoulder again. In my confusion, resentment and bitterness toward the woman guided my emotions. At the same time, I heard the other voice a second time.

"Ignore her. She's a nuisance. Focus on yourself."

I hesitated, but a spirit of Confusion goaded me. I ignored the woman, despite her persistent tapping on my shoulder. Finally, I spun around to face her and stared at her with such anger that it baffled me when I later thought about it. Unfazed by my reaction, she said, "You know, I love my husband so much for finally letting me come here. He's such a good man and an excellent husband."

I knew I should have offered her an encouraging reply. Instead, I found it a struggle in my mind to hold back an incomprehensible rage. Without even acknowledging her comment, I turned away and closed my eyes. I focused my efforts on regaining control over my emotions, thoughts, and actions. What disturbed me most was why these emotions had arisen at all. In my mental turmoil, I could not understand my harsh reaction toward the woman.

Moments later, a deep masculine voice screamed vulgarities. When I turned to look, I saw it was coming from the throat of the same woman. She now stood on the pew next to me with clenched, uplifted fists, her face red, as Rage identified itself as the one controlling her. This spirit, manifesting through her, continued to curse her husband. Another demonic voice announced itself as being Murder and declared its intent to *murder* her husband for allowing her to come to this place. Troubled by what I was seeing and hearing, I gladly moved away, making room for several women to minister to her.

As I sat off to the side, I became very still. At that moment, I felt as if I had dual personalities, each struggling to maintain control over me. As I saw the others helping the woman, one part of me was desperate for someone to help me also. Another side of me felt a Controlling spirit manipulating my mind and body to prevent exposure of the demonic realm's influence over me at that moment.

A short while later, I left the church, and within minutes was on my way down the Interstate. As I drove along, I pondered all that I had witnessed over the weekend. Then the Holy Spirit interrupted my thoughts.

"Son, do you realize what happened between you and the woman sitting next to you? Your attitude and responses to her triggered what you saw."

"I didn't mean to be that way, Lord. Something else influenced my thoughts and emotions."

"*Exactly, and those spirits, affecting you, stirred up another group controlling the woman. Many at that church would have willingly ministered to you also. Fear's prompting caused you to flee. Son, I did not encourage you to come here to observe My Spirit freeing others, only for you to leave unchanged. There are those in this body uniquely qualified to help you, and then to train you to help others. However, as I told you before, you must truly desire My help."*

"Go home to your bride, who eagerly awaits you. Be patient with her, even as I am patient with you. Know that I will ask you to return many times to this church in the future. There is much work to be done, and the sooner we get started on it, the better."

Personally Impacted

Arriving home, I answered several of my wife's questions about the weekend but offered nothing more. She seemed delighted that I had *enjoyed* myself. Still, she backed away from any further discussion, claiming to have other things she needed to do.

Mid-morning the following Saturday, she found me digging through boxes in the garage. I was looking for the materials I had stored away many years earlier at her request. She didn't ask what I was doing. I did not explain, and she retraced her steps back to the kitchen. I opted to listen to an eight-hour teaching series by Derek Prince. I grabbed my sound-deadening headphones and headed to the barn. I knew it would take a full day to mow and trim our yard, so I figured I could listen and learn while doing so.

I finished up as dusk turned to dark. After putting all of the equipment away in the barn, I took a quick shower. Long after my wife and children were in bed, I remained alone on the front porch, drinking iced tea. Tired but not sleepy, I thought about all I had heard on the cassette tapes. When I finally climbed into bed, I lay awake for hours, praying and asking the Holy Spirit to show me what was next.

My wife remained quiet over the next six days. I was almost hesitant to ask why for fear it would result in another argument. I kept busy every spare minute, once again reading and studying the materials from the box in the garage.

On Saturday, two weeks after my solo trip to that church at the Spirits' urging, my wife approached me when I was working alone, pulling weeds in our garden.

"I've watched you since you came back from Dallas," she said hesitantly. "I can't deny that something has made a big difference in you. It's obvious that you're changing, and it's a change for the better. I'll admit to you that I don't understand this deliverance stuff, and it scares me. I've been praying about it, though, and the Holy Spirit wants me to go to that church with you. Honestly, I don't know how I'll react, or if I'll be able to handle it. Even so, if you want to drive there tomorrow for their Sunday morning service, I'm willing."

Afraid of my enthusiasm scaring her off, I pulled her toward me and held her in a long embrace. As I stood there, I asked the Lord in my mind and heart if this was what He wanted. He didn't hesitate in replying in the affirmative. I hugged my wife even harder while silently giving thanks to the Lord.

† † †

Leaving very early the next morning, the two of us and our three youngest children set out on the long drive north. We arrived at the church about fifteen minutes before the start of the service. I guided them inside, ushering them into a pew in the center aisle near the front. I looked around at the half-filled church and grew concerned. I thought to myself, *Should I have waited for the next scheduled conference to bring them? If I had, they would have then seen more of what I saw.*

As the pastor came to the lectern to begin his sermon, the Holy Spirit interrupted his thoughts. He stood there on the platform, looking down at the floor for several minutes, unmoving. Sensing that their pastor was listening to the Lord, the people remained still while waiting. Finally, having a clear understanding of what the Spirit wanted, he looked at the audience with a visible sadness in his face and explained.

"I had a sermon prepared for today, but the Holy Spirit wants this service to go in another direction. You who are members of this body have given of yourselves for hours on end, week after week, blessing untold thousands who the Lord has sent to us. During the conference two weeks ago, we saw the Holy Spirit move more than ever before. Hundreds from around the world returned home changed, with new hope for a glorious future. That was possible because of how generous you've been in working with the Holy Spirit to set the captives free."

"Yet, I stand here now, looking at you all—my wife included—through the Holy Spirit's perspective. He is allowing me to see how tired and run down you are in body and soul. I know there is not one of you who will complain about it or even readily acknowledge it, but that does not mean it isn't so. There is an inherent danger in this, as the Lord has warned us so many times in the past. When we are physically exhausted, we are more subject to attack from our enemy. Some of you look to have lost your joy, and I am not criticizing or condemning you when I say that. Rather, it is an acknowledgment that I have neglected my primary obligation to shepherd this body, to be aware of the needs and vulnerabilities of this body, and to respond. I have been so involved in helping the endless streams of people coming here, that I forgot this. So, first of all, I apologize and ask your forgiveness."

Some in the audience called out, "We forgive you, pastor." As I glanced around at the others, most were nodding, acknowledging the truth in what he was saying. A few stared down at the floor, somewhat disconnected and unresponsive.

"So, the Holy Spirit told me to dispense with the sermon. We are going to minister to one another, as well as any guests we may have here today. I urge you to be open to anything with which you have not yet dealt. Be alert for spirits that may have latched onto you while you were busy freeing so many others. Allow the Holy Spirit to move in and through you. He will bring us release and a refreshing that we all need right now."

The pastor began a shortened version of the renunciation prayers. Next, he commanded spirits to manifest and identify themselves. His focus was on those that the Holy Spirit brought to his heart and mind. Within just a few minutes, it became evident how right the Lord had been, as many in the church began to grow restless. Without warning, one of the lay leaders bolted from the pew, running for the side door, as the troubled spirit drove him to escape. Several of the men stopped the man, and others gathered around to help. As the pastor continued praying, dozens more began to manifest in various ways. Others responded to assist these also.

While this was going on, my family and I sat unmoving, observing what was occurring all around us. Our children were wide-eyed in wonder, never having seen anything like this before. My eight-year-old daughter snuggled into my side, uncertain of what was occurring. Further to my right, I overheard my wife and older daughter refusing one offer after another for prayer.

Meanwhile, I had scooted to the front edge of my seat and sat staring at the floor. When I glanced at my son, mid-way down the pew, I noticed him acting extremely nervous and chewing his fingernails. As the pastor continued speaking, I found myself struggling to maintain control. The manifestations in my body were becoming ever more evident. Both of my hands gripped the back of the pew in front of me so firmly that my fingers ached. My body began jerking and pulsating. Speaking to whatever was causing this reaction in me, I demanded, "No! No! Stop!"

One of the church members, a man ten years my junior, slipped into the pew next to me. He rested his hand on my shoulder and spoke into my ear.

"The Father loves you, brother, and so do I, and we're going to help you."

At the mention of the Father's love, the spirits wrestling for control reacted in violence. I honestly do not recall what happened to me next. I can only tell you what the pastor, several men who ministered to me, as well as my wife and children said, hours later. That which they described, I confirmed at a future date by watching the video footage, which was very unsettling and hard to do.

As other men moved to encompass me, all hell erupted. Those spirits controlling me caused me to kick and fight to break loose of their holds. Through me, they cursed everyone who came near me. Because of my size, more men joined the effort, moving me into the center aisle and onto the floor. Hour after hour, they ministered to me. The spirits caused me to scream and jerk as they tried to free my body from the men who were restraining me. For a while, the resistance to their efforts was overwhelming for those men. The spirits' combined strength arched my back repeatedly and thrashed my body from side to side. After more than two hours, not much had changed. At one point, the spirits controlling me overheard my wife talking to the pastor.

"He has a list in his shirt pocket of things the Lord's been trying to address in him," she stated. She referred to the list I had written down weeks earlier at the Spirit's leading while I was in Dallas.

Upon hearing this, the evil spirits reacted in a rage. They screamed at, cursed, and threatened my wife and all who were ministering to me. Several more men joined the others in restraining me. Still, the spirits began digging my heels into the carpeted floor and propelling my body backward. Foot-by-foot, I drew ever closer to the doors at the end of the aisle.

Meanwhile, having pulled the list out of my pocket, the pastor read it. Taking the lead, he began addressing the spirits by name and nature. One at a time, the strongholds started to break. Non-stop spasms of coughing, retching, dry-heaving, and violent shaking racked my body. The pastor and the seven other men continued working as a well-trained team. Together, they freed me from the control of hundreds of spirits.

I had assumed our trip would be a general introduction for my family to the subject of deliverance. Six hours after entering the church, they finished ministering to me. The pastor prayed for a heavenly peace to settle over me and watched as the Spirit honored his request. I sat there, sobbing, at the very back of the church. The spirits had lifted and propelled my restrained body the hundred-foot length of the aisle. Perspiration saturated my underwear and outer clothes. Every muscle burned from the hours of exertion while the spirits tried to break me loose. My previous attitude of false self-confidence was gone. Brokenness, genuine humility, and sincere gratitude were now evident in my actions and demeanor.

The pastor and I sat alone for an extended time as he spoke with me. He explained what had just occurred over the previous six hours. I listened and wept. The pastor then spoke to me with a tenderness I had never before experienced. He asked me how I thought the various groupings of spirits had gained such a stronghold over me. Sensing the presence of God's love emanating from the pastor, I felt safe to let down my guard. For the first time, I spoke of the sexual assault I endured as a young boy. That incident was something I had never revealed to anyone, including my parents and wife.

I recounted the fears, insecurities, and shame originating from the attack. I told the pastor how the demons seemed to overwhelm my mind and imagination with vivid sexual thoughts by day. Nightmares of the assault caused broken sleep for years. I confessed to that pastor how desperate I was to escape what was occurring. Hoping to feel more accepted, I had joined in with a large group of boys and girls in our neighborhood. These were both pre-teens, as I was at the time, as well as older teens nearing adulthood. Later, I had discovered their brazen involvement in witchcraft and all types of sexual promiscuity. Threatened and pressured by the older teens, I had promised to tell no one. Instead, I became like them. By the time I'd reached my teen years, there was little in the sexual realm that I had not seen or experienced. In my later teen years, I'd begun drinking and developed a fascination with the occult, reading everything I could find on the subject.

After listening without interrupting me, the pastor revealed that a majority of the spirits cast out of me had involved Lust or Sexual Perversion of one sort or another. He prayed with me, asking the Holy Spirit to fill those areas of my soul that the Lord set free that day. The pastor then gave me a strong warning to be alert to any attempt by Satan's demons to reclaim their former influence over me. He urged me to call upon the name of Jesus Christ should this occur. Additionally, he said to plead the Lord's cleansing blood over my body and soul daily, or even hourly, if necessary. He further encouraged me to study the Word of God, non-stop. He said I needed to use Scripture to halt the influence of Satan over my mind and imagination. Next, he gave me a list of hundreds of Scripture references, circling those pertinent to my situation. Last of all, he suggested I inquire of the Holy Spirit daily about any other spiritual influences my enemy might still have over me. "Address them as soon as possible—on your own, if you're able, or by returning to this church in the future," he said.

After hugging and thanking everyone for all they had done in helping me that day, my family and I headed home.

For more than an hour, no one in the car spoke. My wife watched out the side window most of the way home. Our older daughter did the same in the rear seat. After thirty more minutes, my youngest daughter leaned forward. She then said, "Daddy, when you got mad, you almost kicked me in the head, and you were cussing a LOT! You said some REALLY bad words!"

On hearing this from my little girl, the tears began flowing down my cheeks once more. She reached her small hand forward, wiped the tears from my face, and said, "It's all right, Daddy. I love you, and Jesus will help you."

It was at that very moment that I determined to do whatever was necessary to allow God to free me from any remaining evil. However, despite the hours of ministry I had experienced, I had no concept of what the future held, or understanding that this was only the beginning. I had finished the first battle in what was to be a prolonged war to free and restore my soul, followed by training to teach me to help others.

"Do you understand that you created the opening for the stronghold to exist when you repeatedly dwelt on it? Do you further see how your foolish actions of proclaiming your thoughts aloud provided an opportunity for a demon spirit to come into agreement with you?"

Coming Alongside

While in prayer the following week, the Holy Spirit brought up the Saturday men's prayer group. Many of the remaining twelve continued to attend regularly. They all were enthusiastic about the direction in which the Spirit seemed to be leading us. Most sensed that God was bringing us into unity for a purpose. Until that point, none of us had yet figured out what that purpose might be. Nevertheless, the Holy Spirit chose that day to explain that He was going to bring about a dramatic change in our group. He also spoke of how vital it was that this shift in focus began with His ministry to me through the deliverance team. Still, I had not yet revealed anything to the others concerning what I had experienced.

Weeks after that, in Gods' perfect timing, my wife and I received a mailing from that same church. It was the announcement of the next weekend deliverance conference scheduled for mid-October. I had returned there to gain more help on two of the previous three Sundays and saw no reason to visit again so soon. However, my wife then surprised me by asking if we could attend the conference.

"Since the last time we went there," she said, "I've been seeking the Lord's will in this for me. I know there are persistent habits that I still can't break despite years of struggle. When I ask the Lord, He keeps telling me I need to return there and ask for help. He said I'd then know how to join with you in helping others."

Two weeks later, we made the trip north. By this time, I had become much more receptive to the daily help from the Holy Spirit. He exposed issue after issue to the light of truth. I would confess and renounce my association with, or tolerance of, each spirit. When I then invited the Lord to move on my behalf as my Deliverer, He freed me from their clutches.

For my wife, it was a different story. Up to that point, she had observed what had occurred to me but had not experienced anything herself. Now, the closer we came to that church, the more nervous and irritable she became. She and I both understood why.

"It's as if we've upset the demonic realm," she said. "They know the Lord is about to set me free in areas in which I've allowed them control for years."

On Thursday, mid-morning on the first day of the conference, my family and I sat in a classroom. We were watching a video presentation on various forms of fear. While the video continued playing, the Holy Spirit spoke to me about a fearfulness that had been overshadowing me since my early twenties.

I recalled the day my mom had told my siblings and me about the hole the doctors had discovered in my dad's heart. The specialist had encouraged my dad to schedule surgery as soon as possible. The alternative was his having an estimated ten years to live. At that time, my dad was working two and sometimes three jobs to support our large family. He had worried endlessly about what would happen if he didn't make it through the operation. As a result, he had postponed the surgery until well into the tenth year following the warning. By then, the four oldest of us children had graduated and left home. Only my four youngest siblings were still living at home—all who were by then in their teens. Because of my dad's stress level, the surgery had not gone well, with him experiencing a massive stroke while undergoing corrective heart surgery.

My wife and I had visited him in the Intensive Care Unit following the surgery, and his condition shocked me. I could hardly recognize the man who lay before me. My dad appeared to have aged twenty years in a couple of days.

These many years later, the Lord prompted me to recall that hospital scene. As I did, sitting very still and listening, the Holy Spirit spoke to me about it.

"Do you remember standing there watching your dad in the Intensive Care Unit? Do you recall the thought that was on the forefront of your mind?"

"Yes. It both saddened and worried me. My father's hair had turned completely white. He looked so old and helpless. I remember thinking, 'He's only in his early fifties. I'm only thirty years younger than he is. What if this happens to me in thirty years?'"

Then the Holy Spirit responded. *"At the time, you had not yet come to accept Jesus as your personal Savior, but I was there nonetheless. I was watching over you and your dad, aware of what was going through your heart and mind."*

The Holy Spirit then allowed me to see for the first time the extent to which that situation had affected me. Here now in this conference, twenty years in the future, my subconscious replayed every detail of that visit. As I recalled it all, the fear related to that event returned like a suffocating hand.

"Yes, son," the Holy Spirit said. *"Now you're beginning to understand. You did more than think about it at length. You voiced that fear to your wife and others, using those exact words, and dwelt on it for months. As a result, a genuine spirit of fear— Fear of Heart Problems—latched hold of you. That demon prompted your recall of that hospital scene each time you thought of your dad. When you accepted Jesus as Savior, the Lord set you free from this spirit's hold. Over time, however, that spirit regained a stronghold on your mind. Now every time you experience unexplained pain, it prompts you to worry about the health of your heart. Do you understand that you created the*

opening for the stronghold to exist? How? By dwelling on it, and foolishly proclaiming your misguided thoughts aloud. Do you see how this provided an opportunity for that demon spirit to come into agreement with you?"

I had no reason to do anything other than to acknowledge the truth of what the Lord had said. I knew I did not want to wait any longer before confronting this spirit for a final time. I closed my eyes and whispered to the Holy Spirit. "Lord, forgive me for allowing my enemy to influence my soul. Would you please free me from this fear, and fill that place in me with Your love?"

There was no outward physical manifestation. I felt a release of pressure followed by lightness and joy more magnificent than anything I had felt in many years. I turned to my wife and smiled, and with tear-filled eyes, whispered, "It's gone! It's truly gone!"

"What?" she asked.

"A fear of dying at a young age from heart problems," I said, and then went on to tell her about it. When I had finished explaining, we hugged and rejoiced, thanking the Lord together. Even as I did, I could see in my wife's eyes that something was weighing heavy on her heart. Still, she had not yet reached the point where she felt up to speaking about it.

† † †

The hours seemed to speed by day after day, as we continued to learn. We gained a Biblical understanding of the ways of the Holy Spirit as well as of Satan's demonic host and their methods. We also learned our responsibility in preventing and correcting these situations. Soon enough, the Saturday evening service came. My family and I arrived at the church early enough to get seats near the front.

By now, we were familiar with the pastor's usual routine. This time there was no massive disturbance in my soul. Nor did any explosion of fear-generated anger pour forth from me. Instead, for two hours, I found myself sitting on the end of a pew, watching and praying in my prayer language for my wife. Several women ministered to her where she lay on the floor in the center aisle. As the Spirit gave them discernment, they addressed various issues. I watched with joy as they joined with the Holy Spirit in setting her free. When none of the women discerned anything further, the one who had taken the lead turned to me. Knowing that I was her husband, she asked, "Is there anything else you're aware of that we need to address?"

"Yes," I replied, without hesitating. "My wife's been complaining about having trouble hearing with her right ear. This difficulty happens most often when she is in church, listening to our pastor's preaching. Her dad is deaf in the same ear."

Despite the surrounding noise, the demon that was influencing my wife overheard me. The spirit jerked her head sideways, as the now rage-filled eyes stared at me. The demonic spirit began to thrash her body around on the floor, trying to get her free. The women helping her now struggled to restrain her. The one who had sought my input began looking in nearby pews for a bottle of anointing oil to apply to my wife's ear.

Meanwhile, the influencing spirit grew more disturbed and violent. The other four women were losing the battle in their attempt to hold her still. Praying as I watched this, I finally moved to obey the prompting of the Spirit. While my wife was looking in the opposite direction, I knelt next to her, speaking to her and the spirit in a loud voice.

"We're going to anoint your ear with oil. Then we'll command this generational curse and spirit of deafness, in the name of Jesus Christ, to release its hold on your body."

I reached my hand toward her right ear. The controlling spirit swung her face toward me, glaring at me with what I knew were not my wife's eyes. It then caused her to begin lunging and biting at my hand. Avoiding her mouth, I slipped my hand underneath her hair. Touching the ear, as the Holy Spirit had directed me, I began praying aloud in my spirit language. I knew there was no anointing oil on my hand. Even so, the spirit of Deafness let out a blood-curdling scream through her in a roar.

"IT'S BURNING! IT'S BURNING! GET IT OFF OF ME!"

Surprised by this reaction, the women intensified and focused their prayer. After a few minutes of this, the team leader rejoined the others, resuming the lead in ministry. Next, she gave a final command to the spirit of Deafness to release his hold on my wife's body. With a prolonged gagging cough, it departed, and her body relaxed. After a few moments, the other women helped her sit up. They began testing the hearing in that ear by covering her unaffected ear while one of them spoke to her in a whisper from behind her. The ability to hear with the ear they had prayed for was now unrestricted. As everyone praised Jesus for freeing her, a peace settled over my wife. A couple of the women helped her to her feet, and they each took a turn in hugging her. The leader of the group sat with my wife for a while in one of the pews, talking and praying with her. She also gave her follow-up instruction from the word of God.

Finally, my wife had experienced first-hand what I had been trying to explain to her for weeks. Now, I knew she comprehended.

At the Lord's prompting, our family returned to that church many times over the next four years. Each time we received more ministry for ourselves. Also, the leadership at that church trained us to minister to others whom the Spirit might lead our way.

The Lord then urged me to invite individuals and couples we knew to attend future conferences with us. Over those same four years, more than thirty persons made the trip. Most marveled at the difference between those ministering and those receiving ministry. The deliverance teams maintained a loving, patient attitude with each person they helped. The contrast between this and the angry, challenging nature of the demons was shocking to them.

Those who went there with a genuine openness to getting free in some areas of their souls received much help. When leaving that place, they also never failed to rejoice at how peaceful and joyful they felt. After those weekends, my wife and I would discreetly observe them for weeks. With most, the initial change following deliverance ministry was still visible. This visible evidence indicated to us that they had retained their freedom from the spirits that had previously plagued them. This result did not come simply by their **claiming** they were trusting in God. Instead, it was **because of their actions** in response to believing in the promises of God.

Even so, a few had reacted with great anger and resentment. One couple had created quite a scene at the church, arguing and snapping at anyone who offered to pray for them. They never considered that their very reactions were a good indicator of a problem. They were hostile to the loving-kindness the church team members demonstrated. A short time later, they left for home without saying goodbye to any of our group. On another trip, a different couple, repulsed by what they had seen, reacted in an even stronger way. They separated themselves from those at our church who had also attended the conference that weekend. Eventually, the enemy of their souls convinced them to change to another church, thereby escaping any future perceived threat through us.

Back at the Saturday men's prayer group, some of the remaining men had been studying me. Their curiosity grew over many months as they noticed how I had changed. Little by little, they began asking questions. It was then that the Holy Spirit told me to invite those interested in attending the next conference with me as a group. Three men joined me in attending the April conference. A fourth man, a brother-in-law to one of the three, lived near that church at the time, and he met us there. The pattern for that weekend was the same as for previous conferences. However, only two of the four men were open to and received abundant help.

The one man's brother-in-law received no help that weekend. Nevertheless, what he heard and saw left a significant impact on him. He knew he needed to begin addressing the tremendous turmoil that reigned in his soul, which he had kept hidden for decades. At the Holy Spirit's later prompting, he made a life-changing decision. He quit his job in Chicago and moved six hours south near his sister's family. There he hoped to find help by joining our Saturday men's prayer group.

Meanwhile, my son and one son-in-law, as well as the sons of other men in the group, began joining us. Additionally, the Holy Spirit sent other men our way, and the group grew.

† † †

Each Saturday, our gathering still started with worship and extended periods of prayer. Everyone was willing to wait on the Holy Spirit to set the theme and agenda for the day. Not a Saturday went by without some in the group asking questions of the men who had attended the last conference. While most were eager to know and learn, these discussions noticeably bothered a few others. Over time, many of the men in the group—but not all—made the trip north.

Those who did so invariably returned home with an altered perspective on the spiritual realm, which the Holy Spirit honored during many Saturday gatherings that followed. As they were willing to change and grow, the Lord searched each man's heart and soul. Only the Spirit knew what needed addressing. He prodded men about things in their lives that they intentionally overlooked. He questioned long-standing behaviors that went unchallenged. He also spotlighted deep-seated strongholds and fears. The men worked together following His lead, helping one another through prayer and deliverance.

Then the day arrived when the Spirit moved in everyone in a far more profound way than at any previous time. He opened our hearts and minds to consider other possibilities beyond our group. We talked about this for weeks, and yet we remained quite uncertain of what the Spirit wanted.

Laborer vs. Co-Laborer

For months, the Holy Spirit urged those of us in the Saturday morning prayer group to take a specific action. We were to offer what He had taught us about deliverance to the world waiting outside the four walls of that pole barn. Still, we hesitated. It was not that we doubted our personal experiences in this realm. Neither had we decided to ignore the Lord's promptings. We understood that there was a universal need, but we were not quite sure how, or where, or to whom we were to take it. We spent an increasing amount of time as a group praying about this. In response, the Lord answered our prayers by bringing a visitor to join us.

As with any first-timer, we warmly welcomed him. One of the men then explained to him the basic guidelines by which our group operated. There was no pecking order, and everyone was free to follow what he felt the Lord urging him to say or do. Even so, with that freedom came a responsibility that the group upheld. We would always wait upon the Spirit for confirmation.

With that out of the way, everyone in the room returned to worshipping the Lord. After a short while, it was evident to most of us that the new man had something stirring in his heart. Prior experience had taught us, however, to wait until he volunteered the reason for his coming—and we did not have long to wait.

"I'm here because I need help for my wife, myself, and our marriage," he began. "I don't know where else to turn. I've talked with my pastor for almost a year about our situation. He prays with me again and again, but nothing's changed, and I'm getting desperate."

One of the other men in the room asked him, "How can we help?"

"My wife has terminal cancer," he replied. There was a long pause before he continued. "Her doctors have treated her for over a year with chemotherapy. Now they say they can't do anything else for her because she doesn't want to live. It's frustrating because they're right! She keeps on attempting suicide." Tears were now flowing down his face. "Shortly after they discovered cancer, she started hearing voices. She says they tell her they're waiting for her last breath—that she has no chance of surviving this." Pausing for a few minutes, he wiped his face with his sleeves. The rest of us waited for him to continue, praying for strength for him and direction from the Holy Spirit.

"She hasn't left the house on her own in a very long time. She doesn't even go to church anymore. If not for me opening the blinds and drapes, they would never be open in our house. I took her to the hospital for each round of chemotherapy. Now I drive her to the follow-up visits at the oncology center. She hides her face as she rushes to get inside the car, and then she tells me to drive away quickly. She doesn't want any of our neighbors to see her. They ask me about her, but she gets furious if I tell them anything. I love her, but feel so helpless and angry. Lately, I get so little sleep. It's affecting my work a lot, and now I'm worried about losing my job."

He paused and wiped the tears from his eyes while glancing around the room at each of our faces. From a heart filled with compassion, one of the men said, "You're here today for a reason, brother. The Holy Spirit Himself sent you our way, and our Father in heaven will be faithful." Several of the others looked into the newcomer's eyes, nodding in agreement with what the other man had said.

Sensing a spark of hope for the first time in a long time, the man took a deep breath and continued speaking. "She used to be so beautiful and so full of joy, so full of life compared to how she is now," he said, looking at the man in the room who had invited him. "A year or so ago, at church, you saw her. She was happy then. And now—." He stared at the floor, weeping for several minutes before continuing.

Tears filled the eyes of a few of those in the room. The Holy Spirit was stirring His compassion in our spirits for this man and woman.

"She no longer wears makeup," he continued. "She won't even comb her hair. She says she can't look in a mirror. She sees faces. Hideous faces! They torment her, cursing at her, telling her she belongs to them, that it won't be long before she is dead." The woman's husband was now sobbing continuously, overwhelmed by brokenness.

"The insurance won't cover the expenses for much longer. The doctors have given up on her and sent her home to die. I take her to the oncology center once a week so they can check her, but she's always trying to end her life, and she was almost successful twice. Every few weeks, I have to call for an ambulance to rush her to the emergency room. Time after time, she slashes her left arm with a knife, and I find her sitting in a pool of her blood, begging me to let her go." Now thoroughly despondent, he stared at the floor, trying to calm his emotions.

"I don't know what else to do or where to turn," he said. "I've had the pastor and elders and many others at our church praying for her, but nothing's happening. I cry out to God day and night, but it's like He's not listening."

"This brother here," he nodded again toward the one who had invited him. "He said there's a possibility that we're dealing with more than a disease. I agree, and I mentioned this to our pastor a while ago. All he ever says is, 'I'll be praying.' I told him I was coming here today, and he tried to talk me out of it. I can't handle this anymore, and I'm hoping –." His voice trailed off again. He sat there, slumped over, staring at his feet.

As a body, we moved from our seats to surround him, our hands resting on him as we prayed. The visitor sat in quiet as we sought the Father above for His direction. Tears pooling in the bags under his eyes overflowed onto his cheeks. A few men prayed aloud in English. Most of us prayed in our spirit language. We waited for the Lord to communicate to our spirits what the Father desired in this situation.

After a lengthy period, everyone grew still, and an undeniable peace came into the room. It became evident that the Spirit had conveyed His heart to each man's spirit, and one of the men spoke forth confirmation.

"I desire to show Myself strong for the sake of this couple. Are you willing to go forth co-laboring, with Me as Deliverer, to set this woman free?"

The Holy Spirit elaborated further, directing us to go to the couple's home early the following Saturday morning. The husband suggested 8:30. Everyone else agreed to gather at the barn ninety minutes before that for prayer. Each of us also promised to be in prayer throughout the week, listening for the leading from the Spirit. We needed the Lord's input about which of us were, or were not, to take part in ministering to the wife. When the morning ended, the husband returned home with a glimmer of new hope in his spirit.

A day later, the Holy Spirit spoke to the man who had invited the husband, directing him to place a call to his—and that couple's—pastor. The Lord did not want us to move in this situation without the blessing and covering of the couple's pastor. When he called him, he explained to the pastor what had happened on Saturday, and asked for the pastor's blessing and covering for what would occur the following week. The pastor said he would pray about it and get back with him in a day or two.

When the pastor called back, it was to say that he and several of his elders would go with us to the couple's home. The man welcomed his pastor's participation. He also invited him and the elders to meet with the men in the prayer group at the pole barn, before going to the couple's home. We wanted to pray together for unity and clear direction from the Spirit on how He wanted us to proceed.

On Saturday, all of the men arrived early, as they had promised. Together, we lifted our focused prayer to the Father. Before long, several of us from the prayer group revealed what the Spirit had spoken to us. There seemed to be understanding and acceptance among everyone present as to the leading of the Spirit.

The Holy Spirit had impressed upon the spirits of many of us that morning the passage in 1st Chronicles 20: 20-25. There, Israel used a unique strategy against their enemy that involved sending the singers and musicians to the battle in front of the armed soldiers. As these singers and musicians sang and praised God, the Lord supernaturally moved. That day, using God's plan, they saw their enemy defeated.

The Lord wanted the same method used against the enemies we would encounter. The word from the Lord was short and precise. *"You will not see victory through your exhibition of might or power. Neither will your many words or great determination produce it. Rather, it comes by My Spirit. I will move through your praise, worship, and sincere thanksgiving."*

Ten of us loaded into two cars—five from the Saturday group, the pastor, and four of his elders. We arrived at the couple's home twenty minutes later and gathered outside of the two cars. The pastor announced that he and his men would take the lead, representing the church. The five of us from the prayer group exchanged glances. We then agreed to defer leadership in this situation to the pastor and his elders.

The husband had told his wife that a few people, including their pastor, would be coming by to pray for her. When he opened the door to greet us, she watched as the ten men entered their home. The spirits inside of her reacted to what they knew to be a significant threat. They drove her to flee to the far side of the living room. There she cowered in the corner by the fireplace—cursing, hissing, and roaring at us as the spirits reacted through her body.

Knowing that the situation might get noisy, the husband had closed the house windows. He had also switched on the air conditioning, turned on the living room lamps, and kept the drapes shut. Turning on a portable CD player we had brought with us, all ten of us began to worship the Lord God Almighty. We ignored the woman, as well as the spirits in her that were cursing and threatening us in many voices.

Within a short period after our arrival, the pastor stopped worshipping. He then began confronting the spirits. His elders also stopped singing and stood there observing. The five of them surrounded the woman who had clawed her way across the carpet to the middle of the room. The pastor began repeating the same command for the spirits to "release this woman." After an hour of using this and other words and approaches, the woman had grown worse and not better. Collapsing into a nearby chair, the pastor indicated to one of his elders to continue. Keeping her corralled in the center of the living room, one by one, the elders took the lead. They pressed the spirits in the same manner their pastor had—with similar results. After an extended period, the pastor resumed the lead. His church elders joined him this time, as the five of them synchronized their verbal confrontation with the demons. This joint assault brought no more success than their previous individual efforts.

Their methods had consumed more than six hours, with no visible change in the situation. For quite a while, they lounged in various chairs around the room without speaking. Several were almost hoarse from talking for so long. Their countenances revealed how exhausted and disheartened they were. Some stared at the floor, avoiding eye contact, unsure of what to do next.

During that entire period, the other five of us did not interfere. Instead, we continued to worship the Lord and intercede in our spirit languages. We remained clustered at the far ends of the living room. A couple of us withdrew to the dining room, seeking the Lord as to how to proceed. One thing was evident to the other five of us from the Saturday men's prayer group. The pastor and his elders had ignored the Holy Spirit's direction. Still, we were hesitant to point this out to the pastor, worried about offending him. As we prayed, the Lord again emphatically repeated His directive to two of us.

"You will not see victory through your exhibition of might or power. Neither will your many words or great determination produce it. Rather, it comes by My Spirit. I will move through your praise, worship, and sincere thanksgiving."

The man from our prayer group who also attended that pastor's church, once again approached his pastor. He reminded the pastor of what the Spirit had said that morning. He then revealed that the Lord had, moments earlier, repeated the same words. The pastor's response was to point at the woman and say, "You're welcome to try."

The woman was still kneeling in the center of the room. Her eyes darted from one man to another like a wary, cornered animal. The five of us from the prayer group now gathered in a loose semi-circle around her. Turning up the music, we began to worship the Lord God Almighty with renewed passion. We declared our love for Him and thanked Him for His love for this woman.

The woman stood to her feet, her body rigid. Next, the spirits inside of her caused her to cover her ears. As she did, the demons screeched, wailed, and cursed at us through her voice. We ignored what was happening, singing even louder. More than sixty minutes passed with no sign of change. Then, without warning, the woman's body fell face-down on the carpet as she thrashed about in a rage. Before long, she became motionless, except for the spirit voices speaking through her. They begged in a series of whiny pleas for us to leave them alone.

At the direction of the Holy Spirit, the five of us fell to our knees. We lightly placed our hands on the woman's back and began praying with a fervency in our spirit languages. Within minutes, without any of us speaking another word in English, the woman reacted. She began to shake, retching and gagging, as though she was coughing up her lungs. Followed this, her body jerked violently. It appeared as though she was experiencing a seizure. Thankfully, the Spirit told us not to be concerned and revealed to us that this was a tactic of Satan. He was trying to get us to back off out of fear that we could be inducing severe physical harm. When the shaking subsided, she lay very still with her face to the floor, giving the impression that it was all over. Once again, the Holy Spirit revealed the deception of her enemy! The Lord gave two men discernment to see the one spirit remaining in her—Death. When one of us spoke this aloud, and the other confirmed it, Death responded with an ear-ringing roar. At the same time, her back arched in the air, as a cat does when it is angry. Unwilling to relent, the five of us continued in intense prayer in our prayer languages. This time the resistance was short-lived. That spirit erupted from her throat in a furious scream that trailed off into silence. With that, the woman collapsed prostrate onto the carpeted floor.

One by one, the Holy Spirit assured the five of us that the battle with the demonic had ended, which became evident a few minutes later as the woman rose to her feet and stretched her hands toward the heavens. With tears pouring down her cheeks, she shouted praise and thanksgiving to the Lord God Almighty for setting her free.

Beholding her unbridled joy, the five of us joined in with her. We rejoiced and worshipped Jesus as Deliverer, Savior, and Lord. As the celebration died down, the woman once again fell on her face on the floor, this time voluntarily prostrating herself in an attitude of prayer and perfect peace. Most of the men gathered at the end of the living room nearest to the dining room and front door. They talked with one another, hugging the husband as he rejoiced. For nearly eight hours, we had declared Jesus to be her Deliverer and Healer. Even so, the Lord knew the work was incomplete.

The Spirit then told me that Jesus wanted to complete the emotional healing she needed. I did not understand, but still, I obeyed what He directed me to do next.

"Lay face-down on the floor, stretch out your arm, and place only your fingertips gently upon the crown of her head."

As I did so, I closed my eyes and began praying aloud in my spirit language once more. Almost immediately, the Spirit overwhelmed me with compassion for the woman. He allowed me to comprehend and feel the damage within her that the pain and suffering had caused. Immersed in this experience, I failed to notice what my friend commented about later—how a holy hush seemed to have swept into the room then. Several minutes after it began, the wailing pouring forth from my spirit ceased. Then a deep weeping arose from within me as the Holy Spirit showed me the love of the Father for this woman. In the end, I lay still for several minutes, whispering thanksgiving to the Lord.

When I opened my eyes, I found the woman staring at me. She appeared to be reveling in the same Perfect Peace that I was also feeling. Through tears of joy, I told her repeatedly how much the Father in heaven loved her, and how pleased He was with her. The woman smiled and shook her head in agreement, her face now glowing with the light of the Eternal One.

As a group, we thanked the Lord in prayer for all He had done that day. We asked the Holy Spirit to fill her and her husband, covering and blessing the couple and their home. Everyone hugged the pair, assuring both of them of our continuing prayers. At four-thirty in the afternoon, all ten of us departed their home, having learned a valuable lesson. It was one which those from the Saturday men's group would recall and apply in future situations. The battle indeed was the Lords' to fight. He did so only when we had stopped trying to labor *for* Him, choosing instead to become a co-laborer *with* His

Spirit. Our part required only two things—a willingness to hear, and faithfulness to obey. Then, and only then, had He moved on her behalf—delivering, healing, and restoring—to the glory of the Father.

On Monday morning, she and her husband met with her oncologist, entering the waiting room with a new-found joy. The excitement they felt showed on their faces. The usual nurse had escorted her to the examination room a few minutes later. As she did, the nurse struggled to believe the positive changes in the patient's demeanor. Where depression and paranoia had reigned for months, she saw genuine peace and joy. It had appeared to radiate from the patient's being.

The doctor's focus was on her medical record when he had entered the examination room. Hearing the woman's cheerful greeting, the doctor had looked up at her in surprise. He had never seen such a dramatic change in all the months during which he had treated her—or anyone, for that matter.

"What happened to you?" he'd inquired.

She had told him why she no longer felt depressed or suicidal. While the doctor had listened and noted her chart, she had concluded by stating that Jesus Christ had delivered and healed her. The last thing the doctor had wanted to do was discourage her. It had been too obvious that something had helped her escape her depression. Even so, his training as a physician had caused him to doubt her conclusions. The doctor had asked whether she would be willing to undergo a series of tests to see what might have changed.

"Absolutely!" she had replied. The doctor called ahead, and the nurse directed them both to the wing of the oncology center that she had come to know too well over the previous two years.

Six hours later, the doctor had sat down once more, with her and her husband, as he thoroughly reviewed the results. The lab had run everything twice. In utter amazement, he had explained his conclusion to the couple.

"There appears to be no evidence anywhere of cancer. All indications point to total remission," the doctor said. The doctor had stopped short of calling her transformation healing. Even so, the couple knew otherwise.

Back in the car, she and her husband had rejoiced. They had thanked the Father in heaven with laughter intermixed with tears of joy. At home, the husband had opened the drapes and windows, flooding the house with the late afternoon sunlight. For the third night in a row, they had slept soundly, she in her husband's arms.

The following morning, she had awakened bubbling over with joy and wasted no time in dressing. A desire had arisen to take her little dog outside for a walk—something she had not done in many months. Now, as the woman walked along, she had studied every little thing with newfound amazement. Colors that went unnoticed in the past had become so vivid. The bird calls were more pleasant to hear. The smell of the morning air had proved to be intoxicating. Above all else, her heart had overflowed with joy at being alive and healthy.

Her brisk pace did not leave her feeling the least bit exhausted. At the end of that time, she'd arrived back at the walkway leading to her home. From a house across the street, an elderly neighbor had called out to her. This neighbor had seen the younger woman's many ambulance trips and prayed each time.

Now that same elderly neighbor rushed to meet her while still being dressed in her robe, with her silver-gray hair askew. While waiting there with her dog, the younger woman had noticed how distressed her elderly friend seemed. The older woman had then stopped in front of her and immediately begun to speak.

"Forgive me for bothering you," the woman said. "I haven't seen you in so long, and when I saw you walking your dog, I just had to come over and talk with you." A moment later, the older woman's emotions had given way to intense weeping.

The younger woman had stood there on the sidewalk in front of her home, embracing her friend. The woman had sobbed for several minutes into her shoulder. When calm had finally overtaken her, she'd explained. "I found out yesterday from my doctor that I have an advanced stage of cancer, and the doctor said it's inoperable. I'm so scared!"

Her love-filled heart had listened to the older woman who was now where she had so recently been. Praying aloud to the Lord, she had thanked Him once again for what He had done for her. Then, with deep compassion not previously experienced, she had followed the inner urging to pray aloud for her friend, as others had prayed for her.

When she had finished speaking, they'd separated. The older woman had thanked her for the prayer and hugged her once again. As she returned to her home, the younger woman had watched her, reflecting on the astounding joy and peace that now flooded her own heart. The more she thought about what had just occurred, the more astounded she'd felt. She whispered aloud, *"It's only been days since You finished healing and delivering me, Lord Jesus. Why, then, did You so quickly bring before me someone who needs help, who faces the very thing that I recently faced?"*

Then the answer to her question dawned on her like the sudden dissipating of a fog. Awed by the lingering presence of the Lord, she now understood that Jesus longed to be for **ALL** that which He had proven Himself to be for her. She rested now in this sweet assurance and the unshakable truth that the Living Son of the Eternal Father was eager to co-labor with ***anyone*** – and that '***anyone***' included her.

Multiple Personality Disorder

Over the next two years, I made a monthly trip to the church conducting the deliverance conferences. I intended to learn as much as possible about the subject. Most often, I went alone, with my wife's blessing and encouragement. With each trip, I continued to receive more personal ministry and training.

Near the end of those two years, the church conducted its first "Men Only" conference. Six others from our Saturday men's prayer group joined me for that weekend. Four of these men had been to the church many times over the previous three years. The other two were first-timers. Although uncertain about what to expect, they were all still curious enough to make the trip. One of the first-timers was a minister at a large non-denominational church in our home city. Over the five-hour drive north, the minister had twice voiced a concern that was nagging at him. "I sure hope this does not end up being something I'll later regret."

On Thursday through Saturday, we attended those hour-long learning sessions that interested us. At dinner break on Saturday, the minister in our group confronted the other six of us in the parking lot.

"If you all want to go to the service tonight, have at it. After watching last night's so-called 'ministry,' I don't see any reason to return. There's nothing wrong with me. I don't have any secret sins, or vices, or anything I need to have cast out of me," he stated, with heavy sarcasm. "I'm not that hungry, so I'd prefer that you drop me off at the hotel. I'm going to grab something out of the vending machines, and spend the evening watching some football."

None of the other six of us knew what to say in response, so we agreed to do as he requested.

The Saturday evening service ran from seven until three the next morning. When the other six of us returned to the hotel, we heard the television on in the room where the minister was staying. The man who was sharing the room with him opened the door, and we saw that the minister was still awake. For a few minutes, we all stood in the doorway, quietly rehashing what we, and other attendees, had experienced. The minister—who had refused to attend the service—could not help but hear our words. Still, he acted as though he was ignoring us, as he remained focused on the sports updates. The conversation finally wound down. Those who were not sleeping in that room moved on to their hotel rooms. Before doing so, we all agreed to check out of our hotel rooms by eight-thirty the next morning with the idea of heading home immediately after the Sunday morning service.

The following day, all seven of us filed into the ends of the first two pews on one side of the center aisle. Following the praise and worship, everyone in attendance took their seats. Rather than preaching a sermon that morning, the pastor spent an hour reminiscing. He elaborated on many unusual circumstances and situations they had encountered. "Through the years," he said, "the Holy Spirit has sent thousands of folks to us for help—men, women, and children. We've recorded each session, as we do in every service here."

"I can say without exaggeration that there isn't much that we haven't seen," he continued. "We've dealt with every type of perversion and sin, and a wide variety of demon presences, attacking people of all ages. Each attempted to impact or control an individual's soul and torment their flesh. As an example, let me speak about two confrontations with demons causing migraine headaches. For one man, the point of influence—**as revealed by the Holy Spirit**—was something as simple as a Masonic ring on his finger. In another case involving a woman, it was a long-forgotten miniature Buddha on the end of a cocktail stirrer, hidden in the back of a drawer at her home. Hard to believe? Well, for her, the cocktail stirrer represented a cherished memory that was sexual and pleasant, but it was also sinful. The man smashed the ring with a hammer and threw it away. The woman also used a hammer to smash the Buddha, which she was amazed to find exactly where the Spirit said it was. As the affected individuals later testified here, destroying the connections totally eliminated the headaches for both of them. Strange? Yes. Even so, both are true. These are a couple of examples of truth revealed to us by the Holy Spirit through the gift of discernment. Answers like these we would never have gained or understood on our own. And, as I said, we preserved recordings of both."

"We've faced, and cast out, many demons that prey on and drive the emotions. These include spirits tied to different Eastern religions and forms of advanced martial arts. We regularly deal with Occult spirits such as Witchcraft, Voodoo, and the like, including what we call the more *exotic* demons. Some call themselves Irish Banshee spirits. Others claim to be American Indian animal spirit guides and even Werewolf spirits. Much of the world is quick to explain these away as complete fantasy. Except, of course, those who create television series and movies about them for profit."

Some of the men in the audience shook their heads in agreement. Others just laughed, until moments later, when it all became real. Someone let loose a long, drawn-out wolf howl, interrupting the undercurrent of chuckling. It shocked us to see that it had come from the mouth of the minister in our group. He was the one who had refused to attend the deliverance service the previous evening. The spirit continued manifesting itself through him with repeated howls. A few of us assisted others from the church in encircling, moving and gently restraining him on the floor. Asking the rest of the men in the audience to pray, the pastor joined us on the floor. He commented later that he thought it would only take a few minutes to deal with this interruption. When notified that the person they were helping was a fellow minister, the pastor's heart went out to him. Forty-five minutes of aggressive confrontation by the pastor brought freedom from the demon. Profound brokenness and peace settled over the minister, as his mind became clear. With the man's permission, the pastor then took a few minutes to interview him before the others. He knew it would help the men attending the conference to understand the reality of what he had been discussing earlier. He asked the pastor how he believed the spirits had found a hold in him, and the minister explained.

"I was very skeptical when I came here this weekend. I came because some of the other men I believed to be godly invited me. Still, I did not come to the service last night. I told myself, after the Friday night session, that this was not for me. I stayed in the hotel room and, I can assure you, had I driven my car, I would have left and been home by now."

"Quite honestly, I thought most of what you were talking about for the last three days was ridiculous. Then, this morning—" At this point, the minister stammered, and then paused. "When you mentioned the Indian spirit guides, something inside of me jumped. One minute I was peaceful, and the next, I had this overwhelming urge to howl. I panicked and tried to resist, but as you know, I could not hold it in. It was like, at that moment, I didn't have control over myself."

The pastor continued listening as the man spoke. He nodded in understanding, having seen similar reactions thousands of times before.

"While you and the others were helping me, the spirits tried to overwhelm my mind. For many years, I researched the culture and beliefs of the American Indian tribes. Indian pictures, figurines, and memorabilia are what I used to decorate my apartment. I've even visited Indian ceremonial sites. If I hadn't come here and experienced it for myself, I never would have believed this. What I thought was a harmless fascination, I now see were demons influencing me. I now know I have some housecleaning to do when I get home," he concluded, smiling sheepishly. He and the pastor hugged. The pastor prayed over him, asking the Holy Spirit to fill the man anew with His presence. When he finished, each man returned to his seat as the pastor remounted the platform.

Standing there on the platform, the pastor then asked every man present to sit back down for a little bit longer, while the women and children vacated the sanctuary. One hundred seventy men (and the late pastor's widow) remained. We gave him our attention, expecting to hear closing comments wrapping up the weekend. As we watched, the pastor pulled a small folding table and a chair up onto the platform and sat down on a folding chair. He looked around at those in the pews for several minutes, as each person waited in silence for him to speak. I sensed in my spirit that he seemed hesitant to begin. Uncertain about what he was going to say, I once more turned on my mini digital recorder.

"Yesterday morning, the Holy Spirit woke me very early," he finally said. "He told me to lie on my face on our bedroom floor. I obeyed without asking why. It was quite a while later before He finally spoke again. When He did, He gave me this command. *'The Father in heaven would like you to present to the men tomorrow what I revealed to you months ago at the library. You have kept this to yourself, as I asked, unwilling My command to release it. Now is the time. Do not preach it or teach it. Instead, read it as I gave it to you.'"*

The pastor paused, flipping back and forth through pages in a spiral notebook. As he did, he occasionally glanced at the audience. About one-third of the men were church members. The remaining men were visiting there for the conference. With a serious look on his face, he began to speak.

"Four months ago, I took my oldest daughter to the local library on a Saturday afternoon. She needed to do some research for a school report that was due the following Monday. I knew it would take her three to four hours, so I found a copy of the Bible from the religious books section and sat down to read. As I did, I asked the Holy Spirit if there was anything in particular that He wanted to speak to me about in His Word. He responded right away. He took me to the passage in Luke in which He led the writer to identify Satan as the one also known by the name of Beelzebub. You may already know the meaning of that name. If not, it means 'lord of flies' or 'fly-god.' The Holy Spirit made a point of telling me to write that verse in this notebook."

"He then directed me to the Science aisle, pulling my attention to a book on flies and other parasites. Returning to my seat, I turned to the pages he mentioned, and added more notes in this notebook, as He guided me. Next, He led me to a book on schizophrenia, then one on paranoia. Finally, He had me read from several books on Multiple Personality Disorder."

"I had no idea where He was heading with all that He was showing me, but I determined to be obedient. He continued speaking to me, and I read and made notes—pages and pages of them," he said. The pastor held up the spiral notebook while flipping through the pages to show how many.

"When my daughter and I left the library, it was still sunny and unseasonably warm outside. The temperature was about ninety degrees that day. When we got home, I made a point of writing that very thing at the end of these notes so that I wouldn't forget it. As we both rounded the corner to the side of the library building to go to my car, it was like entering a walk-in freezer. At the same time, I made a mental note that there was no shade or shadow. I also realized at the time and noted later that there was no sign of a breeze. Nearby trees were absolutely still. At that moment, I discerned through my spirit the presence of evil far more menacing than anything I have ever encountered in this church. Then a loud voice spoke a warning to me."

"*'Don't even think about telling anyone about what you wrote in that notebook. If you do, you and your family will live to regret it.'*"

After a very long pause, the pastor continued. "I'll admit that it shook me up. I stopped, turned to my daughter, and asked if she had heard the voice. She had not, but she mentioned how strange it was that it was cold right there in that spot. Despite the bright sunshine, she said it felt so cold that it caused her to shiver. I had not said a word to her about my sensing the same thing. I spoke aloud, 'Jesus Christ be glorified!' Then we got in the car and headed for home.

When we arrived there, I pulled my wife aside and told her what had happened. She read what the Holy Spirit had revealed to me. We prayed together for God's peace and continued protection, and agreed to leave it in God's hands."

"From that day until now, the Holy Spirit has not mentioned it to me once. Nor did I talk to anyone else about it or even thought about it much—until yesterday morning. That's when the Holy Spirit spoke to me about it for the second time."

"So, rather than talk about it, I'm going to follow the Lord's instructions. I'm simply going to read to you what He explained to me that day, and directed that I present to you men today."

For the next thirty minutes, the pastor read without hurrying. What he presented was what the Holy Spirit described to him as an in-depth explanation of **Multiple Personality Disorder**. "The Spirit elaborated on the correlation between physical and spiritual realms. He also expounded on how this spiritual battle always affected both body and soul."

"The Holy Spirit said, *'Demons hang around, pestering you, much as flies do at a picnic. They wait for the opportunity to gain entrance or influence. That opening may occur in a variety of ways. The obvious is when you disobey the Word of God. Another is when you knowingly and repeatedly ignore the Holy Spirit's instructions. Situations and circumstances beyond your control may also leave you vulnerable. These may include personal or family crisis, illness, hurt, disappointment, depression, and more. Then again, it can often be something as simple as the death of a close family member or friend.'*"

"*'Demons operate by latching on to you, one PERSONALITY after another. They do so in every breach they find. In this way, they act like eggs laid by flies. Flies will lay them anywhere they can—in a cut on an animals' skin or a cut on a tree branch or leaf. Some parasites lay their eggs into cuts or sores in human flesh. As occurs with flies, or any other type of parasite, so it is with demon spirits. One insect finds success* in penetrating the flesh. This successful penetration then becomes the breeding ground and sustenance for others that follow. In the case of demon spirits, their initial aim is to overwhelm the flesh. Even so, always keep in mind their ultimate focus is to influence your soul. Once they overcome your resistance, the number of invading demonic PERSONALITIES rapidly multiplies. Each demon can influence that soul in their unique way. The combined demonic host form a barrier. Their obstruction can often prevent the real personality, deep within, from surfacing.'"

"The Holy Spirit then continued. 'Often, the individuals themselves are so overwhelmed that Confusion reigns and they become uncertain as to which personality is the one that I, their Creator, birthed. Many live out decades of their life having no idea who they are. They often go through life baffled by their actions, puzzled by their thoughtless words, or frustrated by their inability to control their tendency to respond to things irrationally. To those who observe and hear them, these individuals often seem extremely erratic and incapable of controlling themselves.'"

"The Holy Spirit went on to explain even more. 'These demonic personalities act as walls of isolation. Each has a will and an assigned agenda, which they try to exert over the individual's will. Note that these demons are **NOT** always leading the individual into new sinful ways. Often **they coerce you to continue in the way you have already chosen, of your free will, to go.** They strive to affect you at every possible opportunity, influencing your thoughts. It's your responsibility to resist. If you don't, what might have started as a passing interest or curiosity, may become much more. You may find that it has become, for you, a form of compulsion or obsession, which the demonic spirits then fuel.'"

"The Holy Spirit cautioned me about a few other things. 'Too often, men and women defend their actions or words at times like these. They make light of what is occurring, as though it did not warrant their or anyone else's concern. They excuse themselves, saying 'that's just the way I am.'"

"'At some point, some become influenced and misdirected by the enemy of their souls. As such, they never consider if their response might be truer than they realize. They have accepted a lie. Now they live it out day after day without ever questioning why. In a similar, unquestioning way, many tolerate reoccurring headaches, allergies, pain, or disease. Any of these may begin as a medical symptom of a genuine illness or weakness in their body. At that point, it IS a physical symptom or disease, but usually temporary and treatable. Even so, it's also the time when, for some, their thinking and speech begin to change, confirming with their tongue the individual's acceptance of ownership of and surrender to these maladies. These affected individuals speak of THEIR headaches, THEIR allergies, THEIR arthritis, or even THEIR cancer. The opening is then available for invading spirits to come into agreement with them. **When that person has verbally accepted Satan's influence, the demon's task becomes much** *easier. It only has to keep the individual's thinking, speech, and actions going in the same direction. Unfortunately, that direction is the one the individual ALREADY VOLUNTARILY CHOSE.'"*

"When I was writing this out, the Lord told me to emphasize that last part heavily," the pastor interjected. After a momentary pause and drink of water, he continued reading what the Spirit had conveyed.

"*'This acceptance by individuals will always be evident in their speech. Words flow forth from the thoughts now rooted in their hearts. Remember that out of the fullness of the heart, the mouth speaks.* **Each word they ignorantly or wrongfully speak reinforces the strongholds.** *These thoughts, words, and actions are creative forces, shaping their world, determining their future, and establishing their destiny."*

"*Remember also that invading strongholds may effect the physical, mental, or emotional realm. For that reason, men and women should carefully consider the other, not-so-obvious obsessions or compulsions, which* **may not necessarily be demon-initiated, but often transition into being demon-directed.** *When this occurs, evil spirits fuel that person's lust in or for a given area, habit, or realm. Sometimes, things looked upon as "entertainment" or "relaxation" are evidence of a spirit of Distraction at work. Examples of this are often hobbies, leisure activities, or sports. For some, it's a desperate compulsion to work – to fill time with busyness or productivity. It can be an overemphasis on* **striving** *for perfection—a demon of Perfectionism at work, as contrasted with a spirit of Excellence, which glorifies God. At times, it's a compulsive need to prove oneself to others, even when no one is asking for proof. Too often, this is demonic spirits of Pride, Boasting, and Inferiority working together with 'SELF'— one's soulish nature—to strongly encourage a person in the very way in which they had already determined to go or be.*

Moreover, there's the drive to succeed at any cost, fueled by a spirit named Driven. It goads men and women to work to the point of exhaustion. Too often, this destroys families, marriages, your children, and the very future about which you are so concerned or focused . Consider My words well! **ANYTHING** *that causes your life to be out-of-balance or* **'SELF**-*focused' should be suspect.* **ANYTHING!**'"

"The Holy Spirit then got my attention, saying, *'the final thing that I'm about to explain to you is every bit as important to understand as anything else that I've revealed up to this point.'"*

"*'Most of My children can readily identify Satan's visible, and expected, work, which is to captivate individuals through outright disobedience and sin. Even so, his more subtle aim is to distract you enough to lead you astray. The latter is every bit as devastating. His demons will goad you from a simple interest in something to a deeper, more compelling fascination. Furthermore, they will not stop there. Their goal is for you to reach the point of compulsive need or obsession. Once established, this can easily become a stronghold for Rebellion, which makes way for other strongholds of Self-Satisfaction, Self-Fulfillment, and Pride. These strongholds will become just as "vital" to you as cherished idols were to some of the Israelites, so much so that you would not think about depriving yourself of them. As such, they will have supplanted the place in your soul formerly held by your first love, the One True God.'"*

The pastor finished reading what the Holy Spirit had given to him, so he closed his notebook. Moments later, there was a stirring from the back of the sanctuary. A dozen men came forward as a unified force and ascended the stairs to the platform. They were all members of that church body. They tightly encircled the pastor, blocking the congregation from viewing what was occurring. The late founding pastor's son-in-law appeared to be the leader of the group. He reached for and turned off the microphone. He then bent forward and spoke quietly to the pastor, where he sat in his chair. The pastor arose, and the group exited the side door into a hallway. The late pastor's widow (who had been sitting in the rear of the sanctuary with her son-in-law) followed them.

Everyone else remained seated, many whispering among themselves, wondering what was happening. Next, angry shouting came from the door to the church offices, across the hall from the sanctuary. Ten minutes later, the son-in-law returned alone and made his way to the microphone.

"The man who has been acting as pastor for this body has tendered his resignation," he stated. "I will be taking his place as the senior pastor of the church effective immediately. I do so with the full blessing of the other leaders in this body and our departed pastor's widow."

Several church members in the audience loudly questioned, "Why? What possible reason do you have for this action?"

The response was short and final. "What you tolerated for the last hour, in the estimation of the leadership of this church, was not Biblical. It was psychology or pseudo-science, and God had no part in it. We won't tolerate that here, so we insisted he step down."

Having given that brief explanation, he proclaimed the conference concluded. Many other members shouted out questions and statements challenging the actions taken. The son-in-law refused to answer or acknowledge them. Instead, he turned and left the sanctuary.

As we headed home that afternoon, we talked about what had occurred. Everyone agreed that Satan had finally found a way to destroy the Holy Spirit's work there. The leaders had ousted the one man in that church who most demonstrated the genuine love of the Lord in all that he said and did.

After-Effects

Those of us in our Saturday morning men's prayer group who had attended one or more deliverance conferences could not help but think and talk about all we'd learned, seen or personally experienced. The more significant part of our understanding came through the ministering help we had each received. We thanked the Lord for opening our hearts and minds to that area of the spiritual realm. Without the Spirit's prompting, we may never have known about Satan's ways. Now we were no longer willing to settle for our self-imposed spiritual limitations. We'd seen first-hand the remarkable power and authority resident in the name of Jesus Christ, and the Spirit-led results of our praying in unity in our spirit languages. Now, we were open to whatever the Holy Spirit might choose to lead us into, as an individual, or as a group.

Still, for the minister who had accompanied the other six of us on the final trip, it was a different story. For months, he battled Shame and Embarrassment about what had happened to him. He had remained quieter than usual for most of the five-hour return trip to our hometown. In the weeks that followed, some of us reached out to him. We encouraged him to rejoin us for the Saturday morning gatherings. He listened but never would commit.

One of the men reminded him that his reaction was typical for men and women alike. Too often, they hesitated to turn to the Lord for help, having been overwhelmed with feelings of embarrassment, shame, or unworthiness. As the man spoke, the minister remained silent. The only thing he would acknowledge was that he was struggling with some things in his mind. Abruptly, the minister said he had many other things to do, and then ended the call.

After several more weeks had passed, another man from the group tried to reach out to him. Once again, the minister was unresponsive. Not knowing what else to say, the man ended the call by blessing his friend in prayer. As he did so, he poured out his heart to the One whom they both called Father.

A few days later, the Lord spoke to me about the same situation.

"You men are not to grieve about this any longer. Continue lifting your friend in prayer as I lead you. His heart is seeking Mine, and I will answer him."

The Holy Spirit then reminded me how much the Father cared for all His children.

"Son, turn to Psalm 34, verses 4 through 6. This passage is My promise to you, and the other men in the prayer group. Everything will be okay with your friend. He has many concerns stirring in his heart and mind. He is sincerely calling out to Me for help, and I will give him an understanding of this matter."

I turned to the Scripture reference and read it. Immediately, I felt His incredible peace settle over me. Then, I read it a second time, aloud.

"I sought the Lord, and He answered me; He delivered me from all my fears. Those who look to Him are radiant; their faces are never covered with shame. This poor man called, and the Lord heard him; He saved him out of all his troubles."[1]

One year after that conference weekend, that minister finally returned. Several hours into that Saturday morning's prayer gathering, the door opened to the room in which we met. The minister entered and slipped into an open chair without looking around, closed his eyes, and bowed his head. A few of us looked at one another and smiled. No one spoke, and we all returned our focus to the Lord. Thirty minutes later, the man finally addressed the group. As he did, a genuine humility was evident.

"I owe some of you an apology for the way I acted when we went to the deliverance conference last year. I wasn't ready at the time to accept what I saw there. It was even harder to believe when that evidence involved something about me. It honestly scared me. Following that, I began to question what I thought I knew about the spiritual realm. I knew for sure that I didn't understand much of what they spoke about at that church, but I eventually had to admit how real it was—which the Holy Spirit later confirmed."

"For several years now, I've been handling all of the counseling responsibilities for hundreds of couples and individuals in my church who came seeking help. When I met with them, I had always tried to diagnose based on what I was seeing and hearing. I categorize it based on my understanding of the physical and psychological. That was the in-depth training I received. I never considered what they taught at the church we attended for the deliverance conference. **To think about things *beginning* in the spirit and soul level changes EVERYTHING. It made me realize that people needed help, first and most importantly, at the spirit and soul levels.** If I help to straighten out those, the physical or flesh level will heal, and do so much faster."

"I've read the Scriptures, like each of you. I'm aware of that the Word of God warns us that... **'*We do not wrestle against flesh and blood, but against principalities, against powers, against the rulers of the darkness of this age, against spiritual hosts of wickedness in the heavenly places.*'**[2]

"I realize now, as I look back on it, that I never bought into the concept of there being literal demons. So, how was I supposed to believe the rest? You know—that they were terrorizing, traumatizing, and seeking to destroy humanity. How was I

After-Effects

supposed to believe that? I then found myself at a crisis point. I could no longer deny what I'd seen and experienced. It was time for me to evaluate much of my previous training, both as a Christian psychologist and as a counselor."

"I did quite a bit of Bible study on my own and spent even more quiet time with the Lord. I now know that I've spent years putting bandages over the wounds of those who've come to me for help. **My routine had been to talk with folks and pray with them. I never considered a *spiritual* treatment as PRIMARY. It never crossed my mind to <u>attack</u> the SOURCE of the problems, situations, or diseases. However, I understand now that the "source" operates in the spiritual and soul realm and is responsible for bringing forth the physical manifestation.**"

"For a while, I honestly got pretty sad and depressed when I thought back to how many people trusted me to help them. Instead of helping—as I now know—I may have hurt them far more than I helped."

"At some point, I had to know the truth, so I put it all before the Lord, and listened as He explained things to me. He revealed quite a lot and brought peace to my troubled soul."

"So, I came today to thank you, men, for being willing to be the vessels through which he was able to help me. Now that He's helped me, I'm certain that I'll be able to help so many others more effectively."

Each of us had hugged him before he left that morning. We were thankful that our brother in the Lord had been willing to accept the guidance of the Spirit. He never returned to the Saturday gatherings. Still, many of us knew that God had also brought him there for a second reason. His words that morning were one more reinforcement of what the Spirit had taught us. For some, it had also been a source of renewed confidence in the presence of His guiding hand.

Still, there were men in our prayer group who had opted not to attend any of the deliverance conferences. Several showed an increasing level of irritation whenever we spoke of this subject. Even so, the Holy Spirit would not let it rest, as He lovingly brooded over our gathering each Saturday. We had only waded into the shallows, and the Lord was about to urge us to step out into far deeper waters.

Over the weeks that followed, the Lord impressed an idea upon several of us. We were to move the weekly gathering out of the pole barn and into our homes. We prayed about it as a group for several more weeks. Most of us had peace in our spirits, discerning that this indicated change was genuine. Some, while not as sure, went along with the decision to proceed.

This new direction—moving weekly from house to house—was to continue until we had visited each man's home. The Spirit assured us of what would happen if we followed His leading. He said it would allow Him to move in us as individuals, and as the heads of our families, in an excellent way. He also promised to move in each of the other members of our households. Through one of the men, He spoke an explicit command that most in the group acknowledged.

"I want this team to move into carefully-focused prayer against specific spirits. I will reveal these to those open to My gift of discernment who are willing to hear, and will be faithful to obey."

The first couple of weeks seemed to go well. We followed the same routine used at the barn. After an extended time of worship, we would pray and act as the Holy Spirit led. In the first home, many of the members of the man's family joined in with us. We saw immediate results from their willing participation. The second week proved to be the same. We left there greatly encouraged.

By the third week, some of the men were visibly irritated. They were part of the small number who did not want to attend any of the deliverance conferences. They began to express discomfort with what was happening in the homes we had visited. The rest of us were only complying with what we believed to be the instructions of the Spirit. When our group had moved to the fifth home, their questioning had escalated to a challenging. The rest of us persisted in following the Voice of and discernment given by the Holy Spirit. The results proved that we had, indeed, discerned and acted according to God's will. Mid-morning, those same men abruptly left early, departing in unison from the home we were visiting that day.

When I prayed about this that same evening with my close friend and prayer partner, the Lord answered. He showed us both that Fear had driven those men to leave. The Holy Spirit told us that none of the three were willing to have their home visited. Repeated calls that week to each went unanswered. This confirmed what the Lord had stated. Although we later tried once more to contact them, neither ever responded, and they never returned to the Saturday gatherings.

The rest of us continued to see remarkable results as we obeyed the Lord, which proved two things to us. We still heard the Holy Spirit clearly, and we were continuing to fulfill His will. Even so, what puzzled us was why the Lord would allow the group to fracture. When we asked, He did not answer. Therefore, we pressed on until we had spent a Saturday in the home of each man who remained as part of our small body.

Several men later testified with joy as to how the atmosphere in their homes had changed. The positive effect on their marriages and children was also evident to them, and it was all a direct result of the group's obedience to the commands of the Lord.

After-Effects

Back at the pole barn weeks later, the Holy Spirit spoke to several of us in detail about what had occurred in our homes. More specifically, about what we still needed to address. Many of the men shared this with the group and asked for prayer for deliverance from what remained. We joined as a group to confront this and saw more results.

One of the men—my close friend and prayer partner—spoke up next. He said he had discerned a demon oppressing me the day the group visited my home. He admitted that he had been hesitant to mention it or address it at the time, and went on to explain.

"While we were praying as a group," he said, "you fell to the floor, moaning loudly with your eyes closed. You curled up into a fetal position, as though you were in great pain. I didn't know what to make of it at the time, so I knelt and prayed for you in my spirit language. I was hoping to discern what was going on, but I heard nothing."

Some of the other men who were at my home that day nodded their heads in agreement with what my friend had mentioned. However, the problem was not merely about *what* had occurred, or even *why*. There was also the issue of my having no recall whatsoever of the scene he had described.

"I'm open to more prayer," I offered.

Even so, the Lord prompted my friend's reply.

"No. The Lord just said to tell you that He wants to talk to you about it Himself."

I accepted that word as being from the Lord. I figured that the Holy Spirit would explain everything to me in His perfect timing. A moment later, another man at the other end of the room spoke up. He confessed to continuing strife between himself and members of his family. Repenting before the Lord, he asked the Holy Spirit's help to resolve the situation. We all joined in prayer for him and his family. The Spirit gave us discernment to see three influencing spirits. They were Contention, Marital Discord, and Strife. Within a couple of minutes, the man was set free and filled with joy.

For those who remained in the group, the hunger to pursue God grew. There was no turning back now. We had seen and experienced too much. No matter where He might lead, or whatever the cost, we knew we were willing to follow.

*"...in the flesh,
you don't have
anything to offer...
that they truly need.
However,
through your spirit,
surrendered
to My Spirit,
I do."*

Are You Here For You or Me?

The next six months passed quickly for me. My company's primary sales campaign for the year had drawn to a successful close. As in previous years, I attained the level of success I had come to expect of myself. Having significantly exceeded my company's goals, I knew I would receive the usual accolades and awards, including another boost in my annual income. That was the best part. Despite having this to anticipate, I was still struggling with the lingering stress five weeks after the campaign ended. Ever conscious of our sales campaign deadline, I'd pushed myself hard for many weeks, often working sixteen or more hours a day, six days a week.

As I sat at my desk very early that morning, I took long drinks of my second jumbo coffee of the morning while waiting for the additional aspirin I'd swallowed a few minutes earlier to take effect. Once again, a pounding headache had awakened me—this time at three in the morning. Rolling my neck to the left and then to the right, I tried to release the tension I was feeling. Propping my elbows on the desk and resting my head on my hands, I closed my eyes—and that's when it happened!

One moment the tension and throbbing headache were undeniably there. In the next instant, neither remained, and a quiet voice whispered my name. My eyes popped open, and I looked in all directions. Only a handful of people remained in the office. None was close enough for me to have heard them call, much less whisper my name. Shaking my head as though to clear it, I closed my eyes and rested my forehead back on my hands. Once again, a voice whispered my name, and I came fully alert. I realized that the "voice" was that of the Holy Spirit, coming from within my being.

"Call your wife and ask her to spend time with Me, son. Tell her I'll reveal to her how the two of you are to use your fifty-seven-hundred-dollar income tax refund and the four weeks of vacation you have coming this year."

I sat immobile, puzzled. I considered what I thought I had heard. I seemed confident it was the voice of the Holy Spirit, but the more I thought about it and delayed obeying, the more I convinced myself that it could not be God. It just didn't make sense. *If it was God,* I reasoned, *He wouldn't have told me to ask my wife to hear for me.*

Immediately, the Voice responded, answering my unspoken objection.

"Son, I need to speak this to her, for her sake and yours. I need her to be confident that she is capable of hearing My voice. She must learn that she doesn't always have to rely on you to hear for her. Tell her to write down what I speak to her. Then, just

before she tells you what I said, I will reveal it to you also. In this way, you will both clearly understand that this is My will. She will no longer wonder if it is My Spirit she is hearing, and you will both be at peace with what I am about to ask of you. By speaking to your wife first, she will be completely cooperative and encouraging to you, releasing you to obey without worrying about using this time and money for yourself. ***I need you to learn to follow Me even when you don't understand where I am leading or why.***"

Slipping into the conference room, I closed the door and called my wife.

"Sweetheart, the Holy Spirit just spoke to me and told me to call you. He said He wants you to spend time with Him. He's going to reveal to you how we are to use our income tax refund this year. He's also going to tell you what we're supposed to do with the four weeks of vacation I have coming."

"What am I supposed to listen for?" she asked.

"I don't have any idea. The Holy Spirit said it's important that this comes through you, not me. So, please spend time seeking him. Okay?"

As I drove from appointment to appointment that day, I thought about it a lot. Twice that day, my wife called me, probing for direction.

"Has the Lord said any more about this, so I know more precisely how to pray?" she asked. However, I had heard nothing.

"If He said He'd talk to you, then He'll talk. Just keep praying and be patient," I encouraged. Several times on each of the following days, my wife called. She hadn't heard a thing, and I could detect the growing anxiety in her voice.

Wednesday evening, after we'd finished dinner, she asked me, "Did He say anything about *when* He'd talk to me?"

"No. I told you exactly what the Lord said. He hasn't said another word about it since then," I answered, frustration now evident in my voice.

I silently inquired of the Spirit. *What exactly are You trying to show us, Lord?* Still, I received no answer.

Mid-morning on Thursday, my wife called me once more. This time she didn't probe for information. She had heard, and she knew for sure what the Lord wanted.

"You're going to Argentina. You're going with some of the other men in the Saturday morning prayer group," she stated. "But you have to go to Brownsville first, and you have to go now. The Holy Spirit said Brownsville is as important as Argentina."

"He told me the same thing just before you called," I confirmed to her somewhat hesitantly. "But it's already too late to join the Argentina trip. We both prayed about that at length months ago, and neither of us received His direction for me to go. Besides, the money was due more than a month ago, and I may not be able to get airline reservations."

"I know," she said, with a level of confidence I had never before heard in her voice. "You asked me to pray and listen, and God said He wants you on that trip. You need to call the outreach group immediately, but the Lord said it's important to go to Brownsville first."

"Okay! Okay! I know! He didn't tell me, though, where Brownsville is. I've never heard of it. Did He explain this to you?"

"He told me to call our church. They'll have the answer. I left a message on their recorder. I'll call you back when they return my call. Meanwhile, you need to call California. They should be in shortly. Here's their number."

When the outreach coordinator revealed that there had been a last-minute cancellation, all doubt concerning the Holy Spirit's words left me. I arranged to join the outreach, and then I called my wife back to let her know. In the interim, she had also heard from our pastor's secretary.

When I got off the phone with her, I called and made airline reservations for both trips. Then I booked a hotel for the following week in Pensacola, Florida. That was where God wanted me to go first—to attend the revival at the Brownsville Assembly of God.

Two days later, I joined the others at the Saturday morning men's prayer gathering. I testified about how God had moved through my wife to urge me to go to both places. One of the men expressed a desire to join me for the trip to Brownsville. The two of us flew south late the next afternoon, with neither of us aware of what was awaiting us upon our arrival.

Calling the church in Pensacola before our flight out, I discovered that their services started each evening at seven. The woman who answered warned us to arrive early. On Monday afternoon, the two of us got to the church at five. More than two thousand people were already waiting for the doors to open.

That night we both observed from the back row. The worship stirred the people in a more profound way than either of us had ever seen or experienced. The evangelist, Steve Hill, preached with a fiery boldness, and conviction settled over the crowd. We watched in awe as more than a third of the people ran for the altar when the call for repentance came. This ministry period lasted for several hours, with signs and wonders occurring throughout the sanctuary.

Back in our hotel room that night, we both had trouble sleeping. We thought about all that had happened that evening. The following day we arrived at noon to join the waiting masses—already a thousand strong. We were hoping to get better seats that night. We followed this same routine each day. Each gathering seemed to build from where it had left off the previous evening. Saturday's service was a climax and continued well into the early hours of Sunday morning.

As we headed to the airport later that Sunday morning, our bodies were exhausted from lack of sleep. Even so, our spirits resonated with the lingering presence of God that we had experienced all week.

When my wife and three youngest children met me at the airport, they hounded me with questions. I tried to explain all I had seen and experienced. Finally, I told them, "I brought home a box full of videos that will show you an idea of what I saw and experienced every day. I can't wait to see them myself."

That evening we all huddled around the television watching late into the night. The energy level of the worship drew them in and stirred me once more. We watched hours of incredible testimonies given by those saved, healed, and delivered at the revival.

In my quiet time with the Lord the following morning, the Spirit spoke to me. *"Return to Brownsville immediately. This time take your wife and children."*

My children were out of school for the summer, and this was a slow period for my company. When I told my family, they were eager to go. I called work and arranged for another week off without pay. My remaining three weeks of vacation would cover the trip to Argentina. We spent the day packing and left early the following morning for the long drive south. At the last minute, our second daughter's boyfriend asked to join us. [When we returned from this trip, he asked for our daughter's hand in marriage.]

At Brownsville, all that I had described, and all they had seen on the videos, became real for each of them. They marveled night after night as God moved with power and authority in and around us. At one point late on our last night, the senior pastor, John Kilpatrick, was walking down one aisle toward the rear of the church, praying for guests as he went. People filled the aisles, each wanting him to pray for them. As he reached out and touched one after the other, men and women collapsed like bodies without bones. Soon they lay piled one on top of another, blocking his further progress up the aisle. Turning to his left, he began working his way down one of the long pews in the center of the church. He acted as though he was intent on reaching the other aisle. The first half of the bench was empty, but my family and I were occupying the other half. I was standing in the very center of that long pew, facing the approaching pastor. As he drew nearer, I stared at him while wondering in my mind. *Where does he think he's going?*

I glanced over my shoulder at my family to see if they were vacating the pew so I could do likewise. However, people wanting to receive prayer filled the aisle at the end of our row, and there was nowhere for us to exit. As I turned back around, Pastor John Kilpatrick's finger touched me. I felt a power surge through my forehead and body. In an instant, my two-hundred-fifty-pound six-foot-four-inch body flew backward. It was as though something catapulted me over the pew in front of us. I landed in a heap on the floor under the next bench and lay there for the longest time, semi-conscious and unhurt. As I did, power and heat continued radiating through my body.

Hours later, my family and I returned to our hotel rooms to try to get a few hours of sleep before leaving for home. In the morning, we packed and started the long trip north. For much of the return trip, our children talked about what they had seen and experienced. And, of course, they couldn't stop laughing about what had happened to me. As the miles passed, I listened and watched their interaction in the rearview mirror. Awed by the new excitement and visible change in them, I rejoiced in my heart, giving thanks to the Lord.

Two days later, I was back at the airport departing for my trip to Argentina, along with six others from our city. It was my first missionary outreach, as well as my first trip outside the USA. The journey started rapidly downhill with a delay in our connecting flight in Atlanta, which caused the seven of us to miss both of our other connecting flights. In the end, this resulted in an hour delay in Miami, and a much longer delay in Chile. In the Santiago airport, we joined with twenty-three others. Their group—also part of the outreach team—were from the northeastern part of the USA. Like our group of seven, they had missed their connecting flight to Buenos Aires.

While in Santiago, restlessness festered in my heart and mind. I grew irritated with being stuck in a situation that I found aggravating. I couldn't control what was happening and set it right. Meanwhile, the local people seemed to take it all in stride. The terminal had seating to accommodate no more than thirty. The other two hundred waiting passengers sprawled out on the airport terminal floor. They huddled in groups with their carried-on luggage. Many took turns sleeping—and snoring—while awaiting connecting flights. Accessible public facilities included only two small restrooms. There was a coffee and news kiosk offering reading material, but only in Spanish.

All the outreach participants stranded from the Miami flight sat huddled together. No one was certain about what to do next. Only sixty of the three hundred total participating in the outreach spoke Spanish. Those sixty had moved on to Buenos Aires on the scheduled connecting flights that we missed. In Santiago, we had surrendered our passports to the Chilean Customs authorities. None seemed able to speak more than a few phrases in English, and those working the ticket counter spoke no English at all.

After twenty-four hours of idly waiting, an outreach coordinator finally flew back to Santiago to rescue us. He arranged for connecting flights and explained to our group what to expect next.

Even so, the difficulties and delays did not end there. When we arrived in Buenos Aires, it was snowing. A storm that had swept in overnight from Antarctica confronted us as we exited the terminal. Most of us had winter coats. Like me, a few of us had packed them in our suitcase. Unfortunately, the airlines had misrouted our luggage to Lima, Peru. Thankfully, our itinerary was flexible enough to allow for an extra day in Buenos Aires. When the luggage finally arrived, they delivered it to the hotel.

The full outreach group was then broken up into smaller teams and loaded onto assigned buses. The drivers headed in separate directions, each to the towns where we would stay. Six of us from my hometown joined the largest group of men and women, which headed east in two full buses. We arrived near midnight, one day later than anticipated. The camp where we stayed for the next two weeks was four hours from downtown Buenos Aires. Upon arriving, I joined three of the other men in helping the drivers unload the luggage. Everyone else grabbed what was theirs and headed to the shelters to unpack, eager to climb into a warm bed. The four of us who were helping to unload the luggage arrived at the men's barracks last, only to find no available beds. There also were no extra beds to move over from the women's building. Even if there had been, the beds in the men's dormitory were already stacked three high. No extra beds could have possibly fit into the small building. After the leaders pondered over the situation, they concluded that the only space available for the four of us was in a small, detached, unheated base chapel.

Each night for five days, the temperature dropped, and light snow or freezing rain fell. The chapel roof leaked, and water accumulated on the tile floor, forcing us to move the single portable heater to the elevated altar platform, much too far away to be of any use in warming us. The first night we tried to sleep fully clothed in sleeping bags stretched out on wooden pews. After that, we huddled on the poured concrete altar platform, close to the portable heater.

With each passing night, the entire group at that base camp struggled to get adequate sleep. Teams of witch doctors had taken up positions outside the perimeter of the ranch. They shouted over megaphones day and night, cursing everyone staying on the base. The men and women in our group began to grow restless and irritable. Never had any of us experienced the level of evil exhibited by these determined servants of Satan.

Nonetheless, each day, we filled the buses beyond capacity and headed out mid-morning. We went to churches, prisons, parks, orphanages, and towns. In each place, our teams testified and ministered to the local people. We observed hundreds of souls receiving the Lord as Savior, and it encouraged us. We watched in awe as the Spirit moved in situations and the lives of individuals. Signs and wonders occurred—many more than most of us had ever witnessed in our home churches.

During that week, the temperatures hovered below freezing. Head colds, sinus infections, and bronchitis overwhelmed many at the camp. Our buses returned to the base camp well after midnight every night. Each time we found more and more bonfires blazing outside the ranch perimeter. The witch doctors remained, shouting curses over their megaphones. On the fourth day, we saw one of them positioning severed cow heads suspended on tall poles. These they placed immediately outside the four corners of the property. Our leaders gathered teams of prayer warriors to intercede around the clock.

Returning to the base after midnight on the fifth night, we found the place dark. The only light came from the still-burning bonfires. One of the leaders quickly started a single emergency generator. Even so, it only fed power to the kitchen area of the main building. Throughout the night, many spent time in the kitchen trying to get warm. Very few of us found rest that night. Everyone awoke to temperatures that were near freezing and cold showers.

Several hours later, men from the local electric company arrived to restore power. They had to replace a *new,* recently installed transformer, located on a pole inside the base entrance that had unexplainably exploded.

The extended cold weather, compounded by the lack of heat, caused many in the group to become even sicker. Those most affected were the four of us housed in the chapel. Some at the base camp seemed to be walking around in a state of mild depression made worse by exhaustion. As for me, I had developed severe bronchitis, a head cold, and an overwhelming sinus infection.

That sixth evening, our bus had taken us to a local theater. There we were to combine with the members of many local churches for a worship service. While everyone else went inside to take part, I opted to remain with the driver on the warm bus. For those few hours, I tried to catch some sleep despite my non-stop coughing.

The following morning, the sun rapidly warmed the air. Those in charge announced we were taking a day for everyone to rest. One bus driver took many of us to a nearby town to pick up medicine and take care of other needs. I joined them and found a pharmacy. There I loaded up on cough syrup and amoxicillin—available without a prescription.

Back at the base by early afternoon, I sat on my folded sleeping bag that I had placed on the ground. My head and back leaned against the sun-bathed stone exterior of the chapel. The temperature had risen quite a bit, and the afternoon sun felt great. Every few minutes, spasms of coughing racked my body. My close friend and prayer partner from the Saturday men's group quietly prayed for me. Even so, I didn't feel much like joining him. I had no desire to do anything except go home. Accumulated anger and frustration gripped me, and when my friend left, I began venting that anger to the Lord.

"Why did you tell me to come here? Everything has gone wrong since the moment we left home. All I did was waste a lot of money and all of my vacation to come here and get very sick?"

For the longest time, I sat still, sulking, not speaking lest I begin coughing again. Ever so slowly, the anger abated, at which point the Lord spoke.

"Are you here for you or Me?"

I had no immediate response to his question. Shame tried to overtake my mind and heart. For a second time, the Lord spoke, halting my enemy's deception.

"Son, I'm not angry at you, and neither am I disappointed in you. Your enemy would lead you to believe that your actions warrant condemnation from God. The shame you feel is of him. I desire to broaden your awareness of what is transpiring here. With that in mind, think about what I'm asking you, son. ***Are you here for you or Me?*** *If you came representing the heart of the Father, then your purpose here is to be a benefit to these people—My creations who I dearly love.*

At this moment, I know it does not appear that I ordained this outreach for you. Nevertheless, I did. This trip is one more way for Me to further fashion you into the vessel I need you to become. Doing so will prepare you for that which the Father has declared for you. Each adversity presents you with a unique opportunity. Will you seek My direction, My wisdom, and Me? If not, is it because you choose to follow your demonically-influenced thinking?"

"I know your enemy has manipulated circumstances on this trip to attack you. He is hoping to hinder you from fulfilling what I'm calling you to do. However, your purpose here will not draw upon your physical strength. Rather, it will draw forth from your spirit that which I've been pouring into you for years. Much of what you've learned, you've not yet put to use. Some of this, at times, you believe you've forgotten. Believe Me when I tell you now that it all lies like a reservoir inside of you, waiting for My Spirit to draw it forth—but only if you will allow Him to do so."

"Spend the remaining daylight hours here, alone with Me, and I will renew your spirit, which will bring forth My healing in your soul and flesh. Seek Me now, amid this adversity, with all your heart, mind, soul, and strength. In doing so, you will find My purpose for you here."

† † †

The next morning our group awoke to even better weather than the day before. A clear sky and warm breezes chased away the darkness that had blanketed the base since our arrival.

This outreach coincided with winter break for the Argentine schools. With the bright sunshine came the sound of children's laughter as they ran and played in the local parks. Along with the younger children and teens, there were parents and grandparents. All were eager to intermix and talk with the "foreigners."

Outreach efforts that last week accelerated. Our groups began moving from one small town to another. We visited orphanages, parks, and prisons. In the evenings, we joined in with local churches. Other days, we walked the streets in pairs, knocking on the door of every home and business. To those who answered, we asked only one question: "Is there anyone here that needs prayer?"

Without fail, the Argentine people eagerly welcomed the prayers. Many in our group saw the Holy Spirit move through astounding signs and wonders. First thing each morning, men and women were encouraged to testify of these instances to the team.

One of the day trips in which I participated was with a smaller group of twenty men and women. We went to a former jail, used now as a community church. The local people and the twenty of us filled the building until there was little room for anyone to move. Some of the Argentine men and older teenage boys leaned against the rear wall. The rest stood outside, glancing in the windows now and then. It was the women, teenaged girls, and a few children who sat on the rest of the metal folding chairs.

After a time of lively praise, a few from our group gave short testimonies. Next, our team members formed a line at the front as people came forward for prayer when the leader gave the invitation.

I stood, side-by-side with others on our team, waiting to pray for those coming forward, and a thought arose in my mind. *How can I possibly help these people when I feel so helpless?* I watched the women and girls line up for prayer, with the men still holding back. I closed my eyes, attempting to quiet the growing feelings of inadequacy. That's when the Spirit spoke to me once more.

"Son, in the flesh, you don't have anything to offer these people that they truly need. However, through your spirit, surrendered to My Spirit, I do. So, once again, I ask you—Are you here for you or Me? Remember, it's not by might, nor by power, but by My Spirit, moving through you as a surrendered vessel. Only in this way will I be able to help those that stand before you."

When I opened my eyes, an older woman stood before me with her eyes closed. The top of her head was level with the lower part of my ribs. In a moment, as I looked at her, deep compassion and love for her welled up inside of me. Tears began to flow unhindered down my cheeks as I stared at her through spiritual eyes. Unable to speak in her language, I resorted to praying in tongues. I reached forward and lightly touched her forehead. An unexpected surge of heat traveled down my arm to my fingertips, and the woman fell to the floor. I had never before experienced anything like that. Standing there in a state of amazement, I stared at her and wept as compassion for her overcame me. Moving then to my left, I reached out to the next woman awaiting prayer. Once again, I felt heat rush down my arm to that woman's forehead, and she likewise fell to the floor. I continued moving to the next waiting person, feeling intense love for each one I faced. Weeping now uncontrollably, I no longer even prayed. Instead, I whispered Jesus' name and stared in awe at the results. Each time, the Fire of God poured through my being to those desiring their Father's touch.

I spoke to no one on the trip back to the base that night, as I intentionally watched out the bus window, unable to control the tears that continued to stream down my cheeks. As time passed, I marveled at the love I now felt for men, women, and children who were, only a week earlier, total strangers. What I had looked at as a mission trip for the benefit of the Argentine people had, in the end, affected me most of all. More walls of separation that I thought would protect my heart and soul had crumbled in the Presence of the Lord. My spirit had come alive more than ever before. For the rest of my time in Argentina, as well as the trip home, I seldom spoke. Instead, I listened to the Spirit of the Lord as He showed me those parts of my soul that still needed His healing touch.

Gone Away Backward

After five consecutive weeks without working, I returned with new enthusiasm. I arrived at the office earlier than usual on the first day back. It was time to begin planning and prepping for the upcoming fall sales campaign. The office was an open floor plan environment. It was set up as twelve aisles, three desks deep per aisle. My desk was at the far end of the space, the full width of the office away from the vice president's office. Most of the other sales reps had come in within an hour or so after I had arrived. They had gathered what they would need for the day and left. Four hours later, I was still sitting at my desk, having accomplished little. Every time I tried to focus on work, my mind would wander to some memory of what I had recently experienced. Heat would radiate through my abdominal area, and my stomach would vibrate uncontrollably. Each time, I held my stomach with my left hand while sheltering my face with the right. I was hoping to prevent anyone from noticing the tears spilling from my eyes.

I sat that way for the longest time, staring out the glass wall by my desk. Soon, I heard footsteps approaching, and out of the corner of my eye saw the vice president drawing near. I did not know her well outside of the usual employer/employee relationship. She had only been running the local office for about one year. During that time, I had overheard plenty of rumors and gossip from my peers about her ungodly ways. I was unsure of what to expect at that moment. As I watched, she pulled the chair out from the desk in front of mine, turned it around, and sat down facing me.

"Tell me about it," she said.

I hesitated for the longest time, uncertain of what to say or not say. The vice president waited for me to respond, not moving, or saying another word. Realizing that she was sincere, I began speaking. Over the next sixty minutes, she listened without interrupting. I told her of all I had seen, felt, and experienced at Brownsville and Argentina. I spoke of the bad things that happened, the times of weakness and uncertainty. I also talked about the good times of great humility and subsequent joy as the Holy Spirit poured through me to others. I passionately expressed my heightened awareness of increased love for the Lord. I explained how amazing it was to me that He so freely and unconditionally loved me. Throughout the hour, I found myself spontaneously and unashamedly weeping before her. When I had finished speaking, she sat there studying me for the longest time before she responded.

"How can you possibly go back to doing this job after experiencing all that you did?"

I stared at her for quite a while then turned my head, looking out the window to my left once more before replying. "I don't know. It's not going to be easy."

However, as I was soon to discover, **a life filled with activity can often distract from and dull even the sweetest of relationships, and this is almost certain to occur if that relationship is not continuously cultivated, guarded, and treasured.** The Holy Spirit had taught me this once before, but I had too soon forgotten the lesson.

That previous lesson was some thirteen years earlier when the Lord had blessed my family and me by providing me an employment opportunity in the advertising industry. These many years later, I was still with this same firm.

For the first year of the new job, I had thanked the Lord continuously for all He had done for me and looked forward to my quiet time with Him and His Word each day. Fifteen months later, however, I had become thoroughly preoccupied with proving myself to my employer and peers, which resulted in rapid promotions and a tremendous increase in income. However, it also consumed many hours every day. Meanwhile, my time with the Word, or conversing with the Author, had steadily diminished.

Each evening, after our children had gone to bed, I would work on paperwork for orders to turn in the following morning. Periodically, I had glanced at my wife sitting across the room, reading her Bible. When she had begun to occasionally ask me to explain a verse or two to her, I had gladly done so. Before long, it had become a regular part of our evenings. Unaware at the time of what was occurring, the Lord had used my wife's faithfulness to reach me. Through her curiosity, the Spirit had rekindled in me a desire to read and study His word.

Soon after that, I'd returned to rising early to spend time with Him. One particular morning, I was awake and fully dressed by five-thirty, hoping to spend an hour or so with Him before heading to the office. After fixing a mug of hot coffee, I had pulled on a light jacket, grabbed my Bible, and slipped out the door to the front porch. Dawn had just begun to lighten the day, but the sun had not yet climbed high enough to warm the chilly April air. After settling into a sprung-steel chair with my feet propped up on a bench, I placed my Bible on my lap. Sipping coffee to warm myself, I'd sat there doing nothing for a bit. Within a few minutes, a deep peace had settled over me. Eventually, I'd opened my Bible, although uncertain of what to read. The pages had fallen open to the book of Isaiah, and a sudden thought had come to my mind. *I've listened to Isaiah on my Bible tapes but never read the entire book.* Starting from the beginning, I had paused at the last half of verse four in chapter one. For some reason, those few words had disturbed something deep within me, so I read them a second time:

"...they have forsaken the LORD; they have provoked the Holy One of Israel unto anger; they are gone away backward."[1]

Once again, I'd paused, studying it a bit longer. Language had always fascinated me, which made me appreciate authors who had chosen their words with care. I knew what a challenge it could be to convey thoughts or intentions with clarity. I had found this fascination particularly heightened when studying the Word of God. Many times, this had caused me to puzzle over a passage I had read, wondering to myself, *"Why had the Holy Spirit inspired the writer to choose one word or phrase rather than another?"*

When meditating on the Word of God with this same type of curiosity, the Holy Spirit had often goaded me to study specific words further. For some of them, He'd guided me to dig deep into the original language. Often, He'd tell me to consider the impact of the culture and history of that era. Several times, He had even led me to other non-Biblical texts, to works written in both the same period and language, that revealed nuances of meaning that I would otherwise not have understood.

In this instance, what had piqued my curiosity were those words in the latter half of verse four, which I'd rhetorically questioned aloud.

"Why wasn't Isaiah guided just to say 'they turned away' from You?"

An unexpected, deep Voice had responded—much louder than that which I usually heard when God spoke to my soul or spirit. Whether it was audible or not, I would never be sure, but it had alarmingly grabbed my attention.

"No, son," the voice had said. *"They had indeed **'gone away backward,'**[2] even as you have been doing for the last three months."*

When I'd heard that, I'd jumped to my feet, causing the remaining coffee in my mug to spill onto the porch. The hair on the back of my neck had stood on end, and an involuntary shiver had shaken my entire body. My head jerked in all directions as I'd looked to see if there'd been anyone else present at that moment, as my mind struggled to accept what my spirit had known to be the truth. Still, I had needed to be sure.

"Was that You, Lord?" I'd timidly asked.

"You know My voice, son," the Lord had replied without hesitation.

As I eased back down into the chair, my body trembled, and the alertness of my soul and spirit heightened. Suddenly, a moment later, I'd found myself recalling and reliving a specific memory of a day, twenty-four years earlier, when I'd been an eleven-year-old youth. It had been a warm Saturday in July. My mom had allowed me to spend the entire day at a friend's house playing. I had enjoyed myself so much and not wanted it to end. Upon starting the walk home, I had done so walking backward down the middle of the neighborhood street. Determined to prolong the pleasant memories of the day, I'd kept my vision focused on my friend's home with each backward step I'd taken. As the distance between his home and mine had increased, other things had gained my attention. These were men, women, children, pets, houses, and cars to the left and right of me, which I had not noticed up to that point. The farther away I had gotten from my friend's home, the less I'd looked at it, despite it having so filled me with joy and longing moments earlier.

Just as suddenly, the Spirit had redirected my thoughts from the past back to the present. That is when the Voice of the Lord had spoken to me once more.

"Son, My chosen people acted, in their day, exactly as you did that day. The focus of their hearts and minds was on Me. They welcomed and basked in My Presence. They were in awe of me, and I poured the fullness of my love out to them. Too soon, that all changed. It did not start as rebellion. Instead, there were a series of momentary distractions. Added to that were small indiscretions, temptations, and lusts. These they chose to entertain in their hearts and minds. In time, they embraced these in their lives and lifestyles. They never did 'turn away' from Me, as you suggested. They were facing Me. Even so, their hearts and minds became enchanted with that which their eyes beheld—with all that was going on around them. Indeed, they had **'gone away backward.'**[3] and needed a stern reprimand, which I chose to deliver through Isaiah."

"I am pleased that you allowed Me to draw you back, with the help of your wife's actions. Now that you are once more spending time with Me, continue to seek Me with your whole heart, mind, soul, and strength. In doing so, you will discover the kind of fulfillment you could never find in the world."

Interaction with the Holy Spirit soon also began consuming my late evenings. Since returning from the mission trip to Argentina, I could not seem to get enough time alone with Him. I started skipping lunches to have more time for the Holy Spirit to resume where He had left off teaching me that morning. He led me from passage to passage in His Word, to things I would never have seen or understood without His help. I set up a makeshift desk in my garage—the only place where I could be alone with Him. It became a sanctuary for me in which the peace and presence of the Lord resided.

Soon it was early November, three months after I had returned from Argentina, but more than thirteen years since that morning on the front porch when His words had startled me.

Taking advantage of an extended period of warm weather, I was outdoors staining dozens of trim strips. My wife and children had gone shopping and would be away for a few hours. Shortly after they left, a great peace enveloped our property. One after another, songs of worship arose from my spirit. I quietly sang to the Lord as I finished wiping the excess stain off the poplar boarding.

Without warning, the loud, clear voice of the Lord spoke to me, seizing my attention. Once again, I was uncertain if what I had heard was an audible word or only one uttered to my spirit. The message did not come this time as a warning. Still, it reverberated to the very depths of my heart and soul.

"Son, you're twenty-six years late for Colorado."

When He stopped speaking, I waited, but He said no more. I stood still, shocked at the ramifications of what I had heard. During the two to three minutes of silence that followed, I somehow knew in my spirit what the Lord meant. Twenty-six years earlier, I had been a week shy of completing my three years of active duty in the military. Several months before that, I'd acted on a desire I'd had since my teen years, having applied for admission to Colorado State University to study wildlife management. The acceptance notification had finally arrived in the mail. Yet, only days before my military discharge, my brother had phoned me. At the time, he was a district manager for Kentucky Fried Chicken. He offered me a position managing a store, beginning a few days after my scheduled discharge. I was still twenty years old at the time. The salary and bonus structure for the position was outstanding. After thinking it over for a day, I accepted the job and then contacted C.S.U. to withdraw from the fall semester.

Twenty-six years later, the reality of this word from the Lord settled into my heart and mind. The enormity of what I had possibly sacrificed by that one decision unsettled me, as a great sadness tried to grip me. My mind rebelled as I told Him, "I didn't even know You as my Savior back then."

The Voice of the Lord spoke once more, chasing away the sadness, and filling me with new hope.

"But I knew you, son. My Spirit observed you as thoughts and questions began to arise in you. You began to wonder more and more in your heart about the point of your existence. It was true that you did not know Jesus as Lord at that time. That was why you failed to recognize and respond to My leading in your life then. Nevertheless, I still have a purpose for you in Colorado. Listen carefully, and I will reveal My heart to you about this matter."

For several months, I did precisely that. Every day, I asked the Holy Spirit when He was going to talk with me about Colorado. Instead, the Lord continued to speak to me day after day about His Word. February arrived, and still, the Spirit had said nothing about Colorado.

Finally, near the end of that month, I decided to stop asking about it. I resolved that the Lord would talk to me when He knew the time was right. Making that decision freed me to rediscover the peace I had been missing for many months.

At the end of August, the Lord decided I was finally ready to hear what He had waited nearly twenty-seven years to say.

"Son, I want you to know with certainty that I can and will provide for you. You must get this resolved in your heart. If not, you will be of little value toward the plans I have declared related to Colorado. I want you to work for Me. Are you willing?"

I hesitated, a bit puzzled by this. "I don't understand, Lord. What am I going to be doing?"

"The will of the Father, as My Spirit leads you. I have plans for you, of which you are not aware. I want you to begin fasting, so you will hear My Voice and not doubt. I have many things to tell you. Ask Me, son, and I will strengthen you. This intimacy that I am calling you to is necessary."

† † †

Then came Sunday morning, five days later, when I would typically have slept in a bit later than usual. Instead, I awoke at two forty-seven in the morning, fully alert, sensing the undeniable Presence of the Lord. I slipped on a pair of jeans and headed to the kitchen table after closing all of the bedroom doors. Opening my journal labeled *"Conversations with the Holy Spirit,"* I began writing.

"Thank You, Holy Spirit, for once again waking me with a song pouring forth from my heart. Every time I remember to ask, You are faithful to do so the next morning. It's great! The song this morning was, 'I want more, more of You, Lord! More! More of You, Lord! Wanna hold You, love You, not let You go! Renew this fire that's within my soul! I want more, more of You, Lord! More! More of You, Lord'![S-1] Jesus, please do to me as that song asks!"

"I am, My son. But for now, relax and pray in your spirit language."

About half an hour passed before the Spirit of God spoke again.

"Son, you have used excuses your whole life not to seek Me consistently that you might hear Me. But you are hearing Me without difficulty now, aren't you?"

"Yes, Lord. Is this because of fasting?"

"Exactly. It has fine-tuned your spiritual ears. I want to talk to you about your future with Me. For indeed, I have called you to Colorado, and specifically to Ft. Collins."

"For what, Lord?"

"For peace, son. Do you understand that My sending you to Colorado would do what I have in mind by isolating you for a time with Me so that you might learn to depend on Me? You'd have no Christian friends that you could go to or rely on there."

"Lord, what if I become weak and fall. There would be no brother there to hold me accountable."

"I would be there to guide you, to pick you back up, to strengthen you, to teach you how not to fall again from the same thing."

"What about my family?"

"What about them? I am speaking to you about you. Will you heed My call?"

"Lord, I want to, but I am a husband and father. I have a responsibility to look out for their best interest."

"And I wouldn't?"

"Yes, Lord. Of course. Sorry! I mean, what will they think and say if I pull them away from all they know and hold dear to move across the country? I don't even know why I'd be going!"

"Here where you are, you're not at peace. You are comfortable, satisfied. You feel accepted. Consider carefully, though, accepted by whom? Man? In Colorado, I would have you to Myself. Isn't the main reason you're drawing closer to Me now, in fact, because of the increased time spent alone with Me?"

"Yes, Lord."

After a brief pause, I asked a question.

"Holy Spirit, is a demon spirit trying to distract me? My mind seems to want to draw my eyes to the calendar on the refrigerator door. I noticed I circled October 2-6. I thought it would please You that I was willing to take those days off work. Was I mistaken? Don't You want me to attend the "Holy Ghost from Coast to Coast" conference that our church will be hosting that week?"

"I led you to request days off during that time of the month, but not for that purpose. Did you ask Me why, or did you assume you knew why?"

"I thought that You would want to teach me more through these great men of God that will be the guest speakers."

"Do I need a man to teach you? You have asked repeatedly about going to Bible College. Each time, I have said, 'NO.' You need to learn to rest in My will for your life. Trust me to use those individuals to teach you that I choose to use, when I decide to do so. In your case, I did not, and do not, want to use a Bible college—or this upcoming conference. Don't you realize how, throughout your life, you have attached yourself to men who teach you well? You hold them in high esteem to the point of idolizing them. You then begin changing, son. Little by little, you become a man-pleaser rather than a God-pleaser. I want you unto Myself. I want to teach you. I am well able and have always been willing to guide you. The question, as always, is: Are **you** willing?"

"Yes, Lord, I am. Will I be going to Colorado that week in October? That's a long way off."

"Yes, and I want you to continue fasting."

"For how long?"

"Until Friday of that week. That will be the fortieth day. I know that greatly concerns you. Are you willing?"

"Honestly? I'm scared. I've never done anything like this before."

"I know, but I will enable you. Are you willing?

"Lord, I want to be. But I can think of many reasons not to do it."

"Yes, but wouldn't they all be excuses rather than reasons? If you say, 'I am willing,' I will make it possible for you to do this, son. It will be an essential step in your walk with Me. So, I ask again, are you willing?"

For several minutes, I didn't respond. Finally, I said, "Yes, Lord, I am willing. Why am I crying over this? Why was this decision so hard to make?"

"This decision was hard for you to make because your soul has become bound to many earthly pleasures and things. Admit it, son. Over the last decade, you have read the journal entries of our conversations many times. You know those things that still too easily influence you. I need to break loose from your heart many deeply embedded barbs. You've resisted their removal in the past because of the pain you believe you'll experience. You know what they are, son. We've addressed them too many times. Their influence hinders your future spiritual growth."

"My son, the truth is that you're **not** scared, as you claimed. Rather, a spirit called Remorse keeps you from dealing with these. I have been calling you lovingly to this forty-day fast for more than two years. The first time was before you went to Brownsville. You attempted to fast while there but soon quit. Did I condemn you, son? No. You condemned yourself. You then became very hard on yourself, beginning to fast once again for the trip to Argentina. You even told others. Why? Wasn't that your feeble attempt to force yourself to commit? Wouldn't you then have been pleasing in their eyes, and not Mine? That fast was not a pursuit of excellence, guided by My Spirit. No, that was strictly your futile effort. Do you understand?"

"Yes, Lord. I see now how I had the wrong intentions when trying to fast."

"No, you saw it **then**. Even so, you made the mistake of agreeing with Deceit once again. I pointed it out to you at the time, even as I am allowing you to see it now. Renounce your consent with these defeated foes, son, and refuse to allow your heart and mind to go astray any longer. Recall what I taught you, and understand your responsibility in this matter. You were boasting because a Boastful spirit had gained control. Moreover, having boasted, you proceeded with your ungodly fast and failed. You then allowed Guilt to ride your shoulders to Argentina. You became overwhelmed for many days. That opened the door for Sickness, Weakness, and Depression to take hold. Consider this! It all started with My call for you to fast for an extended period. I would have led you through that fast, and strengthened you when necessary. Many times over the past two years, you've started fasting and stopped, each time making excuses. In your times of weakness, you have never been willing to ask Me to strengthen you, and then stand in My strength. Have you?"

"No, Holy Spirit. I asked half-heartedly, but then gave up, as You said."

"Son, I'm not angry with you, or even disappointed in the path you have chosen to take up until now. I alone am omniscient. I knew the choices you would make to lead you to this point. Therefore, I have redirected your steps back onto the path that I know will most fulfill you. It was also necessary that I make you aware of what has been happening in the spirit realm. My son, what is past is past. Will you release it to Me? Will you no longer mentally berate yourself for your past failures?"

"Yes, Lord. I give them to You. Please strengthen me right now. When I count out the days on the calendar, I'm uncertain if I'll be able to hold out that long. It's easier here in the mornings when I'm with You."

"If you will be faithful to start every morning by spending time with Me, as you have until now, I will strengthen you. Furthermore, be certain of one thing, I'm asking for a commitment from you. Are you willing?"

"Holy Spirit, when You ask me to commit, why do thoughts of my past failures flood my mind?'

"Satan attacks the mind, as you know. Even so, you have within your power the means to resist. With a heart of faith in Me, command your mind, in the name of Jesus Christ, to stay submitted to the Mind of Christ."

"Thank You for reminding me, Lord." I then promptly did as instructed.

"Son, you must begin to apply all I have taught you more regularly."

"Yes, Lord. I will, with Your help. Still, I have something I need to ask You. I beg Your forgiveness in advance, but I have to be sure this is all from You. I've heard some preachers talk about fleeces as though they are a sign of utter weakness in a man's character. To me, at least, that comes across from them as condemnation, as if they are setting themselves above their flock in an attitude of superiority. When Gideon laid out his fleece for You, Lord—not once, but twice—You tolerated him, without condemning him. Would it be wrong of me to ask for confirmation of all this that You said? I'm going to bed tonight at ten o'clock, as I did last night. If this that I've recorded here is truly Your will, then I'm asking You for a specific confirmation sign. Wake me Monday morning at the same time as you woke me this morning. Bring me fully awake, Lord, aware that You've called me, with the same song pouring forth from my heart. I will set the alarm clock for 4:55 in the morning, which is the time I would normally get up. It's up to You, Holy Spirit. Please forgive me, Lord. I don't mean any offense by asking this of You."

"I'm not offended in the least, son. It pleases Me that you would take this seriously enough to consider asking Me to confirm it in so precise a manner. We're finally getting somewhere. Now, what else is on your mind?"

"What about the roundtrip airfare to and from Fort Collins and the car rental costs while there? You know I don't have the extra money right now."

"I didn't say anything about flying there and renting a car. Those are your thoughts. I want you to drive there and back, spending that time with Me. By driving, you will have two full days with Me each way, leaving five days to spend isolated with Me in

Fort Collins. There, in that place to which I'm calling you, I'll show you what I'm preparing."

"Yes, Lord. Does this have to be a complete fast?"

"Continue as you have, restricting your intake to liquids. Let your heart worship Me continually. Stay away from the television and anything else that could tempt you to sin in the midst of this fast. I will guide you—your heart, mind, will, and emotions. I will strengthen you."

"I know You will, Lord. Thank You."

"Son, you hear, but you do **NOT know**. What I am doing with you is something new. You have never been down this path before. Everything will start to become much clearer to you in a month. Talk with Me throughout each day. Involve the Spirit in every decision, every situation, even the seemingly inconsequential ones. Do not worry about the next day or even the next hour. Worship and praise Me while you work. Let the joy of the Lord explode inside of you and multiply. Again I say, stay away from the television, videos, newspapers, and magazines. Resist your enemy when he tempts you in these areas. I will strengthen you if you will but ask."

The following morning at precisely two forty-seven in the morning, my eyes popped open. I was instantly alert once again. I heard the voice of the Lord say, 'Go out to the kitchen table, son. I want to talk to you some more.'

When I had settled in at the table, I asked the Spirit of God the question that was foremost on my mind. "Lord, what happened last night? I kept waking every fifteen minutes or so from twelve-thirty onward. I couldn't believe it. Every time I awoke, I heard a different song. Then the same song I heard yesterday was going through my mind when I awoke just now. I'm willing to concede that yesterday was definitely from You. My spirit seemed to be anticipating Your call—a little too eagerly."

"I've been guiding your spirit and soul throughout the night, and I'll continue now. When you committed your heart and soul to My control, they eagerly anticipated My Voice. They yearn for communion with Me, son. Go ahead and pray in the spirit for a while. I'll interrupt you when I'm ready to speak with you."

For more than twenty minutes, I prayed but seemed to struggle. My mind kept recalling scenes from my childhood years.

"Son, do not doubt," said the Lord. "It was My Spirit guiding your thoughts as you prayed in the spirit. What you remembered was yourself as a small child at eight years of age, didn't you?"

"Yes, Lord. It was a very clear picture. But why, Lord?"

"I wanted you to recall what you were like as a young boy. You were joyful and very in love with life, always singing and whistling. Your soul was still pure, innocent, and undefiled. Your spirit was free from the desires and worries of this world. Your heart was ever rejoicing, and you loved life so much. What a joy you were then to everyone you encountered. I need and want you to return to that state. Will you allow your spirit to return to the state it was in when you were that young child?"

"Yes, Lord, but I'm a little confused. Where is this going?"

"Where I intend for it to go."

"But I thought You would pick up on Colorado and other things related to it, where we left off yesterday."

"I have. What I am speaking about now concerns what we talked about yesterday. Of what value would you be to Me if you went to Colorado, or anywhere else, with a burdened down and restrained spirit? I need your spirit to soar. Yesterday morning at church, the worship team played a song that you love. The chorus is, 'Spread wide in the arms of Christ is the love that covers sin. No greater love have I ever known-' [S-2] *As you sang those words, your heart was like soft clay in My hands. Your spirit was in perfect union with Mine. Wasn't it?"*

"Yes, Lord."

"Do you understand why, son?"

"In that moment I finally reached the point where I gave in to the longing in my spirit. I relinquished all control to You."

"Exactly. And when you reached that point, what happened?"

"I stopped thinking about everyone and everything around me. When I focused solely on You, I lost control of my emotions and began weeping without restraint. I seem to be doing a lot of that lately, Lord."

"Yes, and I wept with you—tears of joy, even as you and I are doing now. I need you to be that open, that transparent, and that responsive to Me all the time. I need you to get to the point where you no longer have to work to allow your heart and soul to be under My control. It should be—naturally, spontaneously, and unashamedly."

"But Lord, if I do, I'll be a crying mess all the time. When Your loving Presence overwhelms me, and I welcome you like that, I lose control of my emotions. That makes it hard for people to relate to me."

*"Oh, My son! They **will** relate, but not in the way that you're thinking. They may not relate in the flesh, or even in their minds. Nevertheless, **they will be unable to deny the pull upon their hearts**. You will then be, in those moments, far more real in their eyes."*

"You love the Psalms because you love the way David's heart expresses them. It is important to understand that David's heart never stopped thirsting and hungering for Me. David had placed his heart in My hands and kept it there. David was transparent.

He was also honest with himself and with Me. From a heart filled with sincerity poured heartfelt worship. Think about that when you meditate on the Psalms in the future."

"Yes, Lord."

"You must also start realizing the great importance of **knowing** what My Word says. It's not enough to believe you know based on your own or others' thinking. There is great danger in that. When I bring a check to your spirit, pause, and do not revert to your mind for clarification. Seek Me in your prayer language. I will explain it to you and with the explanation will come peace to confirm it. Many times up to this point, you thought you knew what My Word was saying, yet there remained some hesitation. Would you go into battle with an uncertain sword? Neither should you attempt to wield My sword, My Word, with uncertainty. I want you to begin to read my Word even more than you have been and read it with care. Continue asking Me what I want to teach you at that moment. Allow My Spirit to give you His perfect explanation for each passage."

"I know you have an extensive library of Bible study resources, and, yes, I inspired men and women to write them. Nevertheless, is anyone able to give you more understanding and insight than the Spirit of Christ Who dwells in you? Son, you would be of much more value to others if your heart were so full of My Word that it overflowed out of you. It should pour forth like oil to the wounded heart and soul. That is what those to whom I send you will be. Their wounds are wounds unto death and damnation from the Deceiver. I love them all with a love that knows no bounds. For you to be My vessel, pouring forth My balm to their wounds, you likewise must be full of My boundless love. To become so is a two-fold process involving **saturation** and **surrender**. Not one or the other, but both. Not one, and then the other. No, this must be a simultaneous action. Therefore, I urge you to saturate yourself with My Word. Did you notice that I said **'saturate yourself'**?⁴ This move is the beginning step to surrender. Many are unwilling to be faithful to do this, or they do it only half-heartedly. By their actions, they are saying that they do not believe they need My Word. And indeed, if they do not need My Word, then they have rejected Me, for My Word and I am One."

"Yet, it is more than saturating yourself with the seed of My Word. **There must also be a surrender to the transformational power embodied in My Word.** If you choose instead to allow weeds to remain in your soul, won't they eventually smother My good Seed?"

"When My Fire has destroyed the weeds, and your surrender has broken up the ground, then I will plant My good Seed. Only then does My Living Water bring forth life, and an abundant harvest."

In the weeks before leaving for Colorado, the Holy Spirit continued to lead me through the Word of God. He moved from one unrelated passage to another. Then He would astound me by unifying those passages into one cohesive explanation. Some gave me greater insight into the Father-heart of God. Others showed me the true nature of Jesus' character. The rest expounded on the misunderstood or overlooked workings of the Spirit of God. He also had me read many testimonies of how the Lord moved through those who had fully surrendered. As I read one book after another, I could feel expectation building in my spirit.

Late in the evening on the twenty-eighth day of the fast, the Lord reminded me of something. Twice before, He had spoken about the same subject. This time, the Holy Spirit asked me to note it in my journal, so I would have it to refer to later.

"Do you understand that the littlest things often make the biggest difference? It takes more than one day, or one week, or one forty-day fast to build a mighty temple. Rather, day by day, hour by hour, decision by decision, I perfect it. It is stone upon stone, one at a time, and all dependent on a sure foundation. Do you see, then, how vital each decision is? Do you understand why even little distractions, inconsistencies, or exaggerations can be so devastating? Do you perceive how what seems inconsequential can often be most impactful? Everything is a factor in determining the required results. Will you, indeed, be My temple—trustworthy, upright, pure, and holy? Or will you, instead, be corrupt, unrighteous, impure, and defiled—unworthy of My habitation? Son, the final result of anything is always dependent on the commitment and effort put into it. Are you willing to pursue Me relentlessly? I promise you that it is worth it. Seek Me with your whole heart, mind, soul, and strength. Do so daily, hourly, thought-by-thought, act-by-act. Remember this when you get to Fort Collins."

'As you recall, I explained that there are tasks that the Father has ordained for each person to fulfill. If that individual is unwilling, those tasks often remain unfulfilled.'

Isolation and Intimacy

After driving eleven hours the first day, I arrived late that evening in Des Moines, Iowa. I checked into my hotel and, having already called my wife shortly after dark, immediately fell asleep. During the night, the Lord woke me to pray for my family. Not wanting to wake my wife in the middle of the night, I went back to sleep when the burden for prayer seemed to have lifted. As we'd agreed upon, I called her early the next morning before checking out of the hotel. She answered on the first ring, and I could tell that something was wrong.

"Are you okay?" I asked.

"Yes, but I had to call the sheriff last night," she replied. She sounded as though she was about to cry.

"What's wrong? What happened?"

"I am so glad you listened to the Holy Spirit about installing the central air conditioning," she said. "Late last night, two guys from the high school tried to break into the girls' bedroom windows. The girls saw and heard them, called me, and I called the sheriff's office. The sheriff arrived ten minutes later, but the boys had already run away. The girls recognized the guys, and told the sheriff who they were."

"Is anyone hurt? Do you need me to come home?" I asked.

"No. We're okay, but it scared us all. If you hadn't insisted on putting in the central air conditioning, the windows would have been open. Those boys could have gotten in through the screens without a problem. I don't even want to think about what might have happened to our girls," she added.

"If you want me to come home, I will," I offered.

"No. We're fine now. God has you there for a reason. I stayed awake for quite a while last night praying until His peace came. The Lord said this was an attempt by Satan to distract both of us from what the Lord called you to in Colorado," she said.

"Yeah. I had no idea what was happening, but the Lord woke me up late last night to pray for you all. I praise God that I listened and obeyed—by having the central air conditioning installed, and by responding when He woke me to pray. Join me now, sweetheart, and let's thank the Lord and pray His blessing and covering over our family," I said.

A few minutes later, I headed out for the second day of driving. I entered the city limits of Fort Collins mid-afternoon on the first day of October. The hotel where I had arranged for my five-day stay wasn't fancy, but I knew I hadn't selected it for the amenities. My room was on the top floor at the far end of the building, facing away from the street and the noise from the traffic. Unpacking took only a few minutes. I hadn't brought much with me. Setting up the portable speakers, I connected the CD player and started the worship music once more.

Standing at the window, I studied the foothills and mountains. Finally, I knelt at the side of the bed and lifted my voice in prayer.

"Father, I thank you for getting me here safely. Right now, I plead Your precious blood over this physical room, and my body and soul. Direct the atmosphere in and around this room. Fill this room with Your angelic host, my God. Continue to direct my spirit as You desire, and guide my heart, mind, will, and imagination. Direct my path, Father, and order my steps each moment of every day. Speak to me, and I will obey, Lord, through the strength and direction that only You can bring. My time here is Yours. I have no agenda, and I don't know what You have in store for me. That's fine with me, Holy Spirit. Have Your way, Lord, over these next days, and glorify Yourself in and through me."

As soon as I finished speaking, I heard the Voice of God respond.

"Son, I want this room to be a sanctuary of worship unto Me. Unless I tell you otherwise, leave the worship music quietly playing night and day. Do not exit this room for any reason except as I instruct, at which point I will give you clear direction. For now, pray in the spirit. As you do, entrust your thoughts and concerns about your family, home, and work to Me."

I prostrated myself on the floor before the Lord, allowing the Lord to guide both my tongue and my thoughts as I prayed. When I finally arose from the floor, it was dark outside. I stared at the clock, amazed to see that five hours had passed as though they were but minutes.

"I felt Your Spirit guiding my prayer, Lord. It's so much easier now to pray in the spirit and to hear Your voice since I've been fasting like this!"

"Yes, My son. **Prayer—effective prayer—is not hard. Prayer is about you uniting your spirit with the Spirit of Christ, so the Father has His way through you.** *For now, get some sleep. I'll wake you when I want to speak to you."*

At two o'clock in the morning, I awoke to the Voice of the Lord calling me.

"I love you, son! Lie on your face now and pray fervently in your spirit language."

Isolation and Intimacy

I obeyed, praying with an ever-increasing passion. The Holy Spirit directed my thoughts from one thing to another. After another six hours had passed, the urgency to pray lifted as fast as it had come. I arose from the floor, sat on the edge of the bed, and stared out the window at the sunlit foothills. A great peace enveloped me and blanketed the room. For several minutes, I remained quiet. Hearing nothing more from the Lord, I addressed my thoughts aloud to the Spirit.

"When I was praying for quite a while in the early part of the morning, was it You who told me to open up the Fort Collins phone book? Did You lead me to count the number of churches, denominations, and factions of each that exist in Fort Collins, Lord? I resisted for so long because I thought it was a demon spirit distracting me, but I did eventually do what I felt You wanted."

"Yes, My son. It was Me directing you. Sit at the desk, open your journal, and pick up your pens. Pray in the spirit again, fervently. As you do, I'll speak to you. Write down exactly what I tell you. What I need to reveal is vital! At any point of uncertainty, ask Me, and I'll clarify what I've said."

For fifteen minutes, I prayed in my spirit language. The Lord then began to speak, and I began to write His words.

"I'm not pleased with this area, son. There are so many churches, all doing their own thing. Each is eager to show how they are different from the other churches. Insufficient unity exists, even among churches in the same denomination. Most are unwilling to work together toward My purposes. The body of Christ in this region is fragmented and disjointed. It is also very representative of most of North America. Prosperity abounds here, as does a spirit of division. Do you remember, many years ago, when I taught you about division? I explained how it brings death to the Body when instigated by man."

"Yes, Lord, I do. You made a point of telling me that You found it abominable."

"That's correct."

"But how does this involve me?"

"I made My desires known to you as you prayed this morning. You did not imagine it. I want to use you to bring them together as one body, united to do the will of the Father. However, first there must be a thorough plowing of this mission field. That requires targeted prayer, after which My Spirit will proceed with what the Father has determined."

"But Lord, I'm not from here. They don't know me. How can I influence them?"

"You can't. However, I can move through you if you will allow Me. I want you to form a non-profit corporation, son. Call it 'Love Will Make A Way.'"

"Do what? I know nothing about forming a non-profit corporation. I wouldn't even know how to begin."

"I'll guide you. I will send you godly, wise counselors. But first, I want you to go next door."

"Next door? Where?"

"To the Salvation Army church. I led you to choose this hotel for a reason, son—My reason. Go next door and ask for Jerry Atwood."

"Is this You, Holy Spirit?"

After a minute of silence, the peace of the Lord intensified, and the Voice spoke again.

"It's Me, son, and your spirit knows it. Has the peace lifted?"

"No. I'm just confused, Lord. Who is Jerry Atwood?"

"Trust Me and go, son. All I ask is your obedience."

"Yes, Lord. I said I would obey, and I will. But may I ask why am I going there?"

"Tell him what I showed you while you were praying and what I've just told you to write down. Tell him I have mighty plans for this area and the prosperity of this region. I will abundantly supply and bless those who will work for the unity of My church, My body."

"I thought You told me I was going to Fort Collins to find peace?"

"Yes, but did you believe that this was to be a retirement?"

"No, Lord, but You said this was to be a haven, a place of peace. You also said I would be sent forth from here to the nations of the world. Didn't You?"

"Yes, I did, and so it shall be."

"Now I'm baffled. Did You, or did You not, repeatedly tell me that You were going to send me to Ireland, Cambodia, Nigeria, and Quebec? Was that my imagination each time?"

"No, son. It wasn't."

"Then how does this fit in with what You are now saying about Fort Collins and this region?"

"Perfectly."

"How? I don't understand."

"My son, this organization of My creation and design—'Love Will Make A Way'—will do exactly that. It will make a way where no man or woman, in his or her feeble efforts, has ever succeeded, or ever will. I work through those who will be My co-laborers. How many times have I taught and demonstrated this to you? With the help of these saints, I will build this organization. Those I call will know that they have heard My Voice and will feel compelled to obey. They will be men and women filled with My Spirit, broken and humbled vessels. As such, they will pour forth in abundance. Do you recall when I showed you this many months ago?"

"Wow! I just saw a clear picture of one of our Saturday morning prayer gatherings! Is this of You? Are You referring to that day when I thought I heard You say that three of us were going to Colorado?"

"Yes. You heard me correctly then."

"That was a **really** long time ago! Except, it never happened then, so I thought I misunderstood. I didn't know You were talking about anything like this! I thought You meant that You were sending us for some short-term trip. You said, *'I didn't allow this group to bond in My love without intentions of using you together in the future.'*"

"Correct, but what else did I show you that day?"

"Lord, I thought I heard—. Yes! My prayer partner was there, and He confirmed it. Didn't You say that what we would do here would have something to do with spreading the news of what You're doing?"

"Much prayer is needed to birth this effort. Will you believe and trust Me, son?"

"Lord, I have never done anything like this. I don't have the faintest idea of how to do what You're asking. What is this about, Lord? Help me to understand! Please!"

"Son of My heart, listen to Me. Many months ago, I brought forth from your spirit words that you spoke aloud. Those were prophetic words—My words—though you did not realize it at the time. **They were not words you imagined in your mind. They were words I placed in your spirit and allowed to spring forth in My timing.** I told the three of you through those words of this effort's far-reaching impact. It will trumpet to this continent the incredible works that I'm doing through My Spirit as He moves through all denominations, peoples, tribes, and tongues. Those works have begun, and are about to accelerate. The Father has a purpose and a plan. In this region, a divine purpose will come forth to meet the longing in **My** heart."

"How does this all get off the ground? And why Fort Collins?"

"When I spoke to you in your yard that day, didn't I tell you, at that time, that you were twenty-six years late for Fort Collins? I wanted to birth this then. Your heart pursued the wealth and acknowledgment of the world instead. You ignored the need for your spirit and soul to mature."

"Do you also recall, son, when I led you to read the details of how I urged Lester Sumrall to return to the Philippines? He had just arrived back in the USA after a long missionary trip throughout those islands. Even so, I needed someone to help the demon-possessed woman. Everyone was afraid of her, and the authorities had locked her up. Lester argued with me when I asked this of him. **As you recall, I explained to him that there are tasks that the Father has ordained for each person to fulfill. If that individual is unwilling, those tasks often remain unfulfilled.** When Lester understood this, he immediately returned there. Due to his obedience, the woman is now free of all demonic control. The entire region heard the reports of what occurred, and many accepted My Son as their Savior as a result of his obedience."

"As I said before, you did not comprehend that it was Me drawing you to Colorado those many years ago. Even so, I still have this in mind to do in Fort Collins. I have been preparing this area for many years. The region has flourished and prospered, but not for the reasons most believe. I have a purpose and a plan."

"Lord, it sounds like I'll be spending a lot of time here in this area. If this is of You, how does it fit in with Your sending me to these other places? I sense that there isn't a whole lot of time left before Your return."

*"Indeed, the time is of My return is near. Others will be going with you to those other nations. Many of these individuals are already in Fort Collins and the surrounding cities. Others will arrive later. I told you I would send more of like spirit to join you. 'Love Will Make A Way'¹ will be the springboard, son. This organization will publish the exciting news of what I am doing in this end day. It will declare My love, My glory, and My excellent works. At first, it will be My voice to **this** community. It will have a significant effect on Colorado State University, the institution that you had once desired to attend. It will then reach south to Denver and into the hills of Boulder, touching hearts on the University of Colorado campus. Its impact will extend even farther to Colorado Springs. There, it will affect those in the Air Force Academy and the U.S. Olympic Training Center. From this beginning, the report of what I have done, and am about to do, will spread like wildfire across this continent and the world."*

"Lord, what of the other countries You spoke about me visiting?"

"In My timing, you will go—in the Name of the Lord Jesus, as representatives of 'Love Will Make A Way,' as ambassadors and envoys of My love. Doors will open to you that you could not now perceive. You will reveal My compassion to this world. I will pour forth through you, softening the hardened hearts of those you meet. They will no longer be able to deny My Presence. They will welcome that which I have sent you to say, and a new fire will ignite many hearts."

"Lord, there's one other thing that's bothering me. I thought my close friend and prayer partner said he was going elsewhere. He mentioned many different countries in Central & South America. Is that so and, if it is, how does it fit in with what You are telling me here?"

"He will not be in any one of those countries permanently. Likewise, you will not remain long in the countries to which I will send you. While he is in Denver, he will be My ambassador, My envoy to that area. He will be My voice and My vessel through which I will show My power. He will be My instrument of love, there and abroad. I am not sending you three men forth from your hometown to Colorado so that you may continue as you were. It's time to freely give to others that which I have given to each of you."

"Lord, when is this all supposed to take place?"

Isolation and Intimacy

"Son, I have developed abilities in you that the Father wants to use in these last days. Your years in sales and management prepared you for this. I birthed within you the ability to speak to and train others. The many years you invested in Full Gospel Business Men's Fellowship further solidified these skills. Nothing was arbitrary. The years during which you faithfully served as that chapter's leader were training. That equipped you, even more, to speak out, to reach out for Me. Now I am calling on you for another purpose. It will put to use all that I have developed in you."

"Yes, Lord. Forgive me."

"For now, son, pray—fervently. Satan **will** try to prevent this from occurring. So, be diligent in prayer about this matter. Many things need to come into place, all in the Father's perfect timing. When this sales campaign that you're working on ends, you will begin preparing yourself to leave."

"I'm coming back here in late spring?"

"No. I said you would then begin preparing yourself to leave. When I direct, you will come back here, and not before. I have it all worked out. I will provide all you need, as it is needed."

"Lord, I've heard many brothers and sisters in the Lord testify of Your abundant provision. Though inspirational to read about and hear, it's a completely different situation when You're asking it of me. Please increase my faith in You, forgive my unbelief, and remove my doubts and fears. I still feel so inadequate and untrained."

"For that very reason, you'll have to rely on Me. Those testimonies you read were from men and women who met one qualification. They were willing to say, 'Yes.' Although untrained, they preached well as they allowed me to lead them. I drew forth from their hearts all that I had sowed into them over the years of their preparation. I caused My words, My passion, My compassion to flow through them. As willing vessels, they won hundreds of thousands of souls for My Kingdom. They were not mighty men and women of great renown. Still, signs and wonders flowed through them. Have I not shown you this many times as you've been faithful to spend intimate time with Me?"

"Yes, Lord. You have. However, my mind keeps going back to one thing. You mentioned this Jerry Atwood from the Salvation Army church. I'm very nervous about this, Lord. Will he believe and understand everything I have to say to him? Will I even remember it all?"

"Go and find out, son."

As directed, I finally went next door to the Salvation Army church. It was the building to the right of the hotel, which I had failed to notice when checking in. A while later, I returned to my hotel room very distraught, confused, and concerned. I voiced these feelings aloud to the Spirit, but there was no response. I repeated this several times and still heard nothing. Sitting on the edge of the bed in silence for an extended period, I gazed out the window at the mountains. I was waiting and thinking, hoping to hear from the Lord. After more than an hour had passed, I stretched out on the bed, giving in to the deep sleep that overtook me.

Awakening five hours later, I sensed an incredible urging to begin reading a specific book. The book was *'Intercessory Prayer,'* [B-1] by Dutch Sheets. I followed that prompting, and ten hours later, I closed the book and set it aside, having read it through twice. I reclined on the bed, thinking about all that the Spirit of God had to say through the author. Still, nagging concerns about the previous day's events kept surfacing, distracting my thoughts. Longing for answers, I brought my questions once more before the Lord, hoping He would acknowledge them.

"Holy Spirit, I thank You so much for bringing me this far. But I'm afraid I'm messing things up."

"No, you're not," was the Spirit's immediate reply.

"Then please explain to me exactly what the heck is happening here because I don't understand."

"You've been doing My will, son, and I'm very pleased."

"Pleased with what, Lord? I don't see that I've done anything."

"Oh, but you have! You do not see it because you are looking for physical evidence. Do you recall when I taught you that—like Creation—everything starts in the spiritual realm? And then it manifests into the physical, right?"

"Yes. Forgive me, Lord, for being so slow to learn."

"Don't be so hard on yourself, son. You are improving tremendously. In time, I'll explain in greater detail."

"Lord, reading Dutch's book opened my eyes—again. You taught me much of what he covered in that book years earlier."

"Son, I've taught you well, and often. But knowledge unused is worthless."

As I relaxed on the bed in a semi-conscious state for several hours, He caused me to recall one moment in time after another. Each memory was of lessons He had taught me through the years. The next time I glanced out the window, I saw that nightfall had arrived. I drifted off once more into a deep sleep and, when the Spirit next stirred me, I awakened to the dawning of a new day.

As the weighty presence of the Lord increased in the room, I once again prostrated myself on the floor. I prayed only in my spirit language. My surrendered mind raced from one thing to another. When the urgency passed, the Spirit spoke.

"Get dressed, son. Go out the front door of this hotel. Turn left at the sidewalk and begin walking. Listen with care to My voice and do not allow distraction to overcome you. Pray quietly in the spirit as you walk, and I will guide you step-by-step."

Isolation and Intimacy

I strolled along, block-by-block. I turned first one way, then another, and then still another, as He commanded. With each turn, the Spirit of the Lord led me through the streets of Fort Collins. Mile after mile, I continued walking and praying. I did not have the slightest idea for whom or what I was praying. Neither did I know where I was going. Hours later, the Spirit told me to stop. I found myself standing in front of a two-story Christian bookstore at the north end of town.

"Go inside, son."

I wandered through row after row of books, continuing to pray quietly in the spirit. After more than thirty minutes had passed, I still felt no leading or compulsion to buy anything. Confused, I headed toward the front door to leave. It was then that a strong urging arose in my spirit to turn around. I saw a stairway leading to a second floor. Stretched over the staircase was a banner that stated that the books, tapes, and videos upstairs were for small children and teens.

"Go upstairs," the Holy Spirit directed.

Although uncertain, I climbed the stairs. My eyes scanned shelves of books from all genres, unsure which I was to choose, and why. The fluorescent orange binding of a slender shirt-pocket-sized book caught my attention. When I pulled it out from between two other books, the Spirit spoke once more.

"Buy it, go back to your room, and read it."

As I walked to the cashier, I flipped through the book, thinking to myself, *"Why is the Lord asking me to read this?"*

Back at the room, I stretched out on the bed to relax my legs while I read the book. Fifteen minutes later, I had finished.

"Lord, I've never heard of Eastman Curtis, and an unusual name like his I would have remembered. The same with the book that he wrote—*'Kickin' Devil Hiney.'* [B-2] It's awesome! This man has great faith and a great love for You and his fellow man, Lord."

"Yes, he does. Pray, son, fervently, in the spirit. I have much to say to you."

Twenty minutes later, I felt the Holy Spirit's leading to sit at the desk, open up my journal, and pick up my pens.

"Son, go ahead and write out those questions that are on your mind. Your heart is now in a position to hear My answers. Record all My words, for I will refer you to them repeatedly in days and years to come."

"First of all, thank You for waking me with a worship song flowing through my heart this morning," I wrote in my journal. "I sensed You again urging me immediately to get on my face and pray in my spirit language. It was an excellent time, Holy Spirit!"

"*Yes, it was. I accomplished much through you. I guided your mind and heart from one thing to the next at a rapid pace. That works best for you, son. I know your ways. If you pray too slowly, too casually, your mind wanders. Distraction often occurs with you even when you are praying in your prayer language.* **If you do not maintain focus, your prayer language dies off, and you become ineffective.** *Be careful, My son. That kind of carelessness could be costly in battle.*"

"Yes, Lord. When I was praying so fast for those hours, it amazed me. You led me to pray for so many different things. First, there was my family, then it was the men in the Saturday prayer group, followed by my current and former pastors. You then urged me to pray for the churches in Fort Collins, by denomination. Next, it was this city's government and officials, the school boards and teachers, and many major corporations based here. After that, it was Christian organizations, and then businesses, by Yellow Page classifications! I thought I was going nuts, but it was powerful, Lord! I didn't realize how many Yellow Page classifications I'd memorized through my fifteen years in that industry. You then branched out to media, law enforcement, and the military. Later, You led me in prayer for the USA, city-by-city, state-by-state. Last of all were the countries of the world and their capital cities, states, and provinces. Lord, You blew my mind! There is no possible way in the natural that I could so quickly and accurately recall those thousands of cities and hundreds of countries. I remember playing geography quiz games with my four children many years earlier. You never fail to amaze me, Holy Spirit! You're able and willing to use every shred of knowledge I've absorbed over decades for Your purpose, Your good. All I have to do is surrender my will and desires, and allow You to do so."

"*This only occurs when My children offer themselves to Me as willing vessels. When you tell Me that you are freely submitting your heart, mind, soul, and strength captive to Me,* **and I see the sincerity of your heart**, *I take advantage of those times. They are KAIROS times – as you now understand from reading My servant's book.*"

"Yet, You didn't stop there, Lord. I proclaimed my confusion and resultant frustration. I went to the Salvation Army Church on Monday, as You insisted. There was no one named Jerry Atwood there. The church secretary had never heard of anyone by that name. I even telephoned the Salvation Army church when I returned to my room. I asked the secretary whether someone by that name possibly *attended* the church. She said the congregation there was small, and she knew everyone. The answer was still, 'NO.' I felt like a total idiot, Lord. I then began questioning whether I heard You at all. I got so down, confused, and frustrated. I was feeling so weak and light-headed—a combination of the higher altitude and not eating for thirty-six days. As You know, Lord, I was very upset. I began questioning why I'd left my family to come out here. I wondered why I'd been starving myself for these thirty-six days. I drove down the street and bought some fried rice and egg drop soup, and I ate a small amount.

Afterwards, I felt guilty for leaving the room and quitting the fast, Lord. I began condemning myself and broke down crying. I was a mess, Lord. I finally called my wife, explained what had happened, and told her that I was thinking of coming home."

"I know, son, and you need to thank the Father in heaven for a godly wife who loves you and faithfully prays for you. She gave you excellent counsel—to PRAY."

"I did, Lord, and You so quickly and lovingly spoke to me, saying that You already knew that I would stop fasting after thirty-six days."

"I also told you, son, how much I loved you, and how very pleased I was with you."

"That puzzled me, Lord. I felt relief, but I started crying and remained very confused. I couldn't figure out why You would say that.

"Because it was true, and before you could even ask, I told you. I delight in you because you committed to fast and seek Me daily, and you honored that commitment. You have grown tremendously in faithfulness, son. You drove all the way here, not knowing why. <u>*You sought Me fervently, heard from Me, and, most importantly, you obeyed what I asked of you. I knew there was no one named Jerry Atwood at the Salvation Army Church. Nonetheless, I needed to know whether you would follow my request by going there. I also needed YOU to know that you had been faithful to obey. This request was a test, son. You honored My request. I'm very pleased with you.*</u> *Spiritually, much good occurred that day, and it also did in the natural, in the flesh, despite you telling yourself that you'd failed and it was all for nothing. You didn't see what I saw. Had you asked, I would have told you."*

"I'm sorry, Lord."

"I know, son. I don't condemn you for this, so don't condemn yourself. **That test was critical to what was to come next."**

"What are You talking about?"

"Because you obeyed, I knew that you would wholeheartedly embrace My teaching. That teaching I brought through Dutch Sheets, but it was **My** *teaching. After reading it, I urged you to begin interceding in your spirit language for the plan that I am unfolding."*

"My prayer seemed to change then, Holy Spirit. It appeared to go in a new direction, at an even greater intensity level than I've ever before prayed, if that's possible."

"Yes, My son. It did, and it was. For a few hours, you walked upon a plateau that you have never before attained. Moses resided for many days on that plateau. Dutch's statement in his book was correct. Had Moses not stretched the rod over the Red Sea, it would not have parted for My people to pass through to safety. Bear in mind that I knew the heart of My servant was A HEART THAT REFUSED TO DISOBEY. I also knew he would be My vessel of salvation in that situation. ***I am grooming you, shaping you*** *to be likewise,* ***for a situation yet to come. Be patient with yourself. Persevere,***

son. If I waited more than twenty-seven years for you to respond to Me, surely you can wait on Me for forty days. Can't you?"

"Yes, Lord."

Let Me Re-Mind You

"My son, *for you to accept what I'm about to reveal to you, it's imperative that you think with the mind of Christ. This type of thinking does not occur by hoping and longing for it. Nor does striving for this objective bring you into the unity necessary to allow His mind to direct you. It's about absolute surrender to the will of the Father and the leading of My Spirit. Such a surrender includes the possibility of giving up what you count as most precious, which could be your ambitions, desires, hopes, and dreams. It could also be your beliefs and understanding, and even your ministry, should I ask that of you. In other words, it is about your voluntary entry into a covenant of servitude. In doing so, you present your body as an abode for the Prince of Peace. I will not strive with your spirit, nor will I compete with the distractions, things, or ways of the world. My name is Jealous, and I am jealous of you, My child. I alone must be your sole desire, so that I may move in and through your heart and soul. When you allow this to occur, your thoughts will become one with Mine. Only then will you find your purpose founded and unified in Mine.*"

"So, for now, allow Me to release you from wondering about your purpose for being here in Colorado. Let Me remind you of the things we've discussed in the past. Open up your Bible to the beginning of James. Many years ago, we studied this in-depth together, son. *The process of your mind 'being conformed' to the mind of Christ is NOT a one-time event. Neither is it something pursued when you feel 'moved' and later discontinued. It's a continuous process of transformation, involving an intentional reshaping of your thought and analysis processes, which includes reining in your imagination, turning it over to My Spirit, and leaving it there. It's a matter of you having total trust in Me, for each decision, for the remaining span of your existence. Each act furthers the development of your character and solidifies your faith in Me.*"

"James wrote this first chapter at the leading of My Spirit. It contains much wisdom regarding this ongoing progression. Start by writing verses five through eight in your journal. The act of writing the verse out helps to establish it in your memory. There it will have a direct effect on the formation of your character."

"'*If any of you lack wisdom, let him ask of God, that giveth to all liberally, and upbraideth not; and it shall be given him. But let him ask in faith, nothing wavering. For he that wavereth is like a wave of the sea driven with the wind and tossed. Let not that man think that he shall receive any thing of the Lord. A double-minded man, unstable in all his ways.'"*[1]

"Son, I want you to review the many notes I directed you to write in the margins of your Bible for these passages."

"Yes, Lord. The first note was about the word *'ask'* in verse five. There it says *'let him ask of God.'*[2] Again, in verse six, it states *'let him ask in faith.'*[3] I recall Your telling me to look it up in the concordance. It's the Greek word AITEO, pronounced 'Ah-Ee-Tay-Oh.' The complete meaning is: **'insistent asking, without reservation or qualms.'**"

"*Exactly. There is no place for timidity or uncertainty in such an action. It describes activity from a dearly loved son, encouraged and anticipated by a Father. It's a request by one who knows the Father will hear his plea and act upon it.*"

"And even now as I read this, Holy Spirit, I realize that lately, I haven't been very persistent in my asking. I have been asking, but not like I used to when I asked unrelentingly, with passion and confidence."

"It was then also that I most poured into, and through you, wasn't it?"

"Yes, Lord. Please guide me back to that state, Holy Spirit."

"That's what I'm accomplishing right now. This process isn't about condemnation, son. It's about reminding you of all that I have already taught you. It's renewal and restoration that you might begin once again to walk in My ways. What did I show you about My love, mercy, and never-ending kindness?"

"Are you talking about the next note?"

"Yes."

"There, you explained the term 'upbraiding.' You first referred me to the Strong's concordance, then led me to my history and etymology books, and finally to the Oxford English Dictionary. You explained that men and boys in olden days commonly wore long hair. They maintained it by gathering and weaving it into a braid at the base of their neck. This braiding kept the hair out of their faces. You said 'upbraiding' was the means used by one person to control another in a moment of extreme anger. One 'upbraided' another by grabbing their 'braid' and yanking it upward, which restricted the movement of the head and was very painful for the one accosted as such. Further resistance by them proved to be increasingly painful and futile. The practice usually resulted in the accosted one's quick acquiescence."

"*Correct, and because I'm a loving Father, I give freely to all and* **'upbraideth not,'**[4] *as I stated through James. In other words, I'm not looking for blind submission to My will. **I don't want My children to cower before Me in abject fear of a severe and painful reprimand. My longing is for willing surrender and obedience. It must be your action based on your desire to please Me and love Me, even as I love you. So, ask Me anything, in faith, not fear, expecting to receive, as a young child would of*** *his loving father or mother. Remember, I know the end from the beginning. I know the very thoughts and intentions of your heart, so don't hesitate to speak up. You're not going to surprise Me, offend Me, or make Me angry. I am Love, and I will always react as only Love can."*

"Thank You, Lord. I need to hear that repeatedly. My mind has grown so used to the ways of the world that I too often struggle to think of things from Your perspective."

"Yes, My son, you do, but you have been changing. You will continue to change as you develop a habit of coming to Me with a sincere heart. I desire a willing exchange of your conditioned responses for My ways, My thoughts, and My heart. Now, what did I show you about wavering in your faith, son?"

"I was amazed at how much this one word, DIAKRINO, expressed in the Greek. You showed me that the **full** meaning is the following:

'**to judge thoroughly, evaluate carefully, make a decision, and then no longer have misgivings or doubts, hesitating and being double-minded, or wavering between hope and fear.'**"

*"Knowing this, do you understand why My Spirit emphasized His point through James? He stated, 'A double-minded man; unstable in all his ways.'[5] Always remember, My son! That which the mind accepts influences the heart. The heart of a man will shape his character, his actions, and reactions. An unsettled mind results in an unsettled will and emotions. That person's character will make it evident. The transformation into the image of Christ is most dependent on one thing. That is, how often you read, meditate on, and **obey** My Word, which My Spirit made a point of emphasizing. Didn't He?"*

"Yes, Lord. You spoke about that in verses twenty-two through twenty-five. There, You said, *'...be ye doers of the word, and not hearers only, deceiving your own selves. For if any be a hearer of the word, and not a doer, he is like unto a man beholding his natural face in a glass: For he beholdeth himself, and goeth his way, and straightway forgetteth what manner of man he was. But whoso looketh into the perfect law of liberty, and continueth, he being not a forgetful hearer, but a doer of the word, this man shall be blessed in his deed.'*"[6]

"I knew the word translated as 'doer' also means 'performer' or 'keeper of.' This word infers both one who **retains what he learns** as well as **acts on it**. Even so, it surprised me to see two words listed in the concordance as antonyms of 'doer.' These are 'destroyer' and 'Apollyon.' Isn't Apollyon one of the names given to Satan?"

*"Yes. Now, do you comprehend why I've emphasized to you so many times that **there is no gray area in the spiritual reality**? Man's **thinking** will forever look to challenge this. He will always desire a more agreeable position, a compromise. The spirit of a man, however, will perceive the truth in what I am saying. Never forget! **Your***

unwillingness to hear the truth and allow truth to do its work in you will automatically open the door for you to hear untruth. Once untruth enters, it will never cease its striving to do its work in you. **If you are not for Me, you are, by default, against Me.** My Word declares what is necessary to stay on the path of righteousness. If you question this, then you have sided with the enemy of your soul in favoring unrighteousness. You may say, 'I haven't sided with unrighteousness.' Nonetheless, I would remind you that <u>those who walk in My righteousness **build My Kingdom**. Those unwilling to walk uprightly, become one with Apollyon, the destroyer, in **tearing My Kingdom down**</u>."

"Forgive me, Lord. I'm so sorry for those times when my faith floundered. Many times, I realize, too late, that I am operating out of confidence in my abilities, which I could not sustain. Lord, please remind me to look to You to be both the Author and Finisher of my faith. Help me to trust that You **are** willing and able to do that which You promised."

"I will, My son. For now, let's return to what I've been introducing to your spirit over the last couple of days. There's much that the Father is eager to reveal to you."

"Holy Spirit, I would appreciate an answer about one other thing. In the last half hour of prayer, you moved so incredibly in me as I prayed in tongues. My mind filled with hundreds of pictures, and You spoke to my spirit. Right? If not, was that my mind taking control, and my imagination interfering with Your will? Lord, I'm unsure about this because what I saw and heard seems so far-fetched. I thought about this as I walked around town, praying in the spirit as you directed me. I need some assurance that it was You, and clarification about what it was that I was seeing. If it wasn't of You, I need to know that also, please."

"When you were praying, did you break pace? Did you pause? Did your mind wander?"

"I don't believe so. Did I?"

"No. You didn't. You were very persistent, very aggressive in the spirit. At that point, I began to show you that which I wanted you to focus on, to birth, to bring into existence, as you spoke it forth in your Spirit-led language. That was the reason for the intensity with which you prayed in the spirit. You question it now only because you have analyzed it in your thinking and understanding. In doing so, you allow unbelief and doubt to erode that which I had completed in your heart and soul. <u>**When your mind is in harmony with the mind of Christ, then, and only then, will your thoughts be My thoughts. On the other hand, if you persist in maintaining control, then your ways will not be My way because your thoughts will not be My thoughts**</u>. With this understanding, do you now see why I told you to pray in the spirit, rapidly and without ceasing? I did not permit you to do so in English because I knew what would occur.

Once you begin thinking with your mind about what I am asking you to declare, you falter."

"But what I saw seems so unbelievable!"

"My word says, 'Trust in the Lord with all your heart, And lean not on your own understanding; In all your ways acknowledge Him, and He shall direct your paths.'[7] *Now, what else did I show you this morning? Write it down."*

"You showed me a tall building on a large piece of property. There was also a house on the property. The large building reminded me of an air traffic control tower, with large glass windows encompassing the top floor. The tower looked to be at least forty to fifty feet wide, and four or five stories high. I saw the bottom two floors were offices. You led me to call, in the spirit, for donations. First, for office furniture, phone systems, and computer systems. I saw it, Lord! Everything!"

"And I caused you to begin calling in people, My servants, to run the offices and handle the phone centers."

"But You didn't show me what the phone centers were for, Lord."

"Patience, son. Everything must be in the Father's perfect timing."

"Yet, You did show me gardens and several secluded places on the property. There were small buildings where people went to pray and seek Your face in quiet. It was then that I remembered You showing me something like this, about a year ago, while I was at our men's prayer group, Lord. I didn't know at the time where it was to be. Didn't You say then that it would be a ministry center? I'll be honest, Lord. It concerned me when I was seeing this same image again, and I asked myself, *'Are my memories somehow interfering and beginning to take control?'* "

"Yes. I know you did, but they are not. I allowed you to see it once more."

"I must admit this is where I started wondering when I thought about it later."

"Not just wondering, son, but doubting."

"You're right. Forgive me. You showed me the top of the tower as being like the top of a lighthouse. However, the light that was going forth in all directions was intercessory prayer and worship—incredibly fervent intercessory prayer. You showed me names and faces. Some I knew; others I didn't, and most have no idea who I am."

"What else did I show you, son?"

"There were chairs in a circle, with a larger one at the head of the circle. There were words carved into it – 'HOLY SPIRIT OF THE LIVING GOD.' In the other chairs sat men and women."

"And I said, 'This shall be the board of godly, wise counselors.' And so they shall be."

"Lord, I thought about it as I was walking throughout the town praying. I couldn't imagine that most of these people would believe me if I told them about this. They would laugh and think it to be ridiculous. There is no way I could ever convince them that this was from You."

"You're right, son. You couldn't. None of them would even begin to consider that what you are saying could be so, based on your word alone. I know I can trust every one of them to lift it to Me in prayer, as and when I prompt them. They will understand and believe because I will give them My understanding and faith. I will fill their spirits with My peace about this matter."

"Lord, what if those who You showed me are not receptive?"

"Aren't you merely concerned about looking foolish?"

"I'm afraid of not hearing You accurately, of misleading anyone, and yes, I probably would feel like a fool. Who wouldn't, Lord?"

"That is nothing but Pride influencing your thinking at this moment, son, and it's not of Me."

"Forgive me, Lord. It's just that the people whose names You gave me, that I recognize or know, must keep hectic schedules. This thing started two days ago with Your request for me to set up a non-profit corporation. Now, You're talking about a major organization with many people involved. I'm not even in the same caliber as most of these that You've mentioned. What do I know about any of this?"

"Didn't My Spirit speak to you prophetically many times through your prayer partner? Did not several of My visiting prophets who came to your church, directed by Me, speak nearly identical words to you? Haven't I spoken the same message directly to your spirit multiple times? Each time, I told you to hear and accept Jeremiah 1:4-10. I was then, and I am now, declaring to you, son, **'Hear the Word of the Lord. You are to be for Me a voice to the nations.'** This ministry is not to be an organization run by you. That is why I am appointing godly, wise counselors. You are to be one of them."

"Holy Spirit, what in the world do I possibly know compared to these that You've named?"

"Are you playing Gideon with Me again, son? If I'm the Potter, is it not My decision what I will or will not make of the clay? For now, you are to be one of those through whom I will direct My voice. Stop worrying and be at peace. How and when this all comes together, and with whom, is My concern, not yours. I know you better than you know yourself. I am aware of how you will falter if you think about this for too long. That will allow Fear, Worry, Doubt, Intimidation, Insecurity, and Humiliation the opportunity to interfere. They will focus their efforts on convincing you to forget this all as being a foolish idea. Remember, son! I told you on the very first day. Satan **will** work overtime to stop and destroy any move of Mine, and this one is no different. Over the remaining days, until you arrive home, I want you to stay in prayer constantly. Listen very carefully. You may eat, but very lightly, son. Write down everything I tell you. Do not weigh My words in your mind. I will reveal more of My plans to you. If you have questions, ask them of Me. Be truthful with Me. I'll calm your fears, remove your doubts, and elaborate on anything you don't understand."

"Lord, I've been praying in the spirit and writing for over four hours now. May I take a break?"

"Are you hungry or thirsty?"

"No."

"Then why are you asking to take a break?"

"Never mind, Lord."

"No, son. **<u>This is important.</u>** **Your understanding of why you have asked this of me is vital.** Are you asking to take a break because you are tired? Or are you, once again, beginning to doubt what I am saying?"

"Yes, Lord. You're right. I'm struggling to believe this."

"You MUST learn one vital lesson, son. You'll never resist your enemies by denying their existence, especially spirits of Doubt. They are real, as are their strategies and movements. Acknowledge this, and then deal with it. Do so with the swiftness and sureness of the weapon I've placed in your hands—My Word. You're hearing Me now because you're remaining focused. Do not let down your guard. Do not become distracted and drawn away by your adversary."

The following morning when I awoke, an immediate urging overtook me to put on the _Hungry_ [S-3] CD. As it played, I stood at the window looking at the foothills, listening to the music. When the song _You Are a Holy God_ [S-4] began playing, I heard the Spirit speak.

"Get on your face before Me, son."

I prostrated myself on the floor and began worshipping the Lord. A moment later, the song _Breathe_ [S-5] started playing. Deep inside of me, I felt a welling up, then a sudden weeping and wailing poured forth. I did not initiate it, and neither could I control it. In the very depths of my being, I heard the Lord speak the same words to me many times.

"I love you, son! I love you!"

At that moment, I sensed someone kneeling beside me. Gentle fingers brushed my cheek, wiping away my tears. Afraid to open my eyes, I lay still, reveling in what my spirit knew to be the sweet Presence of the Lord.

When I later inquired of the Lord about that moment, the Spirit explained. _"You didn't imagine it, son. The Lord was there, rubbing your cheek ever so softly. Isn't that what you did with each one of your children when they were little, as they cuddled in your loving arms? Remember how it always calmed them and caused them to fall asleep. In like manner, He was there, son, wiping away your tears, and pouring out His love for you as you wept and shook."_

"And then I fell asleep for a few minutes! I love You, Jesus, so much!"

Next, I arose and worshipped the Lord with abandon – with prayer in the spirit, with laughter and weeping, with dancing and great rejoicing. When I finished, I was physically spent but felt more alert in my soul than I could ever recall being. Climbing into bed, I once again slipped into a deep, refreshing slumber.

Positioned to See

When I awoke, it was to the realization that the weightiness of the Presence of the Lord had once again moved into the room. I slid out of bed onto my face on the floor, lying still, fearful, yet marveling at what I was feeling. Abruptly, the Spirit interrupted my thoughts by bringing a rapid series of images to my mind. Shaken by what I had seen, I remained motionless until He spoke.

"That which I allowed you to see is not related in any direct way to the greater scheme of what I am revealing. Still, it could become the seed for Satan to undermine what the Father wants to do. You need to know this, son."

"Lord, forgive me! I let my preoccupation and fascination with the things of the world continue for far too long. Why didn't You show me this sooner?"

"You weren't in a position to see. For this reason, I've been urging you to come away with Me for an extended period. An extended fast from the things of this world was necessary. Sin was not responsible for leading you astray. It was Distraction, influencing your thoughts. In your case, it was a very effective strategy for your enemy to use. *Did you miss anything by not reading books, newspapers, and magazines during this fast? Did staying away from the radio or television deprive you in any way?* ***Understand that your greatest source of strength to resist Satan is your submission to Me. Stay humble before Me, your heart an open vessel for My Spirit, and your mind captive to Mine.***"

"Yes, Lord."

"*Continue praying without ceasing in your spirit language. Listen with care to My Voice. Be aware that your flesh will always attempt to rebel. The world will also never stop enticing you. If you have given My Spirit the reins to your heart, He will not let go* – ***unless you purposefully take them out of His hands.***"

When the urgency to pray dissipated, I inquired of the Holy Spirit about nagging thoughts in my mind.

"You keep bringing more and more names and faces to my mind as I pray, telling me they'll be *'wise counselors.'* Why so many? Wouldn't the potential for discord, disagreement, and chaos be even that much more significant?"

"Remember what My Word states—'***Without counsel, plans go awry; But in the multitude of counselors they are established.***'[1] This organization will not be the work of any single person or group of individuals. I'll call forth, and I'll put into place those who will oversee this. When the time comes, I'll bring forth a continuous flow of servants that I will draw to this work. I will confirm the calling of each person to the spirits of these counselors."

"Make no mistake, son. I say to you again—PRAY, with great urgency! **Satan will attempt to destroy this work. He will try to deceive you, for he is the Deceiver. Beware! His initial efforts to destroy this will come through Doubt, Distraction, Disruption, and Discord. If unsuccessful, Satan will revert to other methods. Intense opposition to what I am revealing to you will arise. There will be much harsh, outright condemnation. His ways never change. The greatest potential for devastation will come through family and friends. Those you respect and admire will assail you the most.** That is why I am both cautioning and commanding you now: **THIS SHALL BE MY WORK AND MINE ALONE.** This move of Mine will not be a democracy. There will be no majority rule vote. Decisions will be unanimous, and those I place in positions of authority must be in one accord. If there is **ANY** dissent, My Spirit has no part in it. A house divided **will** fall. When My servants seek Me in further prayer, I will give them an understanding of My plans. I am Faithful and True. I'll expect these counselors to be likewise. I alone will be responsible for releasing My servants from their part in this calling. Decisions will not be by vote or by whim. It will be through the unanimous confirmation of the will of the Father, as voiced by My Spirit to each. **That is how it was in the upper room on the day of Pentecost.** Similarly, this movement will operate on absolute obedience and unity. Watch and behold as My Spirit moves to fulfill the Father's perfect will."

As night began to darken the early evening sky, I stood there, facing the window, staring without seeing. Instead, my mind remained focused on the seemingly endless images filling my consciousness.

"Holy Spirit, You poured into me so rapidly just now that I didn't have time to think about what I was seeing. The pictures were clearer this time, but what I saw is now stirring up so many questions and concerns."

"I know your concerns, and I'll address them all later. For now, allow me to give you a fuller understanding of what I revealed to you. It was not coincidental that the song _Thy Throne Oh God_ [S-6] played when it did. The words of that song spoke, at that moment, to the heart of what I needed you to understand."

"Lord, I began weeping uncontrollably as the call went forth for RIGHTEOUSNESS—over and over! Then they started singing about Your throne lasting forever. Holy Spirit, when I heard those words, I _know_ I heard a loud voice declare, 'SO IT SHALL BE!' But I don't believe that's on the CD."

"Yes, son, you heard right, but you heard it in your spirit. **My righteousness is part of the very foundation upon which My throne exists.** So also must it be for this organization, and all involved in it. I'll speak more about this to you later. For now, receive My understanding about that which I've allowed you to see."

Once more, my mind filled with one image after another in a rapid sequence.

"Wow, Holy Spirit! I saw the tower a third time! It was even clearer this time. It was a four-story tower, and more octagon-shaped. The first floor seemed to be where a report was being coordinated, composed, and made ready for distribution."

"The faithful that I call will receive and publish reports about the movement of the Spirit of Christ in every city, town and village, both in churches and synagogues, as well as outside of these places of worship. Know this! There will be many Religious spirits set against this work. A demonic power of Non-Cooperation will direct them. If everyone involved abides in Me, this organization will meet its purpose. "Love Will Make A Way" is to be both the organization name and its purpose."

"Lord, You said you would call these others. Will they be volunteers or paid? If paid, by whom? That's a lot of ongoing responsibility and expense."

"I told you this would not be something you would handle. That which I ordain, I bring to pass and provide for abundantly. I own the cattle on a thousand hills, so why would this be a problem for Me, the Lord of all?"

"Forgive me, Lord. My mind doesn't always think of the big plan, and this is a lot to take in."

"It was not always so. There were many seasons when you completely focused on Me. You anticipated and embraced those dreams I birthed in you. Some you pursued with diligence and passion, and much fruit came forth. Others you doubted. Your hesitations and fears became like concrete that hardened around your feet. Those dreams withered, like ripened fruit left to dry on the vine. Their potential was forever lost. **For Me to fulfill My will in this, you <u>must</u> change, with your mind conforming to the mind of Christ. You will represent Me as a chosen vessel of the Creator of the universe. I desire that you would think and act accordingly.** *When the timing is right, I will send laborers worthy of their hire, with a passion for this work. You must love and cherish them, and do likewise for everyone called to this undertaking. As a demonstration to the world, love must flow freely between everyone called to this work. Only then will the rest of My body, and the rest of the world, see and believe that, indeed, love—My Love—***will*** *make a way. Such a possibility will only come to pass through a communion of hearts overflowing with My Spirit."*

Without any warning, I found my thoughts pulled into a new direction. The change was so abrupt that I initially questioned if it was still the Holy Spirit.

"Lord, I just had a sudden flashback to the very first time I observed Demos Shakarian, the founder of Full Gospel Business Men's Fellowship. That was more than twenty years ago!"

"Yes. There is a reason that I brought this memory alive in you, son. It's very much related to all that I've been revealing to you. Think about it. Do you remember your actions that day?"

"Yes, Lord. That was the first Full Gospel weekend function I ever attended. I was still skeptical about what I called the "Holy Spirit" stuff. Forgive me, Lord. From my end seat on the fifth row, at the far left side of the room, I studied Demos as he spoke. I remember how he told some corny jokes, and then laughed so hard and long at his own joke that he had tears in his eyes."

"He had the heart of a child—a beautiful, loving child."

"I know that now, Lord. Still, I remember that I ridiculed him in my mind and heart at the time. I was an ornery cuss. Oh, my God! I realized something right this second when I wrote this. That was the exact name of the demonic force that You told me to break fellowship with the other night, which surprised me because I would never have thought to call a demon by the name of Ornery."

"Exactly, son. Ornery. It was there all along. **Their names always perfectly describe their nature and workings.** *That's why those who co-labor with Me in deliverance must discern by My Spirit. That which they have discerned and confirmed by My Spirit* **will depart** *when they are commanded to do so by My authority and power, in My Name."*

"When addressing the demon spirits, do so **BY NAME, for their names are a direct indicator of their character and nature, as well as the task or purpose that the evil one has assigned to them***. Recall how those at the church ministered to you and your wife, and how they trained you to help so many others."*

"Oh, Jesus! Thank You for patiently waiting for me, and not giving up on me, Lord!"

"I told you I began calling you in your mother's womb. Even as you criticized Demos in your heart on that day, I still loved you with a love that knew no bounds. Do you remember what else happened that day as you watched Demos?"

"Yes, Lord. I will never forget. Near the end of that day's meeting, the chairman announced that Demos would pray for anyone who wanted prayer. Most of the men immediately gathered into a long line, all the way to the back of the room. As they waited for their turn to receive prayer, I remained seated until the line grew shorter. While I watched, I'd carefully studied Demos. In my heart, skepticism and a judgmental attitude lingered. I was confident that he had to be pushing the men over as he prayed for them. Deciding, in my skepticism, to get a closer look, I'd moved to a spot in the room perpendicular to where he stood. With an unobstructed view, I watched for quite a while, unaware of an increasing sense of awe that slowly overtook me. Demos' hand lighted touched some of the men, but for the majority, his hand never came close enough to touch their foreheads. Tears streamed down his cheeks, and he had the most beautiful smile on his face. Each time, he'd lifted his hand and said, 'JESUS' in the sweetest, most loving voice I'd ever heard, and BAM! The one he was praying for would drop like a rock! Oh, my Lord! I just realized how that is the same thing that happened when I prayed for those in Argentina!"

"*Yes, son. It did because you placed your heart in My hands that day. Regarding Demos, what happened to your heart the day you observed him, son?*"

"My heart ached! I was no longer able to deny what my eyes and spirit had seen. I bawled my eyes out as I stood there, watching for a very long time. My heart ached intensely, Lord! That day, I wanted so much to know You as intimately as Demos knew You. And my heart and chest truly ached, Holy Spirit!"

"*For years, you searched for the love that your soul so desperately craved. Still, you'd never seen such a great demonstration of My Love. At that moment, your journey of love began. It has been a journey of many trials and much resistance to change. It has required My periodic disciplining, but only because I love you, and I alone know what the Father has appointed for you to do in the Body of Christ.*"

"O, Lord! I love You so much, and I never get tired of saying it to You!"

"*Son, that day, you saw love flowing unhindered from Demos' spirit and soul. You felt the unbridled passion in his heart. This same passion must flow freely from the hearts of those I call to this new work. Only then will others who observe truly believe that My love will make a way. Once others witness that magnitude of My love, their excuses and doubts melt away. No longer will it matter what religious doctrine they claim to believe. Their hearts will ache with longing, even as yours did that day. Then My Spirit will be able to move unhindered in their spirits and souls. He will win them without resistance into the Kingdom of God. In that type of atmosphere, you will also see My Spirit move in signs and wonders that will astound the world. That which occurred in this country for a brief period many years ago will begin to manifest. Great waves of life-transforming salvations will occur. The timid will be immediately encouraged to rise and step forward—as you did that day, son. They will cry out from a sincere longing in their hearts, and I will send them forth as My army. You will then see deliverances, healings, and miracles sweeping across this land.*"

"Oh, God! That will be a glorious day!"

"*Yes, it will. That is why this work must succeed. Back to the tower, for now. What else did I show you?*"

"Lord, the third floor had no windows. It looked like a large, open conference room. That's where I saw the chairs."

"In that room is where the board that I appoint will meet—set aside unto Me. What did I show you in the upper room?"

"It was incredibly glorious, Lord! I couldn't stop crying—tears of joy! It gave me chills and thrilled my heart. The outer walls on all sides were glass, from floor to ceiling. It appeared to be a sanctuary of intercession and celebration."

"Yes, son, you did not imagine it."

"O, God! I'm so glad that You're confirming this. I thought I was going crazy. You know, I jumped up and began pacing back and forth in this hotel room, pleading the Blood of Jesus over me and my mind. Thank You, Lord. I didn't imagine it!"

"You're quite sane and seeing what I want you to see. Do not doubt. Resist your enemy, and he will flee. Now, what did I show you in the tower, son?"

"Heaven, Lord! Heaven on earth! Incredibly glorious!"

"And so it shall be!"

"Lord, I saw the room filled with people. They were slowly walking around the perimeter of the room, praying in the spirit. Many cried out to the hills and the plains, boldly prophesying in the Name of the Lord. There were elderly and middle-aged folks—and not just women, Lord, but a lot of men!"

"Yes, son, but there were more."

"Yes! There were teens and college students, and they were the most vocal, crying out and praying so boldly!"

"What about the children?"

"O, Lord Jesus! My heart went wild with joy when I saw that there were also so many young children. Some appeared to be as young as six or seven! They were not merely mimicking the older ones. They were crying out in worship and petitioning heaven with such passion! There were many people in that room, everyone intermixed. They moved around the room like a turning wheel, looking out the glass and praying aloud. O, God! My mind is wacky right now. As I was writing this, I thought about how that had better be one solid floor and structure to bear that kind of weight. I am sorry, Lord. I don't know why I'm laughing, but I can't help it!"

*"There's nothing wrong with laughter. It came forth because of the presence of my joy in you. Moreover, what you said is right. The engineer **will** need to consider that issue when designing the building. For now, what else did I show you?"*

"Oh, sweet merciful Lord in Heaven! I saw angels, Lord! For the first time in my life! Huge angels! At least they seemed huge. They appeared like lightning strikes, but without thunder! I don't know how else to describe it, Lord! They entered into that room with a burst of light. Each one slipped right into that procession of intercessors, Lord! I knew in my mind that there wasn't room for anyone else. Nonetheless, they slipped right between every two persons without anyone missing a step. The number of angels multiplied, and the room became brilliant—I mean absolutely, incredibly luminous! Then the people themselves began to glow, each with a unique brilliance! I remember, Lord, it was just starting to get dark outside. One moment I was in the room—at least it felt like I was. In the next moment, I was hundreds of miles away, standing in a valley, looking in the direction of the tower. A brilliance burst across the mountains and plains! It was like a lighthouse! No! Far brighter! In all directions! Then the song began playing, calling for 'RIGHTEOUSNESS! RIGHTEOUSNESS! RIGHTEOUSNESS! RIGHTEOUSNESS!'[S-6] After that, everyone—I mean all of the angels and everyone else—burst into song!"

"Yes, My son. *The people sang with all their hearts, minds, souls, and strength: 'Thy throne, Oh God, will last forever! Last Forever! Will Last Forever! For in Your Hands are Truth and Righteousness. RIGHTEOUSNESS! You reign with RIGHTEOUSNESS! Forever! Forever!'* [S-6]"

"Yes, Lord! Exactly! I was battling so hard to believe and not to doubt because it so overwhelmed me. I thought the song playing was influencing me."

"What you saw was what I wanted you to see."

"Then, in an instant, I was back with them in the tower! It was fantastic! I watched everyone, Lord. As they sang, they spontaneously began dancing and wildly rejoicing! The little children and the teens first, then the others broke, becoming as small children. The angels were right there in the midst of them, celebrating and singing. I remember thinking, Lord—so many people and yet, no one banging into each other. Like one beautiful synchronized waltz, but faster, and more exultant! Everyone was crying tears of rejoicing. Uncontrollable weeping, and laughing, and singing, and dancing! As the song and celebration rose to a crescendo, I saw the Glory of Your Presence fill the room! So bright! So sweet! Oh, Jesus! My Lord and My God! I love You so much! I long for that day!"

"Son, it was but a slight foretaste of what happens without end around My Throne in Heaven. That upper room will be a sanctuary of intercession and celebration, and the Glory of My Presence will periodically fill the room. It will truly be My beacon of light to the hills and the plains, beckoning and drawing men, women, and children to Me."

"Yes, Lord! It also dawned on me that You had shown me the top of this tower in an open vision ten or eleven months earlier. It was at one of our Saturday morning prayer gatherings. I remember that I had seen then, in the spirit, many people crying out to the hills and plains. I hadn't understood at the time what I was seeing. Even so, I felt compelled to join them, to cry aloud, repeatedly. I called for watchmen to rise from the North, East, South, and West. I called them to cry out to the people, to the cities, to the churches, to wake up, to come out of their slumber! I remember commanding Satan and his forces, in the Name of Jesus Christ, to release the people. I demanded his release of their minds, hearts, strength, and souls, as well as their finances. I cried out so loud, and for so long, with such an indescribable sense of desperation, that I began bawling. I remember yelling many times, 'Jesus Christ rebukes you, Satan!' The other men there that morning didn't comprehend how overwhelming it was to me. They did not know how constrained I'd felt to act. While trying to explain what You'd shown me, I'd stopped mid-sentence and just stared at the men. Instead of continuing, I'd sat down and said no more. Broken and weeping, I'd made no further attempt to explain because I had no idea what was happening, or why there was such a burning passion for me to do what I'd impulsively done."

"I allowed you that morning to experience the desire you will witness in My people who stand watch in My tower, son. When you witness it and see My Glory fill that room, you will weep freely as your heart leaps with ecstasy. At that moment, you will rejoice and thank Me beyond measure for encouraging you to believe and resist the inclination to doubt."

"Oh, God! I can't stop crying! Thank You so much! I will welcome that day. I love You, Lord Jesus! I love You, My Father! I love You, sweet Holy Spirit!"

† † †

"Lord, I just looked at the clock, thinking that I must have been writing for a long time because my hand is very sore. I couldn't believe it, Lord! It's one o'clock in the morning. I've been sitting here, praying in the spirit and writing what You're telling me, for over ten hours. Little wonder that my hand hurts! Even so, I won't stop until You tell me to stop. I don't want to miss anything."

"Thank you, son. Do you recall the quiet places and the nearby gardens on the property?"

"Yes, Lord. I asked about them, but You didn't answer me."

"I did answer you, son. I said to be patient. Everything must be in the Father's timing. Now, let Me give you revelation about what you saw. What you saw are places of seclusion, gardens, and benches, where many will go to spend quiet time with Me. Do you recall that I said I would draw men and women, young and old, to the tower? They will have seen My glory or heard of it from others. They will come, son—a few at a time, in a steady flow. Many will be looking for healing for their bodies and souls. Some will arrive longing for release from burdens they have carried for years. They will yearn for peace of mind. The majority will desire to be set free from whatever plagues them, but most will not understand the absolute darkness that has them trapped."

"So, this will be what I saw?"

"No, it will not be a center dedicated exclusively to deliverance ministry. Still, those who come will feel compelled by My Spirit to come. They will long for help, for relief. Most will move on into works I have ordained for them. A few will remain and join in

this ministry. My Spirit will witness to your spirits about those the Lord will call to join you."

"Lord, this is going to take constant bathing in intercessory prayer. And we're going to need continuous discernment."

"My Spirit will guide all of you in the gift of discernment as necessary. As to the prayer, you are correct. In time, you will have grown to where there will be intercessors on watch throughout the day and night, every day. My saints cannot afford to have their enemy find them sleeping because he doesn't sleep."

"Yes, Lord."

"Son, do you realize why I revealed specific names to you?"

"I imagined that You must somehow want to bring together their wisdom and experience."

"Definitely, but much, much more! Look at their names again. Every one of them, including you, have many things in common. You each have an undeniable love for Me that will allow Me to express My passionate love for others through you. You each have a heart for the lost, the hurting, the outcast, the bound—a heart not of your making, but one that I have shaped. Each of you, in your walk with Me, has stepped beyond your comfort zone into my will. Every one of you has heard My call and responded. This response led you to foreign countries and unfamiliar situations. In this way, I stretched you time after time. Moreover, you all, in those times, trusted Me. As you did, you saw My redeeming grace, healing touch, and deliverance. Each has been willing to confront their enemy aggressively, without relenting. All of you, at some point, have stumbled. I was always there to pick you, and them, up and set you back upon My Solid Rock. I forgave you and restored you because I heard the repentant cry of your heart. Those experiences have strengthened each of you. Now, each understands that they are a work in progress, with a heart that cries out for humility and brokenness. All are extremely at ease praying in their prayer language, and boldly do so when necessary."

"But Lord, couldn't this last thing be a stumbling block to everything else. There is sure to be significant resistance for this very reason from many of the churches. They will be suspicious about proselytizing. They'll worry about us leading their members into a way of thinking or acting that they don't endorse."

"Yes, My son. I told you that there would be tremendous resistance, and it will come through the churches. More precisely, it will come through the Religious spirits controlling the churches. That is why the most important thing that must occur is prayer, prayer, and more prayer. **Fervent prayer!** *If you adhere to this, diligently and faithfully, strongholds will come down. Then the love of My Spirit will begin flowing through every one of these churches and their members. My Spirit will go forth as a Mighty River of My love and My redeeming grace. My mercy, blessing, and anointing will flow. My healing, miracles, and deliverance will blossom forth. With affected*

hearts softened, they will long to testify to the mighty acts they have experienced and seen. They will feel compelled to announce to the world the splendor and majesty of the King. This movement of My making—'Love Will Make A Way'—will give them that means. Believe and do not doubt! Pray without ceasing! Implore the Heavens with your cry to see this come to pass! When this is all accomplished, the work will then multiply and expand."

"In what way, Lord?"

"Do you remember the other towers I showed you? It was immediately after My Glory descended upon that upper room."

"I wondered about that at the time. I thought I imagined it, or was mistaken, and then I almost forgot it."

"No, you have been so focused on all that you've heard and written that it was not foremost in your mind and heart. Now, I want to explain. What did I show you, son?"

"Lord, I recall it now, but it's nearly two o'clock in the morning. We've been at this almost eleven hours."

"Son, would you stay alert a little while longer? Then I'll allow you to get some deep rest before you start the journey home."

"Yes, Lord. Thank You."

"The other towers, son. What did I show you?"

"There were several more! I was both excited, because of what I saw in the upper room, and puzzled, when you showed me the second tower. I didn't understand, and I don't think I asked for an explanation."

"You didn't, but now I will explain. What I revealed to you was the second tower on the western side of these majestic mountains."

"But it seemed like it was farther south."

"It was in the southwestern portion of this state. It was up high and viewable at a great distance. It will give the intercessors there an unobstructed view."

"Lord, I don't understand. What is the point of two towers, or any additional ones?"

"Son, the first will be My prayer tower and beacon to those areas and peoples east of the Rockies. This location will reach the English-speaking peoples of this continent. The second prayer tower will be My beacon to those north and west of that location, and into Central and South America as well. It will be like the first tower, except I'm calling a diverse group of intercessors and servants there. They will reach the Spanish-speaking peoples. A separate reporting, from that same location, will go forth to the North, Central, and South American Native peoples."

"But Lord, You then showed me two more towers. The third was high up in the mountains of Brazil. I recognized the statue they always show in pictures of Rio de Janeiro. The fourth tower seemed to be overlooking a greatly populated city in Canada. Was it Toronto?"

"Yes, son. Toronto. The prayer tower in Brazil will reach the Portuguese-speaking peoples. Similarly, the prayer tower overlooking Toronto will reach the French-speaking peoples."

"But don't most of the people in Toronto speak English, Lord?"

"Yes, but this will reach the peoples of Quebec. It will help to tear down walls of pride, schism, strife, bitterness, resentment, and distrust between Quebec and the rest of their nation. Fervent prayer and demonstrations of My love will tear those walls down. Love **WILL** make a way! Later, there will be more towers, son, as more and more churches come together in oneness of accord. But this is enough for now."

"Lord, may I please ask a few questions?"

"Yes."

"I'm trying to absorb and understand all that You said. If I heard You right, the immediate task that I should focus on is prayer. You'll then establish all that You've explained—while we maintain constant prayer."

"No, My son. **The prayer must steadily INCREASE. The results of the prayer will explode into the kingdoms of this world. Only then will principalities, powers, and strongholds of all types lose their impact. Barriers will shatter. Great walls of resistance will come crashing down. Doors will open, and opportunities will arise in many different areas. I alone will direct each step of this move. All I ask for is a humble, broken people willing to follow.**"

"But at what point do we begin reporting on the move of your Spirit?"

"This will come forth when prayer has broken resistance. **Only then will the rest begin to materialize.** It will pour forth abundantly from the bosoms of men and women of like spirit, whose hearts I will stir. It will all come together in the perfect timing of the Father."

"Holy Spirit, where and when do the foreign countries come into the scheme of things?"

"When the time is right, invitations will come from nearby countries and beyond the oceans. As I told you, I will send you to strife-filled and war-torn nations and peoples. I am preparing your heart and the hearts of others, birthing in each an incredible compassion for these nations. When the time is right, you will go."

"Lord, I'm sure there are thousands of small details that I haven't even begun to consider. I am glad this is Your responsibility!"

"Son, there is a multitude of details to work out and arrange. **First, before anything else, there must be prayer—fervent, prolonged prayer.** I want you to mail this to each person I named, and to other faithful prayer warriors whose names I will provide. Then wait on My Spirit, and continue praying. Do not burden yourself with concern as to if, when, or how these others will respond. Do not make an effort to contact any of them. When they have heard from Me, I will encourage them to communicate with you. Relax *and go to sleep, son. It's nearly 3:30 in the morning. On your way home tomorrow, worship the Lord with all of your heart. Sing to Me of your love for Me. Be open to My leading. I will cause those two days of driving to pass quickly and fill you with abundant joy as I interact with you. I love you, son, very much!"*

"I love You too, Lord Jesus! Thank You so much for these past forty days. It's been the hardest thing I've ever attempted."

"Yes. You persisted, and together, we accomplished much. This discipline will become invaluable for you later, son."

"Lord, a picture just popped into my mind from my days in the Marine Corps nearly thirty years ago. It was about the drown-proofing training that was part of basic training. Is this a demon spirit trying to distract my mind?"

"No, son. I caused you to recall it."

"Why? Staying afloat for an hour in full combat uniform with pack and helmet was incredibly hard. It isn't a memory I enjoy recalling. Why would You bring this up?"

"That struggle is an excellent comparison to what has occurred over the last forty days. In the Marines, they were training you to be an overcomer. They created in you a discipline that would be imperative in a time of war. **You discovered the power of a willing spirit. You found that you were capable of much more than you had initially believed possible.** *My training is exactly like that, except that I prepare you for spiritual battle. With Me, You confront principalities and powers, and boldly face rulers of the darkness of this world and spiritual wickedness in high places.* **To be effective, you must first bring your flesh, your mind, and your soul into submission. You must die to the will of the flesh. It's a yielding unto Me, as one alive from the dead, with you becoming an instrument of righteousness for Me to direct.** *Remember what the angels cried out in the upper room that I revealed to you, son! Always remember! The cry of the Father's heart will shake the heavens. It will one day reverberate throughout this land. That cry was for RIGHTEOUSNESS."*

"Yes, Lord."

Evidence of Love

By mid-morning of the following day, I was four hours east of Fort Collins on Interstate-70. Six or more hours remained before my planned overnight stop in Kansas City. As miles clicked by, I alternated between listening to my Bible on cassette and worship music CDs. My spirit was joyful as I loudly sang along with the song currently playing. <u>My Deliverer</u>[S-7]—by the Calvary Temple of Indianapolis Praise Choir—had become my new favorite.

My car crested a hill in the stretch of I-70 on which I was currently driving. I noticed a Kansas Highway Patrol vehicle on my side of the Interstate, about two miles ahead. I had been traveling for hours with my cruise control set at the sixty-five mile per hour limit. Still, out of habit, I glanced at the speedometer to verify my current speed. My gaze returned to the KHP vehicle, and I now saw the second car in front of it, both pulled over onto the right berm. Less than a mile away and closing the gap fast, I observed as the door from the patrol car opened. The officer stepped out and walked toward the driver's vehicle.

Steering into the left lane to safely pass both of them, I guided my vehicle back to the right about two hundred yards later. Glancing in the rearview mirror a minute or two later, I saw the officer's car pull back onto the Interstate. His cruiser rapidly closed the distance between us. He then drew even with and alongside my car. I observed in my peripheral vision as the officer matched my speed while staring at me. I ignored him as I continued down the road singing. A minute later, he slowed, swung his vehicle in behind mine, and turned on his flashing lights.

Frustration grabbed hold of me as I turned on my signal and pulled over onto the berm. In seconds, the frustration morphed into anger. I thought of the blatant harassment this officer might be about to unleash on me.

I spoke aloud to the Lord, a noticeable edge in my tone of voice. "I didn't do a single thing wrong!"

"Do not allow yourself to lose your peace over this, son," the Holy Spirit responded.

I turned down my music and waited. The officer approached the passenger side and tapped his flashlight on the window. I pressed the button to lower the powered window. He glanced at me, at the interior of the car, and then spoke.

"Where are you heading, sir?"

"Kansas City," I replied.

"Where are you coming from?" the officer asked.

"Fort Collins, Colorado," I answered.

"What were you doing there?" the officer probed.

Without hesitation, I told him, "I spent five days there just worshipping and talking with the Lord." In the next moment, everything changed. Before I even understood what was happening, I started weeping uncontrollably.

The KHP officer stared at me for a moment, confusion and suspicion evident on his face. He then asked, "Why are you crying?"

Uncertain about what to say, I opened my mouth, and an answer came forth. "I just love the Lord so much!"

"May I search your car, sir?" the officer asked, abruptly.

"Sure," I responded and pushed the button to unlock the vehicle doors.

"Please turn the engine off and step out of the vehicle," the officer requested. When I'd complied, the officer crouched down and searched under the car seats with his flashlight. He then checked the glove box in the dashboard and looked into the rear seat. The only things in the interior of my vehicle were some bottled water and a case of worship music CDs.

"Would you mind opening the trunk?" the officer asked.

I pushed the button to open the trunk. I knew the only things in the car trunk were a couple of gym bags. They contained my Bible, journals, speakers, and the few clothes I'd brought with me. I watched without saying a word as the officer looked through the little he found there.

Closing the trunk, the officer explained, "We've had a lot of people coming through lately, claiming to be religious when, in fact, they were hauling drugs."

I didn't respond, and the officer said, "Please return to your vehicle and wait. I'll be with you in a few minutes."

I did as he'd ordered. While sitting there waiting for the officer to return, I asked the Holy Spirit, "What's going on? You know I haven't given him any cause to pull me over."

I glanced in the rearview mirror at the officer, still sitting in his patrol car. Thoughts bombarded my mind as I battled against the anger that had returned to overtake me.

"He's going to issue you a citation, son. Take it, thank him, and don't argue."

I sharply questioned the Lord. "A citation for what? I didn't do anything wrong! I hate cops like this!"

***"Son, I've spent many hours teaching you about My love. How can My love reign in you if you knowingly side with Hate？** Please let My peace abide in you at this moment, and accept the citation. I'll explain later."*

"Fine," I responded begrudgingly. I saw the officer once again approaching the passenger side of my car and lowered the car window.

"I have to cite you," he said. "A warning, this time. You were swerving back there. If you're tired, pull over in a rest stop for a while. Otherwise, stay alert and maintain better control," the officer stated. I signed the citation without looking at the officer. He tore the offender's copy out of the book and handed it to me.

At that instant, I heard the Holy Spirit prompt me again to thank the officer. I did not feel right in doing so, yet I obeyed. One minute later, I was back heading east, my cruise control set to the posted speed limit, as before. In frustration, I left the worship music off. Now I rode along in silence, wondering why the Lord asked me to accept blame for something that I knew to be a lie. After five minutes had passed, the Holy Spirit spoke to me.

"Thank you for obeying, son."

"I didn't have much choice," I replied, still somewhat upset. "I didn't do anything wrong! I end up looking like an idiot to him, and get a ticket out of the deal!"

"My son, I didn't do anything wrong either, and they scourged and crucified Me."

Overwhelmed by His offered comparison, I said nothing more.

"Now, let Me explain what just occurred. My Spirit inside of you caused your emotions to well up. Seeing you crying, the officer became suspicious. That was My doing."

"Why? I don't understand," I said meekly.

"The officer would not otherwise have given you that citation, son. **I needed to request something of you, and I had to be certain that you could not doubt in your mind that you are hearing Me.** *Now, pull the citation out of your shirt pocket."*

I did as the Lord requested.

"Read the officer's name on the bottom of the citation."

Still not understanding, I complied, stating the officer's name aloud.

"He and his wife are My children, son."

"What about the fact that he just lied, Lord? I wasn't swerving, as he indicated in justifying the reason for the ticket!"

"Son, you have lied, at times, to justify your actions, and caused harm to others of which you were not even aware. Neither the police officer nor you were right. Even so, I never condemned you because of what you did. My Spirit extended grace to you while also convicting you of the error of your ways, making it possible for you to confess and repent. It then was no longer a hindrance to us communing. Isn't it right that I extend the same grace to the police officer? Shouldn't I allow him the same opportunity to confess and repent as I gave you?"

"Listen now to what I'm about to say. As I stated, I set into motion what occurred for a divine purpose of which you are not yet aware. That officer and his wife are My

children, and they are desperately in need of My help. Both of them are going through some very trying times right now. Each is thinking of ending their marriage. I brought that marriage about with a far greater purpose in mind. It is one which neither of them is yet aware—with the potential to help millions of individuals."

"**What I seek at this moment is a surrendered vessel willing to petition heaven on their behalf. That will give My Spirit grounds to respond.** Leave the music off. Pray in your spirit language for the next thirty minutes. *I want you to allow Me to pour Myself through your intercession, for their sake.*"

My immediate response leaned toward shame at the way I had acted. However, the Holy Spirit interrupted my thoughts. *"That feeling of shame is not from Me, son. Remember that I arranged this divine appointment. Ignore your enemy. Pour out your heart to me. Be My prepared vessel at this moment through which My 'love will make a way' for Me to reach the officer and his wife."*

For the next thirty minutes, I opened myself up to the intensity of the Spirit moving through me. I prayed in tongues and wept as He burdened my heart and soul for that couple.

After checking into my hotel room that evening, I felt led to sit in quiet before the Lord. About forty-five minutes later, the Spirit prompted me to open up my journal and pick up my pens. I began writing as He spoke.

"Son, this afternoon, about the seventh hour of driving, you came under great attack. You were oblivious about what was occurring. Your mind was no longer following the music in worshipping Me. Instead, you were again beginning to follow the path of doubt and worry."

"I realized it when You told me," I acknowledged.

"Yes, but it had been going on for quite a while before that time."

"That's when I asked You if You would object to me calling my close friend and prayer partner that he might pray with me. I knew he'd most likely be at home."

"And I said, 'NO.' But, you persisted," the Spirit stated.

"Lord, I knew then that I was beginning to doubt again. I asked if I could ask him to pray for me and say nothing more."

"No, that's not what you said, son. You said, 'I'll tell him I'm struggling over what I believe You're telling me to do. I'll ask him to lift it to the Lord in prayer to see if he gets a confirmation that this is Your will. I'll have him leave his response on my answering machine at home. That way, he won't know what it's about, leaving him unbiased in his praying.' Isn't that what you said, son?"

"Yes, Lord. It is," I sheepishly agreed.

"Then I said to you, 'NO. Turn on your Bible cassette. I have some things I want to teach you.' Didn't I?"

"Yes, Lord. I'm sorry. You're right, and when I went back to the tape, it happened to be at Luke 7—the section where the centurion sent someone to plead for Jesus to come and heal His servant. I recall that You had me replay verses seven and eight several times. It was where the centurion said, '...*say the word, and my servant will be healed. For I also am a man placed under authority, having soldiers under me. And I say to one, "Go," and he goes; and to another, "Come," and he comes; and to my servant, "Do this," and he does it.*"[1]

"Yes, and I say to you now, My son, *I am the One in whose hands the Father placed ALL authority.* One day you will understand the authority I give to those placed under Me, and you will then speak as the Centurion spoke, without wavering."

"You still need to learn what it means when I tell you to call things into existence. You are, at that moment, acting as *'a man placed under authority.'*[2] You are fulfilling My command. It is *My* responsibility, *and only MINE*, as to when and how those things will come into existence, not yours. I select vessels of My choosing to fulfill My will. All I ask is obedience. You were in the Marine Corps, son. What did they teach you about obeying commands?"

"To obey first and ask why later, or someday in combat, you may not be alive to ask why."

"Exactly. There is much to gain by an immediate response. I'm aware that man too often abuses this principle. I am not one to abuse. Trust Me. Stop second-guessing your Commander-In-Chief."

"Yes, Lord. Forgive me."

"Because I love you, I am always ready to forgive you. Now, what about My stopping the funeral procession and calling that widow's son back to life? Didn't I tell you that the key was loving compassion? *Remember this! A passionate faith is not enough. To be a chosen vessel, one must FIRST have a compassionate spirit.* My children must do today as I did then in restoring life to that woman's son. The Father needs **His** compassion pouring forth through His children. In this case, however, it will be to spiritually dead churches. Then the 'sons' of these churches, likewise, as with that widow's son, will come alive—*in Me*. The 'sons' that I refer to are the spiritually dead and asleep church leaders and church members. When this occurs, great rejoicing will result!"

"And the reason for this is simple. Love *NEVER* fails! I say to you again, son—Love *WILL* make a way. *I am Love.* You did *not* imagine it. I ordained it to be so. Now, turn to Luke 8:16 in your Bible, and allow Me to give you an understanding on this part once again."

Turning to the indicated chapter and verse, I read it aloud.

"'*No one, when he has lit a lamp, covers it with a vessel, or puts it under a bed, but sets it on a lampstand, that those who enter there may see the light.*'"[2]

This Scripture is another one that You had me listen to many times, Lord."

"*Write it down in your journal, son.*"

When I had finished, He continued speaking.

"*I then asked you, son, 'Who lit you?'*"

"Yes. And I immediately realized what You were getting at."

"*Yes, son, but you did so **because** of the understanding I gave you. I did not light you—My lamp—to watch your light fade or disappear. Neither did I light you to set you in a place where your light would be of little value. No, I've chosen to stir you now with My Breath—My Holy Spirit—so that My Light in you might burn brighter. I'm placing you on a lampstand of My choosing—one fashioned for you alone. I do so, not that others might see you, but rather that they might see My Light shining forth from you. As more and more of My children come to understand and open themselves to this, so will My Light increase—first, in that region, and then across this land. That is what you saw in the vision of the prayer tower, son. They were all My chosen vessels, burning with My Holy Fire, placed up high upon the lampstand of My choosing. The final impact will be glorious! The brilliance of My Light changing this continent and the world!*"

"Yes, Lord. Please cause me to burn even brighter for You! Increase my fervency and passion, O Lord!"

"*I will, as you seek Me and, having heard, obey Me. Do you recall what I showed you next?*"

"Yes. It was when You appointed and sent out the seventy disciples, in chapter ten." I added that Scripture reference to my journal also.

"*I said I would always send my laborers out two by two,*" the Lord continued. "*Likewise, when I send you, I will always send someone as a companion and support. I will do this for all those that I call to this work. I will send each group, here and abroad, as My ambassadors. They will go in advance to those cities, churches, and peoples where I, in the fullness of My Spirit, am about to arrive. I am calling you, and everyone called to this work, to be My vessels. Allow Me to fill you with My Love, shining My Light through you into the darkness, **preparing the Way of the Lord**. Those who will hear you will hear Me. They will look into your eyes and witness My Light in you, and My Light will draw them as a moth draws near to the flame. When they do so, they will discover what you have discovered. My Fire does not harm, for My Fire is the all-consuming passion of My Love, which transforms the hearts of men and women.*"

"Yes, Lord. Please don't stop changing my heart!"

"*I won't, as long as you remain a willing vessel. Now, what was the final thing I showed you concerning this work, My son?*"

"It pertained to the story of the Samaritan helping the robbed and beaten man who others ignored and left to die." Those verses I also quickly copied into my journal.

"Listen again, **very carefully**, son. **This next lesson is one of the most crucial. It is a lesson that anyone who chooses to represent My heart and Spirit <u>MUST</u> learn.** *The Samaritan saw an opportunity to be a blessing to his fellow man. As such, his first thought or action was **NOT** to question the man about his beliefs. Instead, his **LOVE**— which was My love working through him—made a way to heal that man, restoring him to health. Likewise, when he committed himself to help, he did so **FULLY**. Additionally,* **he did this with no idea of, or concern about, what the final cost of his commitment would be.** *This type of dedication is what I require of everyone called to this work. I will present each of you with many opportunities to be a blessing, to show forth My love, and to shine brightly for Me. These opportunities will come as I send you to communities, churches, and the people in both. Some of those will have a **TRUE** relationship with Me. Others will think they do, but do not. If you will pray and follow the discernment and Voice of My Spirit, I will guide you. I will show you, in each situation, how My Love **will** make a way. I will heal those to whom I send you. I will restore their health—their souls and bodies. I will nurse them back to vibrant life. I will fitly join them together with a local body so that My Body can function as a whole. I will daily add to My Body.* **It will be My Love that will make it happen**, *My Love working through those I have called."*

"Lord, this could be an overwhelming task."

"*Son, if pursued in the flesh, this is a work destined for failure. The key will be abundant prayer. I will present the opportunities. Always bring these before Me in prayer to confirm. As I explained before,* **'there is safety in a multitude of counselors.'**³ *Likewise,* **the will of the Father can be most easily discovered through the unified petitions of a myriad of faithful intercessors, all pursuing the heart of the Lord.**"

"Thank You so much for both guiding me and teaching me these things, Holy Spirit. I'd love it if my time with You would always be like this."

"*Son, this is the way your time with Me should be* **EVERY** *time we meet,* **EVERY** *time you draw close to Me. It really can be this sweet all the time!*"

*Understand that My most significant work involves molding and shaping YOU.
I need your heart and mind conformed to Mine.
To the extent that you allow Me to work IN you, to that same extent will I work THROUGH you.*

Holding On, While Letting Go

In the two weeks following my return home, I used every spare minute to do what the Lord had asked of me. I mailed an explanation of what the Holy Spirit had shown me, and spoken of, to those He had designated. On my way to the Post Office to send them, the Holy Spirit reaffirmed His previous instruction to me.

"*Remember, son. You are to make no effort to contact these individuals in any way. When the time is right, I will quicken this to their heart, and they will contact you.*"

One month later, I received an envelope in the mail from a couple who lived an hour north of me. I did not recognize the name on the return address. The envelope contained a single page with one handwritten paragraph. It read, "You don't know us, and we've never met you. A friend of yours, who prayed for you during your trip to Colorado, allowed us to read what you had sent to him. We have been praying about this for over a week, and the Lord spoke to both of us independently. He said that we're to support what He wants to do through 'Love Will Make A Way.' We'll be praying for you."

Along with the short letter, they had enclosed a sizeable check. It amazed me that folks that I'd never met would send that kind of money. I wasn't quite sure what to do with it, so I sought the Lord in prayer about the situation for days. The Holy Spirit led me to request the advice of a specific pastor. He suggested that I deposit it into a bank account opened in the name of "Love Will Make A Way." The Holy Spirit confirmed this with me the following morning, repeating His directive.

"*As with the others, so also are you in no way to contact this couple. They have responded at My prompting with the offering toward this cause, son.*"

I complied without questioning. Even so, curiosity about the whole thing nagged at me.

Thirty more days passed without incident. One late afternoon on a cold day in December, I was outdoors, trimming some of the trees on our property. Next thing I knew, my wife opened the rear door and yelled for me.

"There's a phone call for you," she urged. "It's Gary Klein, and he's calling from Virginia."

Are You SURE God's Not Talking? (Or Are You Just NOT Listening?)

Gary was an evangelist that my wife and I had heard speak at a church that we'd attended some ten years earlier. At that time, the Holy Spirit had encouraged us to help finance his ministry. We'd done so, but we'd never personally met or spoken with him. Gary was also one of those to whom the Holy Spirit had directed me to mail a package about Colorado. I'd obeyed, making no mention on the cover sheet to our having been supporters of his ministry in the past. I'd wanted to be sure that he, like the others, would respond only when and if the Spirit directed.

"I just returned yesterday from an extended trip of several months in Europe," he told me. "I was going through my accumulated unread mail and came across what you sent to me. The last two weeks of my trip, I was in Israel, and the climax of that trip was a seven-day prayer conference in Jerusalem."

At this point, the evangelist began telling me about that prayer conference. I listened, even as a question bothered my mind. *Why is he telling me this?*

"The function was a World Conference on prayer," he continued. "There were people there from dozens of nations. On the first day of the conference, while I was worshipping the Lord with the others, the Holy Spirit spoke to me. He told me to sit down and write out exactly what He was about to reveal to me. I filled up seven notepad pages as He poured into me. When I asked Him what I should do with it, the Holy Spirit told me to take it to the conference Chairman. I obeyed, but the Chairman would not accept it from me, or even read it. Instead, he asked me to type it up so they could make copies for distribution should the Lord prompt him to do so. As requested, I found a typewriter and typed it out. I then carried the pages with me to each day's gathering, but I was never able to get a moment alone with the Chairman. On the morning of the last day of the conference, I began to doubt myself. I questioned if what I'd written was truly from the Lord."

"Then, a few minutes later," Gary continued, "the Chairman walked out onto the stage. Along with him was another man attending the conference. That man had a word from the Lord that the Chairman believed we all needed to hear. He then added that the Lord had instructed the man to sing it as a prophetic word from His Spirit. The man with the message closed his eyes and began singing it forth. As I listened, I immediately realized that I knew each word before he sang it. His words matched word-for-word with what the Holy Spirit had told me to write down six days earlier. I hurried from the back of the room to the area in front of the stage without disturbing anyone. Gaining the Chairman's attention, I handed him the typed pages. Pointing to the man singing the prophetic word, I then pointed to the typed pages. When he saw that the words the other man was singing matched my typed words, he excitedly followed along. After the man at the microphone had finished singing, the Chairman stepped to the microphone. He told the audience of the written confirmation given by the Holy Spirit to me six days earlier. Everyone erupted in praise to the Lord."

I listened as Gary related what had occurred, still puzzled as to why he had called to tell me this.

"When I got home and read what you'd sent to me," he continued, "I got excited again and had to call you. You described what the Holy Spirit revealed to you in Colorado. It exactly paralleled what the Holy Spirit revealed to the other man and me in Jerusalem. In short, the Holy Spirit declared that there would one day be a prayer tower built on Mt. Zion, like what you described. From that tower, fervent intercessory prayer would rise to Heaven. And He also said that, at times, the Glory of the Lord would descend to that upper room!"

Now I became excited! After a month of not hearing anything more about Colorado, finally, the Lord gave me a fresh jolt of hope. It caused my faith to grow to a new level. Gary then greatly encouraged me. He urged me to feel free to contact him in the future with anything else the Spirit might reveal regarding this.

That evening I lifted the whole thing to the Lord in prayer. As I lay in bed beside my sleeping wife, I thought again about the phone call. I also dwelt on all that the Spirit had shown me in Colorado. The more I did, the more excited I became.

"Is it going to be soon, Holy Spirit?" I quietly asked. I listened for quite some time but heard no reply.

Later that same month, the Lord directed me to move my family to another church. This new church, Heritage Fellowship, would be a full hour south of where we were currently living.

At the church from which we were departing, things had become unbearable. My wife and I had both seen too many instances in which the leadership restrained or ignored the Holy Spirit. We'd prayed about the situation at length. The Holy Spirit had revealed that a spirit of Control was directing the leader's actions. We had watched each month as more and more members left, never to return. We had seen on our trip to the Brownsville Revival how mightily the Spirit of God would move if permitted. We grieved at this refusal by our home church to allow Him to do so there. It reminded us of a similar church situation eleven years earlier, and the leadership there also knowingly chose to restrain the Holy Spirit. In that instance, a remarkable work of God fell apart in a very short period.

Following my trip to Colorado, my spirit seemed to grieve over our current church's resistance. I'd begun feeling as though I was spiritually suffocating there. For months, I'd prayed and begged God to either change the situation or allow us to move to another church. Finally, He'd released us to go to Heritage Fellowship full time. Before leaving there, however, my wife and I had met with the former Senior Pastor (now acting in the capacity of a bishop) and his wife. We'd explained the leading from the Holy Spirit to move. We'd thanked them for their pastoring, friendship and love, and departed as friends. We had called that church home for nine years, but now it was time to move on to what God had waiting for us.

During our first Sunday at Heritage, the pastor announced an upcoming four-day conference. My wife, youngest daughter, and I decided to attend. The guest evangelist, Debbie Keil-Smith, was from The River Church in Tampa. She was part of the ministry team under Rodney Howard-Browne. Each of the four days she spoke, her message focused on releasing God's blessing through giving. After the second day of two services a day (with offerings received at each), I began to become irritated. We already regularly gave tithes and offerings, many times sacrificially. The more I listened to her, the more her words bothered me. It felt to me as though she was pressuring the crowd to give, rather than allowing the Spirit to move. By the third day, I began to question whether she was capable of preaching about anything other than *giving*.

In the evening service of the last day, before the guest speaker had even begun preaching, the pastor announced that there would be two separate offerings. A moment later, the Holy Spirit interrupted my thoughts as I sat in the audience listening. He gave me specific directions about how He wanted me to respond to each offering call, giving what **He** requested, rather than what **I** decided. I'd already given a sizeable amount each of the previous three days. Now, the Holy Spirit was asking for more. I tried to ignore the Lord's request, but I couldn't. That night each offering period seemed to last forever. The evangelist called for everyone to bring their offering forward to her personally. Each time, I resisted, remaining in my seat for the longest time. I thought of what the Lord had asked of me. Then, once more, the Spirit repeated His request.

"There are three things which you have come to value, son. Each has become a source of pride and a symbol of self-assurance for you. I want you to release them to Me tonight. The first is the new watch you recently purchased for yourself. Present it to this evangelist as an offering to Me."

Again, I struggled in my mind with what I knew I'd heard. My initial reaction was HUGE resentment, as I talked to the Lord in my mind and heart. *Why are you taking away my watch, Lord? You know how long I've waited to buy a nice one! I just bought it, and it was expensive! What will my wife think when I tell her I'm now going to give it away? Besides, this evangelist doesn't need my watch!*

Ten more minutes passed as I fidgeted in my seat. Meanwhile, my pastor's son-in-law walked forward and gave his watch as an offering. It was an antique he'd inherited, and possibly of more value than mine. A thought immediately came to my mind. *Great! Now she **doesn't** need my watch!* A minute later, the Holy Spirit interrupted my thoughts.

"Son, would you please present your watch as a representative offering to Me? This presentation will be an offering of obedience, surrendering not just the watch, but also

your pride in the ownership of it. To Me, son, this also represents something far deeper. It's proof of your willingness to surrender your ability to acquire those things that you **want**. *It also represents your willingness to allow Me to meet all of your* **needs**, *and not just some of them."*

Finally, I turned to my wife and begrudgingly told her what the Spirit had asked of me. To my utter amazement, she joyfully encouraged me to give it. Going forward to the evangelist, I handed her the watch. I returned to my seat, struggling to ignore evil thoughts that bombarded my mind. A demon spirit laughed at me, telling me what a fool I was to give it away. I sat there for the longest time with my eyes closed. I asked the Holy Spirit to free me from the continued hold that the pride of ownership of that watch had over me. SLOWLY, the sweet presence of the Lord took control, as the peace of God gained ground in my soul. Near the end of the service, however, the Spirit again interrupted my thoughts.

"Son, the second thing I'm asking both you and your wife to do is to give the digital piano to this church body."

Again the struggle within arose, even more fiercely than before. For years, my wife had hinted around that she'd love to have a piano. We didn't have room in our home for a full-size piano, which led me to shop around and instead buy an expensive digital keyboard. On Christmas morning, six months prior, I had surprised my wife with it. I'd watched with pleasure the joy it brought to her. Now, He was asking me to tell her that we were to give it away?!

The more I thought about it, the more worried I became as to how she might react. A sudden thought, prompted by the enemy of my soul, crossed my mind. *Will she think that I'm now expecting* **her** *to give up something* **she** *treasures? Will she wonder if I'm saying this out of spite because she'd been so eager to have me give away my watch?"*

"This doesn't make sense, Lord," I whispered to Him. "Is this truly You speaking?"

Without hesitation, the Holy Spirit responded.

"Yes, My son. This sacrifice goes even deeper, drawing upon both you and your wife equally. **It addresses not only your ability to buy what you want for yourself but also others.** *I need you both to begin to rely on Me to supply all, in the manner and timing I choose. Tell her now what I've requested."*

I leaned over and repeated His words into my wife's ear. I sensed the change in her attitude, which was also readily visible on her face. I turned away and waited with my eyes closed. I felt horrible and couldn't bring myself to look back at her. I wanted to be confident that this was something that she was at peace about, without any pressure from me. When the service ended, and the audience dismissed, my wife leaned over and said, "Okay. Let's do it."

Together we approached the church leadership and explained what the Holy Spirit wanted. We arranged for a convenient time to drop it off at the church later that week.

We said our goodbyes to those around us and gathered our coats to leave. It was then that the Spirit spoke to me for the third time.

"Son, I want you to approach the evangelist and tell her that you'll be mailing her a check. Turn over to her ministry the entire amount that I prompted that couple to sow into 'Love Will Make A Way.' Get Debbie's address so that you can send it to her in the morning. I'm asking you to do this so that you understand one other relevant matter. **What I give to you and your wife in the future is for the purposes that the Father declares.** *I need your heart and mind to remain free from any concern about the funding of My work. Too often lately, your thoughts have dwelt on the funds sitting in that account.* **Understand that My ultimate focus involves molding and shaping YOU. I need your heart and mind conformed to Mine. To the extent that you allow Me to work IN you, to that same extent will I work THROUGH you.** *Moreover, when I see that the fallow ground of your heart stands tilled and ready, I will pour abundant seed into this new work. I will do so knowing it will take root and multiply. So, for now, bless the ministry I am bringing through Debbie."*

That evening, I immediately wrote out the check, emptying the account. After dropping it in the mailbox the following morning, I voiced aloud the question that lingered in my mind.

"Holy Spirit, what's next?"

Once more, I waited and waited, but heaven remained silent.

Several more months passed without the Lord giving any more direction regarding Colorado. Meanwhile, I felt Frustration trying to overtake me. My wife began telling everyone that we would be moving shortly to Fort Collins, Colorado. I had heard nothing about this from the Lord. Due to my wife's declarations, I began to feel pressured. I felt as though she expected me to come into agreement with her, and then we would move. Doing so would disregard the apparent lack of clearance from the Holy Spirit to proceed. I reminded her, each time she questioned me about our future, "All He said was, *'Soon.'*"

Late that spring, a guest preacher visited Heritage Fellowship. Leon Price was in his eighties and walked in the Office of a Prophet of God. He'd been ministering through the Word of God and prophecy since he was nineteen years old.

Three years prior, during a Friday evening service at this same church, my wife and I had observed him as he spoke rapid-fire words of prophecy to many individuals. By the reactions on each recipient's face, it appeared evident that the words he gave had been right on target. That night, while driving north to our home, we'd talked about what we'd observed. It was amazing to me how quickly the prophetic words had come to and through the man.

Now, three years later, Leon had returned once more. However, we had already made plans to visit our eldest daughter and her family in Chicago. Wanting to make it to at least one of the weekend services, we agreed to drive home late Saturday night. That would allow us to arrive back in time to get a few hours of sleep before attending the Sunday morning service.

However, that Sunday morning, the prophet chose to preach rather than give prophetic words. At the end of that service, our pastor invited all who had never received a prophetic word from Leon to come forward. My wife and I, and our youngest daughter, who was thirteen at the time, went to the altar as a family. As I walked toward the front, I spoke to the Lord in my mind and heart.

Holy Spirit, this man doesn't know me from Adam. Would you please use him to speak a word of confirmation about what happened in Colorado?

We stood there along with forty other people in a single row across the front of the sanctuary. Leon walked back and forth in front of the group, praying to and praising the Lord. When he stopped, he was standing in front of my family and me. He asked our names and clarified that we were husband, wife, and daughter. Leon then closed his eyes and lifted his petition to heaven.

"Lord, what is Your word for this man?" A moment later, the Prophet opened his eyes and began speaking to me. "The Lord would say to you, *'Son, I've made you like an eighteen-wheeler, and I've recently loaded you up with a heavy load. But I tell you, son, I'm about to greatly add to that load, and you're on an uphill climb, going all out. Be careful to listen for My Spirit to direct you, for He will tell you when to turn left, or right, and when to slow down. When He does, be quick to respond lest you drive over the edge. Wait for Him. Listen to Him.'"*

Then he continued, "And the Lord would say to you, *'You will prophesy many things in My name.'"* At this point, he paused and asked me, "Has the Lord ever used you to prophesy?" I shook my head in the affirmative. The Prophet then continued. "The Lord says, *'You will begin prophesying more and more, in much greater detail. You will say: "Thus saith the Lord," and you will see it come to pass before your eyes. And you will begin to travel to many places, many countries for Me. Doors will open to you in many places, and finances will be abundant as I bless you, as you do My work. And you will prophesy to many people in those places and see it come to pass exactly as you say. I will strengthen you, and grow you mightily in faith. That which I have recently revealed to you will definitely come to pass. So be not discouraged. Be not impatient either. In My timing, I will make a way. I will open the doors. I will provide the means. I WILL make a way.'"*

Next, the prophet turned to my wife and said, "The Lord says to you, *'Daughter, you are not an eighteen-wheeler. Rather, I have made you like a sports car, and you will ride alongside your husband. You will be his intercessor. You will lift him in prayer. For where I am about to send him, and for the tasks to which I am about to call him, he will need much prayer, constant prayer. For I have made you a prayer warrior, My daughter, a prayer warrior. And I am calling you to seek Me with your whole heart.'"*

Last, he turned to our daughter and spoke. "The Lord says to you, *'I am calling you to come alongside your mother. You are to be a comfort, and support, and strength to her, to lift her in your prayers, as well as lifting your dad. And I tell you not to worry about finding a husband. I have already picked him out for you, and he will be a righteous, holy, loving man, strong in the ways of the Lord. And the two of you will minister as a team, as the Holy Spirit leads you, with signs and wonders following.'"*

Later that week, I called our pastor and asked if I could meet with him. I wanted to discuss the words the Spirit had spoken through Leon Price. When we met for lunch, my pastor asked me what I thought Leon had said. I responded, telling him as much as I could recall. He then explained that he'd listened to the tape from that Sunday morning service before meeting with me. He confirmed that what I'd stated was accurate. He then cautioned me.

"Be very careful to not **EVER** get ahead of God, running to do what He hasn't yet told you to do. And never go forth without a covering, and the Lord's confirmation that it's time to go, with definite signs."

I had hoped the Spirit would take this opportunity to prompt my pastor to speak about Colorado, but he never brought it up, so I stuck to my promise to the Lord to wait upon Him to move in His timing. I thanked my pastor as we departed, and thought once more about the prophet's words as I drove the hour north to my home. The following Sunday morning, I bought a copy of those recorded prophecies spoken over us.

In late May, my wife and I began talking about using part of our anticipated income tax refund for a vacation. She and our daughter wanted to go to Florida. Plans toward that end progressed, and the day in mid-June when we were to head south drew nearer.

Meanwhile, I'd begun having a strong leading from the Lord that we weren't supposed to go to Florida. I sensed that the Holy Spirit wanted us, as a family, to go to Colorado instead. I delayed saying anything to my wife for days. I knew she and our daughter were both looking forward to relaxing on the beach. I dreaded the idea of telling them otherwise.

One week before we were to depart, my wife said she felt like God wanted us to go to Colorado and not Florida. It was then that I told her that I'd felt the same leading from the Lord for weeks. I explained my hesitation to say this to her and our daughter, uncertain about how they would react. That night, we explained this to our daughter, who agreed that we needed to go to Colorado. I changed our hotel reservations and, a week later, we headed west.

We didn't have any particular direction from the Spirit other than to pray and follow His leading. We drove throughout Fort Collins, the surrounding communities, and up into the mountains. I observed how the Spirit opened our hearts further toward that area and the people living there. Additionally, we all seemed to be more at peace and rested than we'd ever felt in Florida. Day after day, we drove up every valley, hill, or mountain ridge that made up N.E. Colorado's Front Range. We prayed and viewed the beauty that surrounded us. Still, I didn't feel any particular leading from the Lord. On our last day in Fort Collins, we drove north on College Avenue. At the north end of town on that road was the Colorado State University campus. We passed through a quaint area of two-story buildings. Small shops and cafes lined the street level, and above each was an apartment.

Without warning, my wife began to cry—not quietly, but loud enough for my daughter and me to hear her.

"What's wrong?" I asked, looking at her in surprise. She turned in her seat and pointed to a building we'd just passed.

"The Lord showed me that exact building in a dream, months ago," she explained. "He told me that one day we'd live on the second floor of that two-story building. It would only be temporary, until the property, which He is going to provide, becomes available."

This revelation surprised me, as she hadn't mentioned one word about it before that moment. Turning around and driving slowly by the building once more, we all took a good look at it. When we returned to our hotel room, we prayed together, asking God to have His way, completing in us what He'd started.

The following morning, we departed for the two-day trip home. Both of us were now intent on prayerfully awaiting the Lord's next direction, curious as to what, when, and to where it might be.

Five more months passed, yet there wasn't a single word from the Holy Spirit about Colorado. In late November of that same year, the Lord finally spoke to me while I was at my office. Weeks before that moment, I'd begun to question in my heart when, if ever, things would happen as He'd said.

When He now spoke, I had been on the Internet looking at the Secretary of State's website for my home state, verifying how a new advertiser chose to register their business name with the state. While I was checking the database for several new company names assigned to me as leads, the Holy Spirit spoke.

"*Check for the name I gave you.*"

I recalled that the Spirit wanted the nonprofit organization registered in Colorado. I located the website for the Colorado Secretary of State's office. Checking for the name "*Love Will Make A Way*," I saw that someone had already registered that exact name. Feeling disheartened, I began wondering to myself if somehow I had missed the timing of the Lord. In response to my thoughts, the Holy Spirit said, "*Dig deeper, son.*"

Placing a call to Colorado, I asked if their documentation was available online. I followed the instructions the state office gave me. When I found the documents, I read them. Someone had formed the non-profit three years before the Holy Spirit spoke to me about the same thing. Their stated purpose was almost precisely what the Holy Spirit had said to me. I studied the list of the three persons on the registration as a non-profit corporation. All three individuals lived in Fort Collins. Their homes and corporate office were no more than a mile or so from each other. The hotel the Holy Spirit had led me to stay in both times was in that same area.

As I sat there, wondering why the Lord had brought this information to my attention, He spoke again. "*Look even closer, son.*"

A sudden chill swept over me as I read the last entry. It reported the dissolving of the corporation **just two days prior**. The realization hit me that the name was now available for use by anyone else who wanted to do so. At this point, the Holy Spirit spoke one last time.

"*I told you the first time you were in Colorado, and I'm telling you again, I have people in place waiting to join you when the time is right. Trust Me, son, and continue to pray.*"

† † †

At another point in time, the Lord had talked to me about the importance of us leaving everything behind to follow Him. Months later, after mulling over what He'd said, I wondered to myself if my ardor had somehow diminished. I searched my heart for the answer to that question, wondering if I was as prepared as I'd believed myself to be. Would I easily give up that to which I'd grown accustomed if He were to ask it of me? Would I eagerly make room to receive what the Lord was about to bring into our lives? He'd spoken several times about my wife and me "*continually serving the Lord.*" I wondered more and more, was some part of me still resistant?

It was a struggle to restrain my imagination and not speculate. Even so, my thoughts too often drifted to the many possibilities my wife and I had discussed. In actuality, I had no concept of what "*continually serving the Lord*" might entail for the two of us.

I'd enjoyed and come to expect the above-average income from my current employer. My position also included four weeks of paid vacation, twelve paid holidays, as well as a company car of my choice. Each year there were also several four-day sales award trips to resorts in the USA and islands in the Caribbean. My wife and I had attended dozens of these. Over my fifteen years there, I'd become highly proficient in advertising design and sales. Best of all, I thoroughly enjoyed my current occupation. Thinking about it in those terms, I couldn't honestly say that I'd be thrilled to walk away from it if the Lord asked that of me.

Despite my hesitancy, the Lord knew He had to begin to shake me free from the comforts and things of this world. Most importantly, He said He needed to change my heart. He desired to release me from the hold of Arrogance, Pride, and Boastful Self-Confidence. Even I knew that I'd operated in conjunction with these spirits for far too long.

The day came when my wife and I addressed the first part of this issue at length. We considered well all the ramifications such a total surrender could entail.

"I want to trust Him for everything," I told my wife. "I know that neither of us has the faintest idea of what that could involve—as a couple, or for each of us individually. However, if I'm honest with the Lord and myself, I know things have to change. Are you sure you are willing to stand with me through this, no matter what?"

She assured me she was, with more enthusiasm than I felt. We prayed as one that day. Both of us expressed aloud to the Lord and to one another, our willingness to pursue His leading. We also invited Him to do whatever He felt He needed to do in our lives to complete in us the work that He had begun.

Nevertheless, the series of events that occurred in the months that followed significantly affected me, far more than my wife. They shook me physically, emotionally, and mentally, and left me thoroughly confused and uncertain.

"I have yet to see a human who finds smooth sailing through life. In fact, the ones He seems to use and love the most must go through deep valleys. The Sovereign loves them infinitely, but allows them to pass through trouble. This keeps them from complacency."

Excerpt from *Almost Heaven*
by Chris Fabry

Confusion, Confirmations & Change

The Sunday morning church service was over. People were saying their goodbyes and leaving. I stayed sitting in my seat, giving my wife and daughter time to visit with others before we drove home. When I stood to gather my things, my pastor approached me.

"I know you've wanted to talk with me for a while now," he commented. "Let's have lunch this week."

Although I had not been thinking about it at the time, even so, I welcomed the opportunity. A question came to my mind. *Is this the Holy Spirit prompting him?*

We agreed to get together the following Thursday, exchanged phone numbers, and each promising the other that we would call if something arose to prevent us from keeping the appointment.

† † †

We met at a restaurant, placed our orders, and the server departed. Then my pastor immediately began speaking. "I read what you sent to me. Has anyone else talked to you about it?"

I mentioned in detail the call I had received from Gary Klein.

"What have you done about this so far?" my pastor asked.

"I've been praying about it daily, waiting for Him to tell me what to do next, as He said to do," I replied.

"You've got to take some action, and He'll meet you," he said. "If it were me, I'd do everything I could do. What about the man He sent you to talk to? Did you try your best to reach him? What was his name?"

I hesitated in responding. I would never forget the name of *Jerry Atwood*. The Lord had brought up that name when I was in Colorado. Now, as I sat there listening to my pastor, I questioned the Lord in my mind and heart.

Holy Spirit, back in Colorado, you told me explicitly that there was no one at that Salvation Army church by the name of Jerry Atwood. You said it was a test of my willingness to obey, and that You were pleased with me because I did as asked. Didn't my pastor read beyond the first few pages of what You had me send to him? If he had, he would know that.

While awaiting my response, my pastor had already dialed for directory assistance. "What was the name?" he asked again. "I'll show you how I'd do this."

"Jerry Atwood," I answered, still baffled by what he was doing.

I sat there listening as he spoke with the operator. He asked her to check for that name. Many listings existed in Colorado for individuals with that name, but none anywhere near the Fort Collins area. Satisfied that he had done all he could do, he ended the call. "If God gives you something like this, you pursue it as far as you can," he said. "God will meet you there."

I sat there without responding. I was somewhat intimidated by my pastor's actions and wondered to myself why he was acting the way he was. I didn't yet feel comfortable enough with him to point out what I'd addressed in my mind with the Holy Spirit.

When we prepared to leave, I offered to pay for our lunches, but my pastor graciously insisted on doing so. Neither of us said anything more about the subject, and we parted, each in our vehicle.

As I made the trip north to my home, I kept rehashing in my mind what had transpired at our lunch. The more I thought about it, the more irritated I became, talking aloud to the Lord.

"I question now how much of what I sent him he read. I don't understand what just happened, Lord! Does he think I'm making this up? Besides, why didn't he offer to pray with me or for me about this whole thing? That's what I wanted. Instead, it was all about action, action, action—and how **he'd** pursue it! That day in Colorado, You told me the most important thing was fervent prayer and waiting on You, and **NOT** action. You said the same thing through Leon Price to my family and me. My pastor himself also warned me **NOT** to get ahead of You when we last met. Now, this time, his advice was the exact opposite! Was I even supposed to meet with him today, Holy Spirit? Please talk to me about this, because I'm thoroughly confused right now, and a little disheartened!"

Still, the Spirit didn't speak right then. By the time I'd arrived home to greet my wife and daughter, I'd calmed down, squashing the frustration and disappointment that festered beneath the surface.

The following Monday, at my company's weekly sales meeting, several guests were on hand. Before the end of that meeting, upper management made a significant announcement. An overseas conglomerate had purchased our parent corporation. The "guests" were the new management team assuming control of our local office effective immediately. The new vice president gave a short introductory speech. In it, he assured everyone that little would change. In his words, "those changes that do occur will prove to be beneficial to all."

In the weeks that followed, the new vice president met with each employee, breaking us down into small groups. He explained the effect that the acquisition would have on each of us.

I had fifteen years invested with the firm at that point, and each year I had reaffirmed my value by my superior performance. As one of only four account managers, I had worked some of the largest and most prestigious accounts for nearly ten of those years. I felt confident that I didn't have any reason to worry about my position, and expressed these feelings to my wife that night, assuring her that this could be a good thing. Still, on meeting with the new management team a few days later, I found out otherwise.

They explained that there would no longer be account manager positions. I would lose my core clients with whom I'd developed a rapport and trust over the previous ten years. Now they would base our assigned accounts on a designated territory, focused on where each sales representative lived. The stated aim of the new owners was to reduce travel time and distance between appointments, allowing each person to schedule more appointments per day. The new Vice President also said that it would reduce car expenses, as well as mileage accumulated on our leased vehicles.

That line of thought sounded reasonable. Even so, the reality of how this would affect me became evident when I learned what new territory I would work. I lost all but a few of my previous larger clients. My base assignment also increased from ninety accounts to over four hundred.

The new VP then requested that I go on calls with those reps assigned many of *my* prior select accounts. He expected me to *introduce those clients to their new representatives joyfully*. Beyond that, what irritated me most was immediately having my salary cut in half. Salary increases in the previous fourteen years were meritorious. Before this cut, my salary made up forty-three percent of my six-figure annual income.

Over the next nine months, I tried to cooperate and maintain a positive attitude. I called on hundreds of new small clients. Many of my previous clients had *willingly* "invested" thousands—and some, tens of thousands—of dollars ***a month*** for their advertising. They trusted that my word and guidance would greatly benefit their businesses in the end, which nearly always proved to be true. Now, to the contrary, most of my newly assigned, smaller clients were very hesitant. Too many balked at "spending" hundreds of dollars ***per year***, nervous about whether it would pay off. As time passed, I became more and more disgruntled and frustrated. My monthly bonus checks were far smaller. We started getting behind on our bills for the first time in sixteen years. I began squeezing in even more sales calls per day. Many days, I left home before sunrise and returned well after dark. I hoped that things would eventually improve.

The following year, management announced that they were cutting salaries once more. To counter this, they were raising commission rates. They assured everyone that we should be able to make up the wage loss through increased commissions. For most, it did not prove to be true. I watched as many seasoned sales reps tendered their resignations. I'd thought about doing the same thing more than a few times but resisted the urge. I wasn't ready to walk away from what was now a seventeen-year career that, until recently, I'd thoroughly enjoyed. Therefore, I hung on, hoping that things would somehow turn around. In the interim, my wife and I refinanced our mortgage again, consolidating our accumulated debts. At the same time, we once again borrowed against the remaining equity in our home. I wanted to be sure that we'd have funds to meet our financial obligations until my income improved.

In our third major sales campaign under this new ownership, I became very disheartened. I requested a meeting with both the new regional VP and the office general manager. I explained to them how I'd been faithful to call on the assigned companies in my territory. Even so, most were small retailers and commercial businesses. I complained about the lack of opportunity now as compared to my previous assignment. I reminded them of my success during my fifteen years with the previous owner. I had also retained documentation to back my claims of having generated tens of millions of dollars in previous sales for the company. I was hoping they would realize that my abilities were being grossly under-utilized. The vice president, however, offered me only two choices—work the territory assigned to me, or quit. Since my annual income was now nearly one-third of what I'd made two and a half years earlier, I didn't see any point in remaining. Following a heated exchange with the vice president, I resigned.

When I arrived home that evening, I explained to my wife what had occurred. I encouraged her not to worry, confident that I'd find another source of income. She was nervous about the whole situation since I was our sole source of finances. Even so, she supported the action I'd taken. She requested that I refrain from putting in applications or mailing out resumes. She encouraged me first to take a few days to seek the Lord about what He wanted me to do next.

On the third day of fasting and praying, the Holy Spirit spoke to me.

"I'm going to open up an opportunity for you to work in the mortgage industry as a loan officer for a season."

I waited for Him to explain in more detail but heard nothing else. The following morning's paper had help wanted ads for entry-level positions as a loan officer. I prayed about which firm, if any, I should call. I felt the Holy Spirit leading me to speak with one company. Another large (and very appealing) advertiser was a significant employer in that industry. He openly identified himself and his business philosophy as Christian. I'd recently heard an interview on a local Christian radio station with this company's CEO and founder. His reputation for integrity preceded him. All of his company's media expenditures reinforced this idea. I knew the Holy Spirit had directed me toward a particular firm. Still, He never said I couldn't talk with other companies.

To be obedient, I called and arranged an interview with the firm the Holy Spirit indicated. I also arranged for a meeting with the Christian-owned lender. I went to the first interview—to which the Spirit had directed me. There I found the majority owner/CEO of the company to be a loud, obnoxious, demanding, Jewish man. His partner was younger and quieter. He was also of Jewish descent. After that interview, the junior partner told me they would give me an answer within a day or two.

When I arrived home, a message was waiting for me on my recorder. I returned the call and scheduled an appointment to interview at the Christian company. That interview seemed to go well. One hour later, I received a call from the founder of the Christian company. He asked to meet with me for a second interview that same afternoon at his corporate headquarters, ninety minutes north of where I lived. The meeting proved to be very promising, and I left there encouraged. I felt confident that he would offer me a position. That evening at the dinner table, I told my wife about what an opportunity it would be to join that firm.

As I'd predicted to my wife, the following morning, one of the Christian firm's local managers called. He extended an offer of employment in the local office. Even so, three hours earlier, as I sat quietly before the Lord listening, the Spirit had spoken to me about this.

"Shortly, you will be getting an offer from the Christian-owned firm, but I want you to turn it down. A second offer will come from the other business a few hours later. That is the offer I want you to accept."

I chose to obey, even though I didn't understand the reasoning behind what He'd told me. However, when I joined the other firm, I got a pleasant surprise. The partners offered me a salary-plus-commission structure that would help me through the learning and licensing curve. Ninety days later, I would transition into a commission only structure. The Christian-owned firm had made no such offer. I related the terms of my new employment to my wife that evening. We both rejoiced and thanked the Lord for His faithful provision.

In my first nine months as a loan officer, I closed many loans, replacing nearly two-thirds of what I had been earning three years prior. Still, in that same three-year period, we'd exhausted all available monies, including the funds from my 401K plan. We struggled to pay our creditors on time. I had to buy a car to replace the company car I no longer had. Health and life insurance coverage were now 100% my responsibility. The deductible part of several significant new medical and dental bills was overwhelming. Despite these, little by little, I accumulated some savings.

The Lord then spoke to me once again—through my wife. I was to commit to an upcoming ten-day mission trip our church was taking to the United Kingdom. The Lord confirmed it to me the following morning while I was praying about other things. Still, I delayed acting on it for days.

"I can't afford to take off now," I argued with the Lord. "You know I've only been at this new job for nine months. We barely have enough in savings to cover the cost of the trip. Moreover, what will the owner think of me wanting to take time off already? Besides, I don't have the faintest desire to go to England!"

Nevertheless, the Lord continued to prompt me about it day after day. Finally, I spoke to my employer about it. To my surprise, he encouraged me to take the trip. His only stipulation was that I return committed to also exceeding my fourth-quarter goals, as I had in the previous three quarters. The next morning, I called the church's secretary and added my name to the list of those who would be going. That evening I paid the required deposits, emptying our savings.

The ten-day trip was to at a sister church located in Bradford, in the northern part of England. Everyone on the team helped with the maintenance needed in the ministry's building. Some painted and installed carpeting. Others performed numerous repairs. By the third day, I began questioning in my mind why the Lord had insisted that I make the trip. Several nights I sat alone in the dimly lit coffee shop that the church operated, talking to God, asking for His direction, long after the shop had closed and most had gone on to bed. Very late on the seventh evening, another man walked into the café. He saw me sitting alone in a semi-darkened room and pulled up a chair to join me. Introducing himself as Jerrell Miller, he said he was from Mobile, Alabama, and had joined the group from Heritage Fellowship at the leading of the Spirit. He explained that he was the founder and editor of The Remnant International, "a newspaper that reports God's moving in revival, signs, and wonders throughout the earth."

"The Holy Spirit woke me up and told me to come down here with you," he said. Uncertain about why he was there, or what to say, Jerrell began telling me his story. He elaborated on exactly when, where, how, and why God called and led him to travel the world as the Lord's reporter. He talked for over an hour, also explaining where and what he thought God was calling him to in the future. I listened without interrupting, wondering if God had honestly arranged our meeting. If that was true, then what was His aim? I knew *about* Jerrell, having seen him once before. He'd visited Heritage Fellowship to report on the move of God happening there. I had never spoken to him before this day. Now, the longer he talked, the more I realized that he had no idea who I was. All he knew was that I was part of the group from Heritage. He concluded that night with a statement. "God told me that He would be relieving me soon of this responsibility and burden for reporting the moving of His Spirit throughout the earth. He's going to send me in a whole new direction." With that said, he returned to his room to get some sleep, leaving me alone in the café to ponder what had just occurred.

Having returned from England, I headed to the mortgage company's office early enough that Monday to be there when it opened at eight o'clock. I arrived to find the building in a state of absolute turmoil. When I asked what was happening, I learned that several of the employed loan officers had been submitting fraudulent loans. Within days after I'd left for England, these three skipped town and disappeared, attempting to avoid Federal authorities. Before leaving, they'd emptied all files from their desks, the company archives, and the company servers. When I entered the office, the U.S. Treasury authorities were questioning the two owners and the president of the company, having already seized computers and loan files.

Only a few months before, there had been a similar occurrence in a nearby city. It was the lead story on the local TV stations for more than a week. I thought about all the direct mail that I'd sent out with my picture on it—all tied to this lender's business name. The actions taken by the Feds in the nearby city crippled that firm. My only thought was how what was now happening could affect my income.

I discussed this with the owners later that morning and with my wife that evening. I prayed about it at length the following morning. Distressed about the situation, I decided to move to another lender. Having reviewed my loan closing performance, the new broker eagerly welcomed me to his team. That same day, I completed and mailed the required state forms to transfer my license. However, the Lord hadn't told me to take this action. Worry and concern had driven me to make the decision. I had justified it to my wife, and myself, by stating, "God didn't say that I *couldn't* move to another lender."

Soon an even bigger problem began to surface in the mortgage industry, one that I could not have foreseen—the sub-prime loan debacle. I had never felt comfortable about recommending sub-prime loans to borrowers. My previous employer had allowed me to choose the type of borrowers I wanted to pursue. After transferring my license, the owner at the company I had moved to was now requesting that I promote **only** sub-prime loans. He justified his demand by pointing out how fixed loan rates were rapidly climbing. When I refused to cooperate with the lender's request, my source of leads dried up, and my income was once more crippled.

I struggled to regain solid financial footing for my family and myself. Despite my efforts, I kept losing ground. Leaving that firm two months later, I launched out on my own. This time I refocused my attention on a new borrower group that I felt had great potential—brokering commercial loans to small businesses. Looking back on it later, I had to admit one thing. I had asked the Lord to bless my efforts, but never actually sought His guidance or approval.

I sent out an initial direct mail solicitation to five hundred local business owners. That resulted in a single call two days later from a regional firm in the moving industry.

The impact of the 9/11/2001 terrorist attack in New York City had crippled that industry and their business since that event.

When I met the company president, he and I recognized each other. We'd sat and talked together at a Full Gospel Business Men's Fellowship breakfast years earlier. He introduced me to the two other officers of the company. Both were sons of the company founder (and the president's brothers-in-law). I could sense the tension in the room when the two other men entered. We discussed their needs at length. I explained the loan process and timetables. They said they understood the appraisal process and environmental approvals needed. I reviewed some possible interest rates, terms, and payment amounts. I assured them that loans of this sort normally closed within sixty days—if everything went well—and I then agreed to give them a couple of days to discuss everything without feeling pressured by me. On the scheduled date, I returned with a formatted loan application that all three signed. That afternoon I submitted it for consideration to many lenders. Only one lender expressed interest.

The processing, appraisal, and EPA inspection all went well. The potential lender called to say they were willing to underwrite the multi-million dollar loan. The borrowers had a choice between several possible combinations of rates and terms. After presenting these to the company officers, the president asked me to wait in his office while they discussed it in private. When he returned, he told me which option they had chosen. He then said the two brothers were on the way out the door for scheduled appointments. We arranged a time later that afternoon to meet again to sign the modified loan documentation.

As I drove home to prepare the paperwork, I thought about the potential commission. The proceeds from that one loan would be more than a third of my highest previous gross annual income. The other good thing was the lender's expressed confidence that the loan would easily close in sixty days.

When I returned at the agreed-upon time, the two sons of the founder did not show and were unavailable. I waited in the president's office for ninety minutes. Finally, he apologized and rescheduled the meeting for a time three days later. However, before that date had arrived, the president called again and left a voice mail message that the loan was not going to happen. The other two officers didn't feel comfortable about it. He agreed that the terms were fair, considering the lender would require no proof of income or assets. I tried many times to reach the president, to no avail.

Meanwhile, I prayed and fretted and prayed some more. Later, I realized my prayers amounted to nothing more than repeated begging. I needed God to move on my behalf. My wife began having panic attacks from the stress, often finding it hard to breathe. In desperation, I called my close friend from the Saturday morning prayer group. We prayed together in the spirit for quite a while before peace finally came, and then the Lord spoke to me through my friend.

"I, the Lord your God, will grant your request by moving in the hearts of these three men. However, I will require of you two things. These are a listening heart and absolute obedience to what I tell you when you meet again with them. Ask the president to arrange one final meeting. Together you will work to reach an agreement that will be acceptable to all."

I thanked my friend, disconnected from that call, and immediately called the company. The president himself answered the phone. One hour later, I was sitting in their company conference room with all three men present. That's when the Lord spoke to me in an undeniably clear voice.

"Son, I want you to look each man in the eye and reiterate what you said to the president over the phone. The other two need to hear from you that you are here to find a solution. Tell them that you'd like to start by lifting the purpose of this gathering to Me in prayer, and then invite the Holy Spirit to dwell here. Ask Him to direct all that occurs and to bring forth My solution, to the Father's glory."

I was a bit shocked. I had never had a problem praying aloud at church, in Full Gospel meetings, or when gathering with brothers and sisters in the Lord. I also prayed one-on-one for healing, or help, or salvation with non-believers, but I'd never prayed openly, or boldly, with customers about business situations. Besides that, I wasn't sure if the two brothers even believed in God.

A demon spirit pounced on my hesitation and doubt. It filled my mind with thoughts of how these two might laugh at and ridicule me if I even suggested praying. The three men sat there waiting, looking at me. I made no move to bring the documentation out of the manila folder. Instead, I chose to obey and trust in the Lord. I looked at each man's eyes, as the Lord had indicated, and spoke in a calm voice.

"As I said to your brother-in-law over the phone, I want to work out a solution that you all will feel comfortable with when you walk away from this table. But before we get started, would you mind if I bring this meeting to the Lord in prayer?"

As I said this, I looked at the company president. He smiled and nodded in agreement. The other two looked puzzled but didn't object. I closed my eyes, opened my heart, and lifted my voice in prayer.

"Holy Spirit, I invite You to have Your way here in this room as well as in our hearts, as You direct our thoughts. Help each of us to be open to Your perfect solution to the situation we are now addressing. Help us all to walk out of this room today with an assurance that we've been in Your presence. Give us Your peace about the final solution through which You will bring us all into one accord with what occurs here today, bringing glory to You, Jesus, and the Father. Amen."

Without looking at any of the three, I pulled the documentation out of the folder, giving each of them a copy of a spreadsheet to review.

"The Lord spoke to me earlier today before I called back to request this meeting. He told me to put together a comparison of three different choices for you to review. Each is at a different rate, term, and payment amount. Please take a few minutes to look it over. If you have any questions, do not hesitate to ask. I want to be a blessing to you."

In less than ten minutes, two of the three men came into agreement on one option. It was what they felt they could most tolerate without straining the company budget. The only objection came from the third man, the company vice president. He had been the most negative from the beginning.

"I'll agree with the two of them if you're willing to cut your commission," he said.

I had a feeling that this was the decisive factor. I explained how I determined my compensation, in an attempt to justify what I felt my time and effort was worth. Even so, the third man sat there quietly, staring at me. I wanted—no, I needed—this to work, and I thought about appeasing him by cutting my share by two thousand dollars. Looking the vice president in the eyes one more time, I said, "Would you give me a minute to ask the Lord about this?"

The vice president nodded at me with a smirk on his face, saying nothing.

Closing my eyes and looking down at the table, I spoke in my mind to the Lord. *What would You have me do, Holy Spirit? You know what it will take to make this happen. Please direct my thoughts and my actions right now, and I promise I will obey You.*

Without a moment's hesitation, the Holy Spirit answered me.

"Tell him you'll reduce your commission by seven thousand dollars if he agrees to it in writing now."

That shocked me, and I knew my face was showing as much when I opened my eyes and glanced at the vice president. I waited a minute longer while I gained control of my emotions, then spoke to him.

"The Holy Spirit said I should offer to reduce my commission by seven thousand dollars. But only if you agree to it in writing now."

The defensive look on the vice president's face vanished as a smile broke forth.

"Perfect! That is the exact amount I had in mind before I would agree. Go ahead and make the changes, and I'll sign," the vice president said.

Sixty days from the president's initial response to my direct mail piece, the loan closed. I had combined and refinanced their several million dollars in loans. The income from that one new loan gave my wife and me some much-needed breathing room.

Feeling burned out from what we'd endured in the previous year, I agreed to my wife's request to take a short vacation one week later. She wanted to relax on the beach in Naples, Florida. At the last minute, our youngest daughter asked to accompany us, with her paying for her share of the expenses. The next morning, I felt a repeated prompting from the Holy Spirit. I needed to contact Jerrell Miller at his home in Mobile, Alabama. I made the call as directed, but he was not home, so I left a voice message. Before I heard back from Jerrell, the Holy Spirit spoke to both my wife and me—individually—to change the destination for our vacation to Destin, Florida. Neither of us had ever heard of or been to Destin. We found it on a map, located in the northwest part of the state, on the Gulf coast. While I was searching the Internet for hotel accommodations, the Spirit spoke to me again.

"I want you to arrange a meeting with Jerrell while you are in Florida. Tell him I want him to lay hands on you and pray that My mantle, which he has carried all of these years, will rest upon you. I then want you to pray for him and his wife, blessing them with the words I will give you at that moment."

A short while after the Spirit had spoken to us about going to Destin, the telephone rang. It was Jerrell, returning my call. After reminding him of who I was, I told him what the Lord wanted. We arranged a date to meet for lunch the week we would be in Destin.

I drove alone that day to Mobile, while my wife and daughter spent the day on the beach. Jerrell, and his wife, Vivian, met me for lunch at a local restaurant. When we had finished eating, I followed them back to their home. There the three of us acted on the instructions from the Lord.

Late that afternoon, I returned to Destin. My family and I enjoyed the remaining two days in the sun before heading home. Early in the morning on the day that we departed for home, my wife and daughter slept in the car as I traveled north on I-65. While driving, I meditated on what had occurred when I met Jerrell and Vivian. Finally, I whispered the question to the Lord that nagged at my mind.

"Did this somehow have something to do with what You said You would bring to pass in Colorado?"

In silence, I waited for a response, but none came.

*"It's in the soil
that is watered by the
tears of brokenness,
and enriched by
the decayed loam of
a surrendered self,
that trust finds
solid rooting.
There it blooms forth
abundantly."*

Broken Stallions Carry Kings

One week after returning from Florida, Leon Price was back at Heritage Fellowship for three days. I made a point of attending all the scheduled services. Additionally, on Saturday morning, he taught a two-hour session on the prophetic. More than one hundred individuals attended. Following the teaching, there was a period of personal prophecy. The guest speaker prophesied as, and to whom, the Holy Spirit directed. For fifty-five minutes, he'd selected one person after another and delivered the word of the Lord to them.

"Okay," the prophet said. "The Holy Spirit said for me to call one last person forward." It surprised me when Leon pointed to me, asking me to join him at the front of the church. As I went forward, I wondered to myself if he recalled prophesying to my family and me three years earlier. As the prophet began giving forth God's word, I listened carefully to what he said.

"Thank you, Lord, for this man of God who can bear the waiting, and carry the burden, and overcome his enemy. *'For your enemy has not overcome you,'* saith the Lord, *'but I have overcome your enemy on your behalf. And you're a big man in the physical sense, but regular-sized in the heart of God. But you're regular-sized, full of love, full of peace, and full of power. The power of the Holy Spirit is on you. The glory of God is with you. I'm preparing you for works. I want you to begin to study the Word of God more and more and allow me to give you much more revelation. I'm going to shine the Light of the Revelation of Jesus Christ on the Word of God for you. Then you will emerge as a man who can teach others and lead others because there is going to be a great work for you to do. If you give yourself wholly over to Me, I'm going to let you teach. And in the past, you felt like you were inadequate. Now, I'm going to make you a wholly adequate man. And you're going to know that My grace is upon you, and you're not going to rely on your own strength. You're going to rely on My strength. And you're not going to rely on your own wisdom. You're going to rely on My Wisdom. And you're not going to rely on your own faith. You're going to rely on My faith. And I'm going to put faith in your belly as a spiritual gift. And I'm going to put wisdom and knowledge in your mind as a spiritual gift. And I'm going to give you a prophetic word so that you can speak to My people and cause them also to prophesy the Word. You are to speak the Word of God when it rises up in you. The Word will bring clarity and righteousness and glory to those you speak to.'* The Lord says, *'Rise up, O man of God, and bear the weight of the kingdom of God that I have laid upon you! The day is coming when many will require your strength and grace. That is going to be spiritual strength and not the physical. And it's going to be My grace that will see you through. And you shall serve Me with a heart of gladness and a heart of strength and joy.'"*

Once more, I was greatly encouraged that the Lord had not forgotten me. I felt reassured that He was continuing to direct my path and order my steps. The only thing that still puzzled me, I voiced aloud to the Lord in my car as I drove home that afternoon.

"Lord, why is it taking so long for everything that You showed me in Colorado to come to pass, or have I missed Your timing on that?"

I waited and waited, but no answer came.

Two days later, at four-thirty in the morning, the Spirit of the Lord finally spoke. He called me from a night of deep sleep to spend time with Him. For an hour or more, I quietly prayed in the spirit while sitting at the kitchen table. As I did, I listened to the Voice I had longed to hear and wrote in my journal what the Spirit told me. Right before dawn, the Lord presented me with a new request.

"Put on your shoes, go outside and begin prayer-walking the perimeter of your property."

I didn't understand why He'd asked this of me. Still, I obeyed. As I did so, the Voice of the Lord directed me.

"Son, I want you to call forth with boldness and confidence everything I revealed to you in Colorado four years ago."

Slowly, at first, I began proclaiming aloud as I walked. Thoughts nagged at me as to what people might think if they drove past my home on the way to work and saw me walking around talking to myself. Little by little, this self-consciousness fell away. I increased the pace at which I was walking, and the volume of my voice, as my boldness and confidence in the Lord grew. This 'prayer-walking' continued for over two hours. The tears that came were a result of joy over finally hearing something about this from the Lord.

The next morning, the Holy Spirit once again woke me early. He told me to go outdoors and begin prayer walking immediately. I obeyed with much joy, declaring things aloud as the Spirit prompted me. At one point, however, I paused, thinking that I'd misunderstood the Holy Spirit.

"Why are you stopping, son? You heard Me correctly. I told you in Colorado that there would be more, and promised to reveal it to you at a later date when the time was right."

I resumed walking the perimeter at a slower pace while I listened carefully to the Lord. The Spirit spoke in detail about the four prayer towers. As I knew, there would be two in Colorado, a third in Rio de Janeiro, and a fourth in Toronto. He then posed a question to me.

"What about Mt. Zion, son?"

"Gary Klein said that You talked to him about a prayer tower, Lord! Will there be one there also?"

"Speak it forth, son."

I did as He requested, with joy and confidence. Several more minutes passed in silence as I continued walking, and then the Spirit spoke again.

"Have you ever considered the Scottish Highlands?"

I hesitated and slowed my step, uncertain as to why the Lord had asked me that question. Finally, I replied.

"Are we still on the same subject? Are you still talking about prayer towers?"

"Yes," the Lord responded.

"Do You want one in the Scottish Highlands?"

*"Yes. **Send forth the seed of proclamation that it might be so, son. Remember, My word never returns void. This assurance applies to My written word, for anyone who believes and acts on it. It is also true of My revealed word. It stirs the soul and comes alive through the voice of a surrendered and obedient vessel.**"*

With great enthusiasm, I added the Scottish Highlands to the other locations I was calling forth.

"What about the Alps and the Pyrenees? What about Mt. Fuji and Mt. Kilimanjaro?"

I began laughing, overwhelmed with the joy of the Lord. I loudly and confidently called each forth. As I did, I walked faster and faster around my property. When I later told my wife about what had occurred that morning, she praised God with me, sharing in my excitement.

Yes, I had once again begun hearing the Voice of the Lord. Within days, however, my financial situation regained prominence in my thoughts. The loan that had closed before our trip to Florida encouraged me. So, I invested in more mailings sent to targeted areas. In each case, I followed up in person with the business owner. Many expressed initial interest, but nothing resulted. One week later, commercial lending rates started climbing. They nearly doubled in the sixty days that followed, and our only worldly source of income again dried up.

Before long, I found myself doubling and redoubling my efforts and investment. It was my way of trying to hold off cycles of worry and fear by staying busy. I kept telling myself that the potential income more than justified these investments. Several business owners contacted me and later signed loan applications. In all three cases, the appraised values came in too low to meet the loan requirements, and the owners gave up. Still, I felt confident. If I remained consistent and persistent, I would dig myself out of my financial mess. However, nothing else came of my extra efforts other than exhaustion. Meanwhile, my wife became more and more worried.

During this same period, I once again spent less and less time with the Lord and His Word. Accordingly, my spiritual hearing suffered.

Two weeks later, my wife handed me a message that she said the Holy Spirit gave to her for me. I sat alone in my office and read what she had written.

"O, My child, be anxious for nothing! It is enough that thy Father loveth thee. Loving thee, He taketh thought of thy smallest need. Surely, He will not allow thee to be put to shame, and He will not be unconcerned when ye are in any kind of need. Turn to Him always before you look to any other source of assistance. It is His love that shall light thy path so that ye may thus be guided in finding other help. Surely, He hath given thee ministering angels, and these may sometimes be in the form of friends. Accept their ministry as from God, and it shall be doubled in blessings. Then ye may also, in turn, be used in a similar manner to bless others. Look not to the physical alone for the transmission of spiritual energy. Divine life can flow out to others through thy thoughts the same as through thy hands. Use My power, and let it flow forth in any form I choose, as I direct and guide you. Ye may multiply thy ministry a hundredfold in this way. Be not restricted by thy present knowledge, but move in and learn more from me."

This message encouraged me. Still, I could not seem to resist the urge overwhelming me to apply myself more, to work even harder. My driven nature had returned, demanding perfection and success. The lack of it was leading me to the brink of frustration and despair. I had abundantly provided for the needs and desires of my family for more than two decades. My current inability to do so brought my stress levels to a new high. I struggled hour after hour, but could not seem to be able to make things happen. I found myself floundering in a situation that I had never before had to face. An overwhelming sense of inadequacy and failure gripped my mind. Everything weighed heavily on my heart.

Two days later, my wife came to me with another *word* from the Lord. I wasn't very eager to read it or thankful to her for bringing it to me. Anger rose up and grabbed hold of my emotions. I battled feelings of resentment toward her that I knew were not justified. Later that day, I had finally regained some semblance of peace. I went outside on the front porch and sat down to read it.

"I have things I long to say unto thee, son. Listen, write, and hold back nothing of all that I shall say unto thee. I shall speak unto thee in the darkness and shall

make thy way a path of light. I will cry unto thee out of the confusion round about, and thou shalt hear My Voice and shall know that which I do. My way I hide from the rebellious and the disobedient, and from them that seek to walk in their wisdom. But look thou unto Me, and I will be unto thee as a beacon in the night, and thou shalt not stumble over the hidden things. Yea, thou shalt walk in the way of victory, though turmoil be on either hand, even as Israel marched through the Red Sea on a path that My hand hewed out for them. Yea, it shall be a path of deliverance, and My Spirit shall go with thee. Thou shalt carry the glad tidings of deliverance to people that sit in darkness and captivity. Tarry thou not for a convenient time. The moving of the Spirit is never convenient for the interest of the flesh. I shall engineer thy circumstances to conform to My plan and My will, and thou shalt glorify Me. My plan for thee excels all other ways, and in the center of My will is a Perpetual Fountain of Glory. Doubt not. Do not hesitate. For I, the Lord thy God, do go before thee. Thou hast already My promise that the work which I begin, I am able to carry through to completion. Yea, there is already laid up an exceeding weight of glory for those who go through with Me and determine to seize the prize, for I have wealth beyond thy fondest dreams to bestow upon them that have left all to follow. All the glittering enticement of this transient life are as chaff in comparison. For the gifts and calling of God are without repentance. The will and choice of the recipient are all that restricts My giving."

Like the first message she'd brought to me, this one sounded encouraging. Nevertheless, the enemy of my soul worked overtime, urging me to resist letting go of control. I had convinced myself of this need, out of fear of what would happen if I didn't maintain control. With that resistance, also came an unjustified feeling of resentment directed toward the Holy Spirit. Instead of talking directly to me, He'd chosen, for now, to bring His words to me through my wife.

Ten days of stubbornness passed, during which I held to my will. I showed no evidence of heeding either of the words the Lord had brought to me through my wife. Finally, she came to me with a third message but didn't hand this one to me directly, uncertain about how I would react. Instead, she left it on my desk for me to find.

"My son, I say unto thee, that though I am ready and longing to come unto thee, yea, and would have rejoiced to have come much sooner, I say to thee thou are not yet ready. I have wooed thee, and I have warned thee. Yet, ye have spurned My entreaties, and ye have fought against the restraining of the Spirit. Break through your religious curtain and behold Me in My glory. Keep thy vision filled with Me, keep thy life in tune, and thy worship in mutual harmony. For I shall come singing, and what will ye if ye be in discord?"

"O My child, let Me speak to thee and let My Spirit direct thy life. I may lead you in unexpected ways, and ask things of you that are startling, but I will never guide you amiss. Across thy path shall fall the shadow of My hand. Wheresoever I direct thee, there shall ye see My power at work. There shall come forth from thy ministry that which shall glorify Me. Do not walk according to thy natural reasoning. Obey the promptings of the Spirit, and be obedient to My voice. I need those who will be completely flexible in this way. There is a multitude of souls searching for Me that would never encounter Me in a personal way through the channels of the organized church. Ye shall go as Philip went at the behest of the Spirit into the places that are out of the way. You shall bring the light of My Word to those who are in need. Stay in an attitude of prayer and faith, and I will do all the rest."

"O My child, it is not appointed unto thee to know the future, nor to be able to discern aforetime My exact plans. It is enough that we should walk together in love and trust. No doubts need to mar thy peace or anxieties cloud thy brow. Rest in the knowledge that My ways are perfect, and My grace is all-sufficient. Ye shall find My help is adequate, no matter what may befall. Let none say to thee, 'Lo, this shall be, or that shall verily come to pass.' Live in the awareness of the eternal destiny of the present moment. To be unduly occupied with matters of the future is to thine own disadvantage, as so much awaits doing NOW. My command stands, 'Occupy until I come.' Live according to this injunction. Thy life is in My hands. But I can only use what is available to Me at the moment. Others need guidance and help with their present problems. Stay available. Minister in the realm of the here and now, and thou shalt have much fruit in the day of reaping."

I read the words three times, and then a fourth time. I sat for more than an hour, just thinking about it. Something bothered me, but I could not identify what it was. I once again read the previous two, and then the third one for the fifth time. Suddenly, it dawned on me.

At the time my wife had come with a second *word from the Lord* to me, I had read it. However, blinded by my enemy's misdirection, I'd begun considering an idea. *Possibly this was my wife's way of once again trying to **make** something happen.* Before long, enemies I'd formerly fellowshipped with had returned. Frustration, Bitterness, and Resentment regularly bombarded my thoughts. They encouraged me down the path my heart had already begun taking.

Now, sitting in my office, I carefully studied all three of the messages she had given to me. I knew in my heart that none of the words from the Lord—**especially the last one**—could have been something that she had concocted. I'd lived with her for over thirty years at that point, and knew the extent of her vocabulary. I was confident she would never speak or write something like this of her own volition, using the many meticulously selected words that made up the message. It wasn't her style.

"This message has to be from You, Holy Spirit," I finally acknowledged aloud to the Lord. "But why won't you talk to me? Why are you now sending these messages to me through my wife? If I've done something wrong, will You show me what, and help me set it right? Please extend Your grace and mercy my way once more, Lord!"

For more than thirty minutes, I sat still and listened. Hearing nothing, I set the pages aside and returned to contacting prospects. I concluded that maybe God wasn't going to answer me right then. But even as I worked, another possibility crossed my mind for the first time. With it came a different set of truths, and far more concern.

*What if God **IS** talking, and I'm just **not** listening!*

At the end of that week, my wife broached the subject of the two of us discussing our situation with our pastor. Reluctantly, I agreed. That Sunday, after the morning service had concluded, I spoke with him and scheduled a time to meet.

On the day of the appointment, we drove a few exits down the Interstate in our pastor's car, where he stopped at a small restaurant. Seated in a booth across from my wife and me, our pastor wasted no time in trying to find the underlying cause of what was troubling us. At his prompting, I gave him a quick summary of the last few years' events in our lives. When I mentioned that I was now working in the mortgage industry, he proceeded to challenge me to tell him what the payment would be for a specific amount, term, and rate. I stared at him and didn't respond, all the while wondering in my mind what the point of his challenge was. What did that have to do with what we'd come to him to discuss?

In the next moment, my pastor started telling me what he thought I needed to do to improve myself. This 'improvement' included what I needed to learn and how I needed to dress and act. He even suggested changes to the style of glasses I'd worn for years. The irritation I had begun feeling toward my pastor quickly escalated. I listened out of respect for him as he continued speaking. Even so, I couldn't keep from wondering why he was lecturing me about success habits. He had not referenced God whatsoever or the leading of the Holy Spirit. Finally, he looked at me and asked, "What's God saying to you lately?"

Since he was one of the forty that the Spirit told me to mail a package to when I returned from Colorado, I began by talking about that.

"The Lord's been talking off and on about Colorado but hasn't said anything about moving there yet," I stated. I then expressed some of the pressure I'd been feeling from my wife. "She keeps bugging me about when we're leaving for Colorado. The Holy Spirit told me very clearly that He'll tell us when it's time to move, and we're not to go until then. I'll be honest with you, pastor," I continued, "sometimes I wish He'd never spoken to me about Colorado."

Without a moment's hesitation, my pastor looked at the two of us and made an emphatic statement. "Not one bit of that stuff about Colorado was from God. Forget about it."

When I heard his comment, I stopped talking and stared off to the side. I was unwilling to look at him for fear of saying something that I'd later regret. The irritation inside of me rapidly converted to anger. I struggled to squelch the bitterness and resentment I was now feeling toward him. We'd come to him looking for spiritual discernment, understanding, and guidance. Once again, all he'd offered was practical advice and opinion. There was no offer to pray with or for us. He discounted the one time in my entire life that had the most significant meaning and impact, a time when I'd experienced the most profound, most intimate fellowship and unity with my Lord and Creator. In conclusion, his "advice" was to forget about it. He acted as though it was some concoction of my imagination, that it had no basis in God!

I wouldn't! I couldn't unless God Himself told me so! I knew what had occurred, and I was not about to let anyone convince me otherwise, including my pastor. I didn't understand why God had permitted some of the things to happen. I didn't know where it would all end up either, or when everything would begin to make sense. Even so, I knew with an unshakable certainty what I'd experienced, and I wasn't about to deny it. How could he say what he did to me? Didn't he repeatedly say, "a man who has had an experience with God is never at the mercy of the one who simply has a doctrine?" Yes! He did.

The three of us left the restaurant, and fifteen minutes later, our pastor dropped us off by our van. As my wife and I drove home, we didn't speak to one another for a while. I had no idea what was going through her mind during that time, but with me, it was a different matter. The Holy Spirit immediately began speaking to my heart and soul.

"Son, I orchestrated today's meeting with your pastor. I allowed him to stir you up by his actions and words so that YOU might gain insight into YOU. Think back to when you were in Colorado those many years ago. Do you remember how surprised you were when I identified for you a spirit named Ornery? Do you also recall that I told you to break fellowship with that spirit?"

"Yes, Lord, and I did," I answered the Lord in my mind.

"Indeed, you did, for a season, until it returned, and you fell right back into companionship. Son, listen now as I reiterate a vital lesson that I taught you in the past. You wrote it down then, but never acted on it."

*"**Where you find one spirit, you will ALWAYS find companion spirits.** In this case, where you find Ornery, you invariably find Stubborn, whose purpose is contrary to*

what you and most others believe. **Stubborn does not simply affect one's personality through interaction with Arrogance and Obstinacy. Rather, it manipulates through a more devastating collaboration with Fear and Pride.** These two spirits, working in unity with a Stubborn spirit, persuade you to hold on with a death grip to the known. You do so, even when the known has been a source of great torment. **A Stubborn spirit will try to convince you of how much worse the unknown COULD be. Not IS, or even WILL be, but COULD be.** The self-same combination preys on the poor and oppressed in this world. Together they convince them to accept 'their lot in life.' In doing so, they also discourage them from hoping for something more. They deter them from wanting something better out of life than what they currently have or are. Nevertheless, out of fear of losing what little they now have, the individuals too often cooperate with Pride, claiming 'satisfaction' with their current way of life. Regrettably, this further binds them to the very existence that they secretly despise."

"Do you recall the day not so long ago when you remained in your seat after the Sunday morning service at Heritage? Covering your face with your hands to hide your tears, you asked Me repeatedly, 'Why am I so afraid?'"

"Son, parts of your soul still need healing and are heavily influenced and directed by various spirits of Fear. Permanently removing Fear's effect on your soul and future is possible. But only when you allow My perfect love into your life to do its FULL work. **That starts with surrendering to Me those fears, hurts, and worries. It also means ceasing your struggles to determine your future, <u>which is directly contrary to surrender.</u>**"

"Always remember this! **It's in the soil that is watered by the tears of brokenness and enriched by the decayed loam of a surrendered self, that trust finds solid rooting. There it blooms forth abundantly.**"

"Consider also, My son, the ways of the wild stallion when a man captures it. It is of no value to anyone until someone gentles it. That process is a battle of wills. It is the stallion's will versus the will of the one attempting to bring the animal under control. The horse bucks and resists with a fury, desperate to once more run free, doing what it pleases when it pleases. As its resistance dissipates, the stallion begins to learn. It also starts responding to the man's gentle commands. The man knows the reasons for the actions and reactions of the stallion. The desire to resist is still inherent in the very nature of the animal. Even so, the two begin to communicate. Trust develops between them, and the horse bonds with the one to whom it has chosen to surrender. Throughout the transformation, the man breaks the stallions' past habits and responses. He **never** breaks the horse's spirit. Its master patiently works with the creature until he gentles and lovingly constrains it. He brings it into one accord with himself. When the stallion responds to his commands without hesitation, the man rejoices. The longer the two are together, the deeper the bond of trust between them grows. Each becomes so familiar with the other that they anticipate one another's desires. The stallion accepts that this 'trusted one' will take care of it like none other. It eagerly responds when its master draws near. Having grown to cherish the stallion, the man looks forward to spending time with the animal. To him, the horse has become like the dearest of friends."

"As you consider what I've just explained, remember the following, My son. **Broken stallions carry kings. Moreover, where there is genuine brokenness, you find two things. The one is unequivocal surrender. The other is an undeniably loyal and loving bond.** I desire that you would allow Me to gentle and transform you. I long to direct you even as the stallion comes under the direction of the master's hand. I want to bring you under the constraint of My Gospel. I long for your spirit to be in accord with Mine. I desire for you to become familiar with and trusting of **Me**. Then you will be able to anticipate **My** desires and respond eagerly. But, once again, son, the first step is complete, genuine, and lasting surrender."

When the Holy Spirit had finished speaking to me, my spirit had finally returned to a peaceful state, and then I got my wife's attention and spoke with her.

"Sweetheart, I've been quiet for the last ten minutes or so because the Holy Spirit has been speaking to me, and now I need you to please understand a few things. I intend to wait upon the Lord as long as it takes. That doesn't mean I'm just going to sit around and do nothing. However, I refuse to jump ahead of Him, trying to **make** something happen. The Holy Spirit told me specifically not to do that, and this much I fully intend to obey. I know I've slacked off in my time with Him, and haven't spent nearly enough time in prayer or reading His Word lately. I've been so worried at times that I've reverted to doing whatever it took to try to make something happen. Concern for what you'd think, or say, or do if I could no longer provide for you the way I have in the past consumed me. That distraction and preoccupation are much of the reason why I haven't heard His voice, and that's why He's had to resort to speaking through you to get my attention. I'm thankful He did, and I'm sorry for the way I reacted toward you when He reached out to me through you. There was no excuse for my actions, and I ask you to forgive me."

"I've wondered a lot why everything I touch lately starts great then seems to die," I continued. "Even so, the Lord is talking to me now and continues to reach me in His special way. All I ask is that you not lose faith in the fact that God has His hand on the two of us. He promised that He would finish that which He started in us. I don't know when, or how, or even what it will end up being or involving when He does. What I do know, above all else, is that the Lord is faithful. He loves us, He never stops moving on our behalf, and He does so, despite my frustration and impatience. I'm also sure that He isn't offended at times when I've commented aloud about whether He even cares about our current situation. That's just anxiety, fear, and anger spouting off through me. I know it's unjustified, just as it was when I reacted that way to you, and I've asked Him to forgive me also. I love the Lord, and I love you very much. If you do not give up on me, we'll see this through to the end together. We'll do so no matter how long it takes, or what changes are necessary along the way."

When I finished speaking, my wife reached over and took my right hand, holding it gently between her two hands. I looked over at her and saw that she was smiling, with tears glistening in her eyes.

"I don't know why pastor said what he said, or acted the way he did," she replied. "When you returned from your time alone with the Lord in Colorado, you were unmistakably different. In all the years of our marriage, I'd never seen such complete brokenness, tenderness, and love in you. Some of that is, to me, still obviously there. Some, you let slip away or put on the back burner, probably because of all of the pressure you've put on yourself. The Lord wants both of us, together, to release control to Him, and leave everything in His hands. I promise you I won't nag you about Colorado anymore. I want you to promise me that you'll start sharing what's on your heart with me more often – the good and the bad. Okay?"

My wife's response was what I most needed to hear, and I willingly promised her that I would no longer hold things inside of me. Sharing our hearts ushered in the presence of the Lord. Along with it, came His perfect peace that once more possessed our souls.

*"I am the Rock of Offense. Correct?
If My Spirit abides in your pastor,
can't I choose to be, through him,
a Rock of Offense to you?
Offense elicits a response.
How a man chooses to respond
to a given situation
reveals much about the
condition of his soul –
whether he seeks to discover
and follow My will,
or remains self-willed.
It exposes in him that
which still needs to die."*

Uncovered and Exposed

It was Saturday morning, five days after my wife and I had last met with our pastor. I sat quietly in a chair at the end of the room in the pole barn in which the men's prayer group was once again meeting. I kept my eyes closed, soaking in the atmosphere of worship in the room. Six others were also present. Some sang along with the worship music that was playing; others were still. When the song ended, no one moved to put on another music CD. Silence settled into the room, and our hearts. No one could deny that the Holy Spirit's presence had increased. Nothing seemed more desirable than lingering in that atmosphere. Even so, it was that very moment in which the Spirit of God spoke a strange request to me, bringing me alert.

"Go out to your car and bring in your large golf umbrella, son."

I sat there for a minute, wondering if I had heard correctly. Unable to guess the reasoning behind the request, I opted to obey without disturbing the others. I exited the pole barn to the graveled lot. Returning with the umbrella in hand, I settled once again into my chair. I still had no idea what to do with the umbrella. A couple of the men glanced at me with a questioning look. The others ignored me. I closed my eyes once more. His perfect peace reclaimed my soul and continued uninterrupted for quite a while.

"Open up the umbrella, son," directed the Spirit, nearly thirty minutes later.

I opened my eyes and looked around the room. The other men still had their eyes closed. I hesitated, wondering to myself what they would think, but the desire to know what God might want to say to me or show me tipped the scales for obedience. I pushed the button, and the umbrella popped open, as did the eyes of every man there. Once opened, I didn't quite know what to do with it. Some of the men laughed good-naturedly at me. One man couldn't keep from asking, "What are you doing?"

"I have no idea," I replied. "I'm just obeying what the Lord told me to do."

One by one, the men returned to their prior positions—eyes closed, sitting before the Lord. As I held the handle of the opened umbrella, I stared down at the inside of the umbrella where it rested on the floor. My focus was on the Voice of the Spirit as he explained something to me in elaborate detail.

"Look at the construction of the umbrella, son. The design, shape, and strength make it possible for it to withstand the wind that would come against it, without bending or collapsing. You, My son, are like the metal framework and handle of the umbrella.

I've fitted you together carefully. When My Spirit flows through you unhindered, My anointing goes forth. It flows through you as smoothly as this umbrella moves when you push the button to open it. Still, of what use is the finest umbrella framework without its covering? The covering on the umbrella is a perfect fit for its framework and the framework to its covering. When the umbrella opens, the fabric stretches taut over the extended ribbings. The stretchers hold it in that position. Furthermore, the material—or 'covering'—is bound to the ribbings at numerous points. Finally, the ferrules on the ends firmly hold the covering taut. In other words, all of the parts are 'fitly joined' together. The strength and smooth operation of each guarantee the success of the whole. It fulfills its intended purpose."

"*Consider well what I am about to say to you, son,*" the Holy Spirit continued. "*I created **YOU** for a purpose, but the fulfillment of that purpose is not dependent solely on you. The activated metal framework indeed makes the umbrella's purpose identifiable. A secondary truth is every bit as important to understand. Without the covering, the metal structure is unable to fulfill its created purpose. Neither the framework nor the covering is of any value without the other, and **neither** is of greater importance. Nevertheless, think about when the umbrella opens as protection against the storm. The covering takes the brunt of the onslaught. There are times when the storms come against this covering and all which that covering represents to Me. The covering is then dependent on the joined strength of the framework.*"

"*Take note that the framework does not choose the covering which it desires. Neither does the covering choose which framework that it will agree to cover. I, the Lord God Almighty, choose whom to join with whom. I bind two together, even as the covering is bound to the ribbings of the umbrella.*"

"*You have resisted My desire for your pastor to be your covering for many years because you misunderstand the purpose of 'covering.' It is not about your pastor controlling you. You have mistakenly come to believe this about all pastors. Your misunderstanding came about because of the manipulative control demonstrated by a few in the past. Those few called themselves servants to My body, while their actions at the time revealed them to be otherwise.*"

"*Neither is this pairing about you, as the framework, controlling when to open, or not open, the umbrella. If you insist on being in control, you hinder the ability of your 'covering'—your pastor—to fulfill one of his assigned purposes. I designed this interdependency to be a complementary union. **Neither** of you is in control. **My Spirit is**. Your pastor counts on your prayers and unwavering faithfulness to support him. He relies on you to undergird his strength, so the storms will not prevail against him. However, when the storms of life come—as they inevitably will—it is My hand that takes hold of the handle. I push the button, and My strong arm points the umbrella in the direction from which the storm has come. That umbrella is the two of you, working* *in unity with Me. I bring into play your **interwoven** attributes. I activate your **joined** strengths to overcome the storm."*

"*Allow Me, son, to explain this situation further, using a different illustration. In many ways, you are like a fighter jet. I fitted you out with all of the instruments of war that give you the ability to wreak havoc on your enemy. Your jet engines (your prayer language) enable you to soar in the heavens, to change course quickly—as need dictates. You can evade Satan's offensive moves while pursuing and defeating any demonic enemies. However, what if your wings were simply a framework. With no covering fastened to your wing's framework, how would you fly? How much would all of the impressive qualities and capabilities matter then? How will you lift into the heavens where you can fulfill your purpose, and where the Pilot (My Spirit) can employ this might? Consider this also. As long as you remain on the tarmac, you continue to be extremely vulnerable to attack. **Your enemy would rejoice to see you never realize your potential. Your enemy longs to see your power neutralized, and your capabilities nullified.** Would you truly prefer to stay grounded, just because you refuse a covering of My choice? Would you continue to listen to your enemy as he convinces you to trust no one? Do you believe that the covering is there to control you? In refusing the covering I have chosen, are you not then the one who has seized control? Are you willing to accept the ramifications of such a decision? As always, My son, the choice is yours."*

"*One other thing, son. Was your transferring to Heritage Fellowship your desire? You believe this to be so. However, it was My Spirit prompting you. I led you here, over time, in response to your request for Me to guide your path and order your steps. Now that you are here, I desire for Cleddie Keith to be your covering. I alone know the plans I have for you and your wife. Seek me with all of your heart, mind, soul, and strength. I will reveal My plans to you, and I will realize them in and through you, in My timing."*

When the Lord had finished speaking to me, I shut the umbrella and set it to the side. Closing my eyes, I meditated on His words. I knew the only sound response was surrender, and I quietly proclaimed this to the Holy Spirit.

"Lord, I'm willing to surrender control to You. Everything, Lord! My hopes and dreams. My wife and our family. Our finances. Everything, especially those areas of my heart, mind, and soul, where I've been blind to how tightly I've been holding on to control. Please forgive me, Lord, and guide me into Your perfect will."

"*Son, I want you to tell your pastor what I explained to you this morning and ask him to be your covering."*

"Yes, Lord. I will. Please show me the perfect time to speak to him. And give me the right words to say."

"I will, My son. For now, confess your sin to the brothers present here this morning. Instruct them on what I've explained to you. You are not the only man here today that needed to hear this."

The following morning, I sat quietly in the prayer room at our church before the Sunday morning service. One of the doors to the pastor's parlor was also accessible from the prayer room. For one hour, I alternately prayed in the spirit or sat with my eyes closed, listening. I heard not one word from the Holy Spirit. Behind the closed door, I could occasionally hear voices talking. Strangely, I felt a sense of relief that my pastor was busy. *Today is not the day that I'll have to tell him*, I thought. A moment later, the Holy Spirit spoke.

"Son, don't you realize that your very thoughts at this moment are under attack. The culprits are Fear, Resistance, Rebellion, Resentment, and Bitterness. The biggest offender is their ringleader—a Controlling spirit. They are working together, trying to direct your thoughts and imagination. They desire to keep you from walking through that parlor door. You need to resolve this situation today. Do not put this off any longer, as they are trying to convince you to do."

"But, Holy Spirit, the door's closed, and he has people in there with him," I said, suddenly not as eager to speak with my pastor.

Just then, the parlor door opened. Those who had been meeting with the pastor entered the prayer room and found places to sit.

"He's available now, son. Go tell him what I explained to you yesterday before you allow your enemy to talk you out of it."

Quietly knocking on the parlor door, I opened it enough to see if my pastor was alone. He sat alone at the large table that occupied the corner of his parlor. Seeing me peeking in, he motioned for me to enter. I complied, closing the door behind me.

"Pastor, the Holy Spirit has been urging me to come in here and tell you something," I began. I then proceeded to explain what the Lord had shown and spoken to me the previous day. I ended by telling him that the Holy Spirit had said to me to ask him to be my covering. My pastor thanked me for telling him this, and a moment later, I was back in the prayer room.

That wasn't so bad, I thought to myself, happy that I'd followed through in obedience to the Holy Spirit's request.

Ten minutes later, everyone in the prayer room exited into the main sanctuary where the worship was beginning. Those in attendance responded joyfully and wholeheartedly. Forty or so minutes later, worship had concluded, and the pastor invited everyone to sit down. I had barely sat when I heard my pastor call me forward. A sick feeling rose in my stomach as I walked to the front of the sanctuary to join him.

Directing me to face the audience, he said, "Tell the people what the Holy Spirit told you to say to me in the back room."

I hesitated a moment, then complied with his request. When I finished, my pastor thanked me, and I returned to my seat without any other comment from him. The people responded by clapping, but my stomach was in turmoil, and I wasn't quite sure why.

Over the next few days, Restlessness troubled my soul. Wednesday morning, I arose early to spend quiet time with the Lord. I could not shake the irritation I felt whenever I reflected on what had occurred that Sunday morning.

"Holy Spirit, I need to talk with you about last Sunday. I told the pastor, as you requested," I continued. "Why am I so bothered about the whole thing?"

*"Your heart was sincere when you spoke to him in the parlor, son. You told him that I told you to ask him to be your covering. However, you didn't take the next step and ask him to be so, from your heart, **with your words**, not Mine."*

"You then went forward in the sanctuary before the assembly. You complied with your Pastor's request by restating what you'd shared with him. As you did, an Irritating spirit was influencing you, and you didn't resist the suggested thoughts. That is what caused your stomach to sour. Even now, this spirit lingers near you. It goads your thinking and influences your emotions as you recall this."

"But why did my pastor have to call me forward and make a big deal out of it?"

"I encouraged him to, son. The Body needed to hear what you said to your pastor in the parlor."

"What was the point?" I responded in mild frustration, not yet understanding. "You only told me to share it with him, not the whole church."

"First of all, I told you to share it with the men at the Saturday prayer group. Others present that morning needed to hear and understand what I'd revealed to you. These spirits too often influence your soul in this area. In the sanctuary on Sunday, My seed went forth through your words. It will NOT return void. It affected many in that Body who were also fellowshipping with a Controlling spirit. Most importantly, though, is this. It is too easy for one to forget later, or even deny what they have spoken to another in private. I influenced your pastor to have you repeat it before the entire assembly. His action, following my direction, eliminates that possibility. It also further frees you from the influence of that Controlling spirit."

"Nevertheless, an unsettledness lingers in your soul even now because you still harbor ill feelings toward your pastor. Issues remain unresolved, things that occurred in the past that you have not released to Me."

"Did you ever consider this, son? When you've spoken with your pastor in the past, it was My Spirit directing his spirit. I affected his response, as well as his reaction. That includes this past Sunday. I brought forth words from him that you found to be

extremely offensive. You now hold a grudge, allowing bitterness and resentment to wreak havoc on your body and soul. You were unwilling to look beyond the surface each time this occurred. You failed to understand the spiritual dynamics of the situation. I am the Rock of Offense. Correct?"

"Yes," I replied.

"If My Spirit abides in your pastor, can't I choose to be, through him, a Rock of Offense to you—now thrice offended?"

"Why would you do this, Lord? I don't understand!"

"I have your best interest in mind, son. Only I know what drives a man, what moves his heart, and what prevents him from fully surrendering to My will. In your case, many things are so ingrained, so much a part of your ways that you are unable to see the truth. **The easiest way for Me to reveal these things to you is to bring before you select individuals. I permit situations to arise through them that I know will offend you. They are as a mirror held up before you, that you might see your true inner self by your response. This action is what I have done for you through your pastor, and offense elicits a response.** How a man chooses to respond to a given situation reveals much about the current state of his soul. Is he seeking to discover and follow **My** will, or will he remain **SELF-willed**? It exposes in him that which still needs to die. Once again, the choice is yours. Will you choose not to be easily offended, dying to self, thereby allowing My love to reign in your heart? Remember, son! **Only when you decide to obey My Word is My love enabled to do its perfect work in you.**"

"Holy Spirit, I don't want this hatred to continue. Would you please address and remove it?"

"Yes, My son. I will."

"Would You tell me something else, Lord? Was everything about Colorado not of You, as my pastor said? That bothered me so much when he said that. Was the enemy of my soul misleading me in all that occurred?"

"You were **NOT** misled, son. All that led up to the trip, and each experience throughout, I guided. Even so, since then, you have not always been as attentive and responsive to My voice. My working through your pastor to offend you forced you to rise in defense of what your spirit knew to be true, reigniting fires of hope within you that had been steadily dwindling. I succeeded in bringing you back into step with Me, son. **However, hear me now. The primary focus of what occurred in Fort Collins was NOT about Colorado or your ministry to Me. It was about the growth of your relationship with and trust in Me.** Now I once again have your complete attention. Finally, I can speak of other things that I have longed to address with you."

The Spirit of Reconciliation: Grace to Forgive

Weeks seemed to pass in a flash. Before I had realized it, months had accumulated into years. During this period, I often found myself struggling to carry on a conversation with the Holy Spirit. It was not that I didn't hear His voice at all. Instead, I only heard Him at select times or in specific settings. I no longer heard Him routinely, as I had grown accustomed to in the past.

One day, as I puzzled over this very thing, the Lord interrupted my thoughts, raising a question to me.

"Son, what happened before I released you to move to Heritage Fellowship? Do you recall how I softened your heart toward that previous pastor who had so greatly offended you?"

"Yes, Lord. You made me write him a letter every day for thirty consecutive days. You told me to lift him to You in prayer through my words in those letters. You also began giving me Scriptures to proclaim as a blessing over him in the closing for each letter."

*"That is not entirely correct, son. I did not **make** you do it. I asked you if you would do it, for I knew this had to be your choice. It pleased Me that you chose to do as I had suggested. Was it an easy task?"*

"No! The first day was horrible! I felt as though I was writing lies. Everything that made me so embittered toward him came back to the forefront of my mind. I honestly despised him."

"Even so, you were obedient in closing each letter with the words 'Love you' before signing and mailing them to him. Each successive morning, you wrote to him again."

"Yes, Lord, I did. Still, for the first seven days, I found no joy in it and felt as though I was a liar and a total hypocrite. What I wanted was to leave that church—to be anywhere but there—but You wouldn't let me!"

"Yes, I know. There was a reason for My restraining you. When your heart began to soften, you wrote a longer letter on the eighth day, without My directing you to do so. For the first time, you prayed about what Scripture to proclaim over My servant. You didn't wait for Me to tell you what to say."

"That was the first day that I ever really saw him as being simply a man like me. He had similar faults, anxieties, and worries facing him every day. Before that day, I never considered his hurt, pain, or insecurities. I didn't think about the possibility of a demon spirit misleading him, driving him to treat me as he did. I'd also never thought about the responsibility he bore as a pastor. He had to represent that body before You daily. I never considered how that must have weighed on him."

"*This understanding occurred because I'd begun removing the scales from your eyes. They began falling off when you started writing to the man. Each day your obedience allowed you to start seeing more of what you hadn't seen before then. Neither he nor his wife, during those thirty days, ever responded. They did not indicate to you that he'd received and read the letters. Still, you were faithful to continue sending them as I'd asked of you.*"

"Lord, I remember so clearly the thirtieth day, as I dropped the last one into the mailbox. I thanked You for giving me the opportunity for my heart to change, to grow, to shed its weighty burden. That day my heart was so full of love for him. My spirit longed to pray for him, and I did so without prompting from You. Thirty days earlier, Holy Spirit, I never would have believed it could ever have been possible."

"<u>I showed you a pathway to healing that began with your discovery of how easy it is to forgive someone, even if there is deep hurt. The primary requirement is that you are **willing**</u>. Then, having forgiven, I taught you how to love that same person. You learned to do so despite the pain and hurt they may have been responsible for in the past. Son, I will never stop reminding you. Love **WILL** make a way, and I **am** that Love!"

"Thank You so much, Lord!"

"*Son, do you remember when My pastor finally acknowledged receiving those letters, and how your heart became so overwhelmed with love and joy?*"

"It was near Thanksgiving, almost four months after I'd written him the final letter. I remember him finishing his sermon that morning. He then began talking to the congregation about many of the things for which he was thankful. I was astonished when he concluded by talking about the letters. I saw how his expression softened, and I heard the sincerity in his voice. He never said my name, but he didn't have to, Lord. He looked right at me and thanked me. He told me how much they meant to him at a time when he so desperately needed to hear what those letters said. He then asked me to forgive him for any pain his actions or words had caused. All I could do was nod my head once and look down. Lord, my heart so overflowed with love for him that day!"

"*Indeed it did, son. That thirty-day period of faithfulness was crucial. It brought the healing necessary to allow your family to depart there as friends. You moved on to Heritage Fellowship with both My blessing and theirs, and you did so with grace and peace, My son. You allowed My love to remain as a bond of love between the two of you. You were able to walk away from there without carrying any baggage to Heritage.*"

The Spirit of Reconciliation: Grace to Forgive

Three weeks later, as I headed north to a neighboring city for an appointment, the Holy Spirit spoke to me once more.

"Do you remember the misunderstanding that arose between your former pastor's son and you?"

I absolutely remembered it as though it had just happened, and nodded my head in acknowledgment.

*"Son, it occurred **nine years ago**,"* the Holy Spirit said, pausing long enough for what He said next to stir my spirit. *"It festers inside of you to this day, sending forth an unholy stench. The reason you so quickly recall it is because you've never asked his forgiveness."*

I was a bit bothered at what He'd just said, and replied, "Shouldn't he be the one asking for forgiveness from me?"

"My son, you have only one accountability to Me in this matter. Ask for forgiveness for any way in which you may have offended or sinned against your brother. In like manner, be willing to forgive him for those ways in which he has offended or sinned against you. It's not your concern as to whether or not he chooses to reciprocate. I want you to call him now, while it's fresh on your mind, and ask him to forgive you."

I called the church, where he had served for many years as the senior pastor. When he answered the phone, I introduced myself to him and explained why I had called, asking him to forgive me.

"I don't honestly recall the event," he said. "But it's obvious that this bothered you enough to hold onto it for nine years. I don't mean it as condemnation, brother, but I think this has hurt you far more than it ever could have hurt me. I'm sorry that it occurred, and I ask your forgiveness. I also sincerely forgive you. I know that our Father in heaven rejoices for this day, and remembers our sins no more. May I pray for you?"

I welcomed his prayer, and as he prayed, I felt the bitterness and resentment toward him dissolve. The Spirit replaced it with a burst of joy that flooded my soul.

After that, the Holy Spirit brought to my attention the names and faces of many others. He knew I still had anger, bitterness, or resentment toward these also. In each instance, the Lord shined His light on the source of the issue. He allowed me to see what remained buried deep inside, so deep that I was often unable, in my insight, to identify it. Once exposed, the Lord guided me to ask those individuals to forgive me. Those actions further freed me from demonic influences over me.

I thought I was making significant progress in this direction. Even so, one day, the Lord brought to the surface hostile feelings that He knew I held toward some of my siblings. There were also feelings toward others on my side of our extended family. Many arose from their reaction to what they perceived as our "rebellion."

Shortly after marrying my wife, both of us agreed to leave the Catholic Church. We'd each come into a joy-filled relationship with God, initiated by our Baptism in the Holy Spirit. From that moment onward, we had longed daily for more of the sweetness of the Lord and began looking for a church that openly welcomed the movement of the Holy Spirit, which we both felt was noticeably lacking in the ritual of the Sunday mass at our parish church.

When the Lord had led me to the Full Gospel Business Men's Fellowship, it transformed my spiritual life. It had been for me as though a brilliant light turned on in a world previously adorned in shades of gray. My wife and I began interacting with hundreds of other Spirit-filled individuals. They exuded the love, joy, and peace of the Lord Jesus Christ. These were our new friends—brothers and sisters in the Lord. They rejoiced to share how the Lord had recently moved in their lives. It was so great! They were just as eager to listen as we told of what God had done in our lives. Everyone 'welcomed' the idea of talking about the truths discovered in the Word of God. It was like a breath of fresh air to us. We'd finally felt free to talk about what was always considered taboo to our families, relatives, and many previous friends. Our new friends and companions did so without hesitation, embarrassment, shame, condemnation, or feeling a need to prove their belief or any revelation from the Lord. Once we had experienced this new freedom, my wife and I shed religion and the doctrines of men. We had found a dynamic, ever-expanding **relationship** with a Triune Godhead, and He never ceased to fascinate, amaze, and welcome us.

The local chapter president of Full Gospel at that time invited my family and me to his church. It was our first time worshipping at an Assembly of God. From that point onward, church attendance became something we anticipated. It was more than a religious obligation. My new relationship was with this Living Christ. He began shaping and directing every facet of my existence. Soon, my family and I found ourselves at church three to four days a week. Reading and studying the Word of the Lord became a time that my wife and I approached with high expectations.

Guided by the Holy Spirit, we also discovered what a great joy it was to reach out to others. We began freely giving of our time and money, helping everyone to whom the Lord directed us. In like manner, we encouraged our young children to do the same.

As I thought back to that period of our lives, I recalled with joy a particular day. We all had worked together, packing and praying over Bibles. We had committed to mailing hundreds of them to individuals throughout the world. We'd started supporting missionaries and attending Christian conferences. We filled our children's hearts, minds, ears, and time with things that honored God. These were things that we knew our Father in heaven would find pleasing. Years later, my wife and I saw the dividends of those efforts invested in our children. Each of them, of their free will, pursued a ministry of one sort or another. Additionally, they each married spouses of like mind, heart, and spirit.

Even now, the evidence of our combined efforts continues, identifiable in the character, words, and actions of the next generation of our family. It thrills us to see our many grandchildren interacting and walking with the Lord.

During those years, I loved to talk about and share the new relationship I'd found. As a result, for a long time, many of my family had treated my family and me *differently*. The only reason we could see for their actions was our choice to go down another path. It was a path that some of them misunderstood, and a few seemed to outright resent. Granted, after a few years, most of their adverse reactions subsided. There was simply no discussion about it. My wife and I, along with our children and their spouses, prayed regularly for both of our extended families. Making an innocent statement to this effect, however, caused some of my siblings to become defensive. They acted insulted, as though we were somehow trying to convert them to something other than their Catholic faith. This suspicion and resentment hung in the air like an ever-present cloud for decades.

At the direction of the Holy Spirit, I had spoken to my dad before he passed from this world. I confirmed that he understood the difference between religion and having a personal relationship with Jesus. Tears flowed from my dad's eyes that day as he acknowledged that he knew Jesus as his personal Savior. He was prepared to meet Him, and that brought great joy to my heart. Nevertheless, one of my siblings ruined that precious moment forever. She came into the hospital room and observed me quietly talking with my dad. A moment later, she loudly demanded to know, "What do you think you're doing?"

A year or so after my dad's death, my mom had begun calling me on the telephone to talk. Each time, she would ask me questions about the Lord and His ways. I always answered her by referencing what the Bible said, without trying to sound preachy. I had read various passages to her and explained those parts she did not understand. At times, I could almost sense my moms' deepening concern, as though she knew her time was likewise drawing near. We often talked for hours as I shared all that the Spirit had opened my eyes to see. I told her what the Lord had allowed my family and me to experience. When I returned from Pensacola and my outreach trip to Argentina, we spoke once more. She listened without interrupting my recounting of what had occurred there.

One day, she asked why my family and I had left the Catholic Church. I explained the difference between religion and a relationship with a Living Savior. I told her how much my interaction with the Holy Spirit had come to mean to me.

"Mom, the only thing I can say is that I was looking for more. I needed a relationship with a *living* Christ that I knew not only as my Savior but also as the source of joy in my life. **I needed that special *'Someone'* who would freely carry on a conversation with me, even as a close friend would.** I needed to know, when the Bible says **'my sheep hear My voice,'**[1] that it was true. I had to know that His Voice wasn't some mysterious thing that hardly anyone heard unless they were ordained as a church leader. **I needed and wanted a *relationship*, and I found it. Not in the Catholic Church. Not in the Baptist or Methodist churches, both of which we've attended. Not even in the Assemblies of God, or in the church where we now attend. I found it in HIM, in a loving Father, in Christ Jesus Himself, and His Holy Spirit.**"

I then explained further to her, "The more I read the Gospels, the more I see how much Jesus despised religion. All the ritual and exaggeration distracts us from focusing on what matters most, which is Him, as our Lord and Savior. **Jesus always talked about His relationship with the Father. So did the apostles as they followed in His steps. That's what He wants with each of us.** It's not important how many years we've attended church, or what denomination. There is no value in how 'good' we are through our efforts unless we first know Jesus as our personal Savior. When grandma and grandpa died, when dad died, do you know what happened? When you die, when my family and I die, do you understand what will happen, mom? Jesus did not ask them what church they attended. Neither will He ask us what church we attended. He won't ask what dogma we believed in and followed *religiously*. The only things that will matter are these: Did we follow **HIS** commands? Do we have a *relationship* with the Living Lord and His Holy Spirit? Have we sincerely tried to know Him and allowed Him to know us? That word **KNOW** is important, mom. As used in the Bible, it means to be unguardedly intimate with Him. It also means laying oneself bare before Him, as you would with your spouse whom you love."

As in the past, my mom listened without interrupting. Unfortunately, she too often ended our calls with little comment, leaving me wondering what she thought about what I'd said. Even so, I treasured those conversations with her as a blessing from the Holy Spirit. I had never once spoken about these conversations with mom to any of my siblings. At her death, several years later, there arose another time of misunderstanding.

Once again, I was most concerned about my mom's relationship with Christ. The Holy Spirit, knowing that her remaining time in this world was short, had chosen to move through one of my daughters. He urged her to broach a particular subject with her grandma. Initially, my mom (her grandma) bitterly resented having a granddaughter question her actions. My daughter begged her grandma to set her spirit and soul in right standing with the Lord before it was too late. In her anger, my mom expressed this bitterness and resentment to my siblings. My daughter had later told me that she had said to her grandma, "I'm asking this of you because I love you so much, grandma. I want to be sure that you'll be there in heaven waiting for me when I get there."

Right before my mom breathed her last breath, my daughter once again felt the urging of the Holy Spirit. He wanted her to revisit her grandma at the hospice center as soon as possible. My mom (her grandma) had been in a coma for days. When my daughter and her oldest son entered the hospice room where her grandma was, the nurse was the only other one in the room. A moment later, my mom woke from the coma, much to the shock and surprise of both the nurse and my daughter. My daughter then told my wife and me about the conversation she and grandma had.

"Grandma looked at me with a smile on her face and said, 'I've been waiting for you. I asked God to keep me alive until I could talk with you one last time.'"

My daughter then went on to tell us how her grandma thanked her for having the courage to confront her about her sin. She then proclaimed with joy that she'd had a long talk with Jesus, and everything was now okay. She and her grandma had hugged and cried together. A few more minutes had passed in conversation, as our daughter combed her grandma's hair. My daughter said she watched with tears as her grandma slipped back into a comatose state. From there, she passed peacefully into eternity about an hour later.

Upon hearing from our daughter what had occurred, I shared it with my siblings. Out of a sincere heart, I'd expressed to them the relief I felt in knowing that our mom had made things right. I knew that she was now with the Lord for eternity. However, in saying this, I'd unintentionally offended most of my siblings, as well as many in our extended family. Nearly all of them identified with the Catholic Church and their Catholic beliefs. Therefore, their "assurance" that mom was in Heaven rested on three things alone. The first was because of her Catholic faith and beliefs. The second was because she had been, in their minds, a good person. The third was because she had received the Last Rites from the Catholic priest.

None of them found comfort and reason to rejoice in what my daughter experienced and reported. Instead, my words of joyful encouragement set off a firestorm of attacks. Many of my siblings and their spouses, as well as some of my aunts and uncles, condemned my family and me. They believed that I'd questioned my mom's salvation and attacked their Catholic beliefs. They also alleged that, in doing so, I'd judged and condemned my mom before her body was in the grave. Several of them sharply criticized my daughter for "lying" about her "supposed" experience. Still, none of them spoke with the attending nurse who had been present at the time it occurred, as I had suggested.

I knew in my heart that none of what they said was right, but many of them were unwilling to consider otherwise. A few went so far as to express a desire to have nothing more to do with my entire family or me.

Shaken by their reactions, I wasn't sure how to respond, so I'd remained silent, distant, and angry. I didn't want to separate my family and myself from our extended family. Neither did I want our presence at family gatherings to be a point of contention and discord. For three years, my family and I kept our distance. Meanwhile, my wife and I petitioned the Lord to break down the walls between all of us.

In the fall of that fourth year, the Holy Spirit spoke to me. He wanted me to address the resentment, bitterness, and anger that I was harboring toward them.

"Son, I want you to sincerely apologize to everyone in your family for what occurred three years ago."

At first, I denied hearing those words. I convinced myself that God knew that my family and I had done nothing to warrant an apology. Still, the Holy Spirit would not relent. He brought the incident to the forefront of my mind daily. Finally, I gave in, sat quietly before the Lord, and waited to hear what the Spirit had longed to tell me.

"Son, how can you say to Me that you love Me? You've carried resentment and bitterness in your heart over this for three years. It is now affecting your relationship with Me. I want you to apologize to everyone. Once again, it doesn't matter what they say, do, or think. What matters is that you are obedient to the Father's wishes. Then this logjam will finally be broken up, and the river of My life will flow once more in and through you. Will you do this for Me, son?"

I thought about it for several minutes before choosing to yield. When I answered, I said, "Yes, Lord, I will. But You're going to have to fill me with **Your** love for them. You're also going to have to guide me on what to say. Otherwise, they will reject what I say. Besides, I don't feel like doing this, Lord."

"I know you don't. Allow Me to guide you. My Spirit will reach out through your obedience to tear down these walls of separation, as you and your wife have petitioned Me. Pick up your pen right now, and I'll tell you what to write."

I obeyed, and words from the Father's heart flowed into and through my spirit, as I wrote what He wanted me to say.

I typed it up in the form of an email addressed to everyone on my side of the family. I immediately clicked on the SEND button before I could reconsider. As I did, an unseen weight seemed to lift off me. The peace of God flooded my heart and soul, and then the Spirit of God spoke to me.

"Thank you, son! I know you don't always understand My requests. In this case, the first step, humbling yourself and reaching out to them, was necessary. This surrendering of your will to My desire freed you from your enemy's hold on your soul. When the door opens, and your family invites you, I want you all to walk through in the joy of the Lord, and hold back no longer."

A few months later, I received an email from one of my sisters. It was an invitation addressed to my family and me. She invited us to her home for the family's annual Christmas gathering—and my entire family attended.

As I described earlier, the Holy Spirit had spoken to me at length about allowing my pastor to act as His chosen covering over me. He'd explained what it all meant in the spiritual realm. I'd understood what the Lord was saying. Still, knowing it and speaking about it wasn't enough. The Holy Spirit wanted me to ACT on it by asking him to be my covering—in my own words. One Sunday morning, in the middle of the time of worship, the Spirit spoke four distinct words into my spirit.

"Ask your pastor now."

I knew immediately what the Spirit wanted. Without hesitating, I walked to where my Pastor stood. Apologizing for my past actions, I then invited him to be my covering. He hugged me and then replied.

"Do you know why most people won't ask their pastor to be their covering? They don't understand what a covering is all about. It's not about me controlling you and your wife. It's about you both inviting and counting on me to stand before God, petitioning Him on your behalf."

Many weeks later, while sitting quietly in the prayer room, the Spirit spoke to me again.

"Go into the pastor's parlor right now, son. This time ASK FOR AND RECEIVE his forgiveness for the way that you hardened your heart against him in the past."

I headed for his door immediately, as directed. My pastor was gracious and receptive. First, he forgave me, and then he encouraged me. I felt unburdened, and my heart softened toward him as he prayed.

At this point, I thought that I'd confessed and dealt with everything from my past. However, what the Spirit spoke next shocked me into silence. He had shone His light of truth on something else that He wanted me to address. This time the adverse, vile reaction that rose up in my soul verified what the Spirit was telling me.

"My child, there is another offer to forgive that I'm asking you to extend. I'm well aware that this will be the most painful. It hurt you the deepest and affected you the longest. It was your biggest hurdle in relating to Me as a trustworthy, loving Father. I'm asking you, son, to forgive the one who violated you. I know your enemy has tormented you for years about this. You have not seen this person in many decades, and have no idea where he now lives. Even so, a single thought from the enemy of your soul about this incident still overwhelms you. It has the ability—more than fifty years later—

to sicken your stomach with fear and shame. The enemy then floods your heart and mind with hate."

"Do you recall the day the men from the prayer group visited your home? This same incident suddenly filled your conscious mind, and those same spirits caused you to collapse onto the floor, curling up into a fetal position. You still, to this moment, do not recall that reaction that your friends witnessed. Nevertheless, that day in your home, you felt the torment and pain anew. You experienced again the pain your enemy inflicted on you those many years ago. That pain anchored itself deep within your subconscious mind. From that single original event, a multitude of fears arose to torment you, and have continued your entire lifetime. Each spirit's hold on you became an opportunity for still others to do likewise. Your act of forgiving this person will break all of your enemy's power over your soul originating from this matter."

I wrestled in my mind and heart about this for a week. I debated with myself whether that person *deserved* forgiveness. Hatred had a great hold on my heart. The voices of Blame, Hatred, Justification, and Revenge spoke loud and clear to my mind. After a few days of this harassment, my health came under attack. I found myself getting sicker and sicker. Still, I couldn't seem to let go of the extreme anger that drove me. Nine days later, worn out from fighting to resist, I finally called out to the Lord in anguish.

"Lord, please help me! Everything within me wants to refuse to forgive. I know I can't go on like this any longer. I need You to love me and guide me through this, Lord. I don't know that I can do it on my own."

"I have longed to intercede on your behalf, My child, but this was a choice that you and you alone had to make," the Spirit assured me. "I know that your heart is unwilling. However, if you will allow Me, I will bring your will into unity with Ours. Your enemy will lose his deadly grip on you in this area forever."

With my stomach in turmoil and my brow covered in a nervous sweat, I relented. In a barely audible whisper, I begged God to help me. "Please, Lord! I need You! I'm so weary of having this plague my soul. I'm willing to release this to You!"

My heart began softening to the point where I could finally respond to the Spirit's prompting. I addressed aloud, by name, the one who had violated me. As the Spirit urged, I yelled one other thing. "In the love of the Lord Jesus Christ, I forgive you for what you did to me, and I pray God's blessings over you."

Like thick ice affected by the strength of the sun at its zenith, the love of the Lord bathed my heart. On my face on the floor, I cried in relief for an extended time. Every vestige of that personal imprisonment was gone. I felt exhilarated as wave after wave of His perfect peace washed through every molecule of my being.

Despite all that I'd experienced, the Holy Spirit nudged my spirit one more time. When I'd arisen from the floor and wiped my face, He began speaking to me about a final action He wanted me to take.

*"Son, there is one last person you absolutely **must** forgive. This one matters the most. That person is YOU."*

*"When we spend time together, you listen and are faithful to record all that I say to you. However, much of what you hear and write down is never applied. There is nothing wrong with your hearing, son, and you understand what I've explained. Still, a disconnect remains. It is much like a shorted electrical circuit diverting the intended power flow to ground. **Do you recall when I told you that knowledge alone was worthless? I told you that it puffs you up. It inflates your ego and opens you up to the control of a spirit of Intellectualism. Do you also recall how I urged you to persist in your searching until you gained My understanding on a matter?** Well, son, you obeyed My directive, and you're now a depository of both knowledge and understanding. Nonetheless, neither is of much value alone. They often exist in you, like two unconnected portions of an electrical circuit. I designed you to carry a 'high voltage.' In this case, it should be the transmission of My power through you. Connected, you are a 'live' circuit. **The application of knowledge with My understanding becomes a demonstration of My wisdom. Only then does My power flow, benefitting all whose lives it touches. The hindrance to an uninterrupted flow is your unwillingness or perceived inability to forgive. In this case, to forgive yourself.** Your enemy tries to persuade you that you are unworthy of My forgiveness. He is both right and wrong. **No act of yours can make you worthy.** However, I became a substitution for you before the Father. I presented Myself as the only acceptable sacrifice. It is now possible for you to become righteous, **through Me**, negating your enemy's statement. He has no further claim on you, and rightful ownership is in My hands, as the One who paid the price to redeem you. All that remains is for you to acknowledge and accept My sacrifice, in **ALL** areas of your being. You've forgiven everyone else. Now, wholly and sincerely forgive yourself, My son!"*

In that instant, a stream of memories began flowing through My conscious mind. The Holy Spirit showed me all that I'd failed to release to Him. Sometimes, pains were self-inflicted, and some caused by others. He allowed me to remember all of the inspiration and blessings sent my way. I recalled the initial enthusiasm and thankfulness in many of those circumstances, but I also saw how that enthusiasm had dampened and, finally, dissipated. It was like the helium leaking from an inflated balloon. This time, with each recalled memory, at His prompting, I vocally forgave myself. The progressive transformation erupted within me. I felt as though I was standing, feet spread wide, in the fury of a rainstorm. One gust of rain after another pummeled me. It saturated my body and refreshed my soul. The experience was exhilarating!

Quite a while later, the sensation lifted. That's when the Lord spoke one last time.

"My son, for a time, Discouragement dominated your thoughts. My Spirit was faithful to overshadow you. Time after time, He encouraged you. He told you how much

We love you, even as Fear worked overtime to convince you otherwise. He saturated you with Our love so that you might show forth that love to others. My Spirit filled and refilled you with heavenly joy, chasing away Depression, Misery, and Sadness. He blanketed you with His peace that passes all understanding, and drove away Anxiety, Confusion, Turmoil, and Uncertainty."

"Through many trials and tears, you learned how to withstand demon-initiated Adversity. My Spirit then taught you to identify Provocation. He gave you the spiritual eyes to discern the sources behind each instance of the same, which made it possible for My heavenly patience to complete its work in you."

"My kindness drew you near to Me. My compassion bathed your repentant heart. We repaired the damage and inflamed you with a desire to reach out to others, even as I reached out to you."

"You chose to abandon your attempt to be righteous in your righteousness. Instead, you chose to walk in Mine, which made way for My goodness and mercy to follow you all the remaining days of your life. **_Now, you must continuously 'dwell' in the house of the Lord. As you now understand, this 'dwelling' is more than regularly making your presence known in a physical church or place of worship. 'Dwelling' in the house of the Lord is about you inviting My Spirit to have His way. He must reign in your body, soul, and spirit—your 'house.' He does so as you subordinate your desires to those of Christ Jesus—as you die, that He may live._**"

"I have watched you building yourself up in your most holy faith, praying in the Holy Spirit. You have more and more often resisted the voices of Doubt and Worry. Instead, you placed your trust in Me to be the Author and Finisher of faith."

"My calm assurance became for you a level foundation. You welcomed humility, which plumbed and squared your walls. I released My gentleness to rest upon you as a fitting roof, making you a dwelling place for My Spirit."

"You submitted your body and soul—your SELF—for My Word to constrain, which now enables the Spirit of Christ in you, your hope of glory, to move through you, to become the hope of glory for others as well."

"As a result, you now confidently walk with Me, undergirded with My peace. You are, indeed, a new creation! Guard your heart and mind, treasuring that which you have received and learned. Dwell in the present, in each moment made available to you, and trust Me to handle your future. In doing so, each current moment, appreciated and lived well, makes your future that much brighter.

If You Would Be My Voice

The following morning, I spent some quiet time with the Lord. I felt more at peace than I had at any time in my previous fifty plus years, and the Lord chose that moment to speak to my heart.

"Throughout your walk with Me, I've taken you through much purging and cleansing. I've freed and healed you. Afterward, we walked hand-in-hand through seasons of training, necessary correction, and retraining. The completion of this recent season was key. Now you are in a position to experience the fullness of what the Father has ordained for you. We hope that you will permit the Holy Spirit to bring forth that which the Father desires."

"It's important that you remain a willing vessel if I'm to move through you to express My heart and mind. I will equip you for each situation you will face. My knowledge, understanding, and wisdom will be yours for the asking. **If you would be My voice, it's vital that you stay open, teachable, and positioned to receive.** Accept that which the Father would have the Spirit reveal to you. Do so without doubting or questioning, son. Let our relationship be one of absolute trust."

I thought He was talking about some new subject or something He was about to teach me at that time. I waited for an extended period, but He said nothing more. I put my journal away and went on with the rest of my day. I knew, as I'd found in the past, that the Lord would find a way to get my attention when He was ready to continue.

The first period of instruction came on a Sunday morning in early September. Rising before dawn, I sat in our living room, reading several portions of Scripture. At one point, the Holy Spirit interrupted me with a short, intriguing statement.

"Son, I want you to pay close attention to the teaching this morning at church. My servant will disclose special knowledge to the body at Heritage. He will detail what a chosen vessel who speaks for Me must understand and do. Be attentive when he speaks. Buy a copy of his message and study it."

Not even relating to my wife what the Spirit had said, I left for church an hour earlier than usual. I arrived at the church prayer room to allow the peace of God to overtake my heart and mind. I wanted to prepare to receive whatever the Lord was about to say through our pastor. Much to my and everyone else's surprise, our pastor did not preach that morning. He had invited an unscheduled visitor from Shelbyville, Kentucky, to speak. The stranger had made the trip to Heritage Fellowship only because God had asked it of him. Our pastor, discerning God's will in the matter, turned the Sunday morning service over to him.

Roger Teal was a man cut from a different cloth. Taller than most, and in his late seventies, he exuded confidence in the call of God on his life. He stood before the assembly and, in his thick northern British accent, made a declaration. "I'm here at the Lord's request as His prophet."

There was no arrogance or prideful boasting evident in his statement. Unshakable in the fact that God had called him to the office of the prophet, he determined to honor God's choice. In the forty minutes that followed, he attempted to convey what it meant to be a prophet of God.

"It's my experience that there seems to be a vague concept in peoples' minds of what a New Testament prophet does. Most are not sure what their function is. Am I a prophet of God because I'm special? No. Have I done things wrong in my life? Yes. Not often sinful, but still wrong. But thanks be to God! I'm here today as His voice *only* because the Lord has chosen to justify the ungodly."

"As a prophet, sometimes you can feel a little on the outside, a little cold. It depends on what it is that God has called you to do. My ministry is not too popular for a reason. When God shows me something about someone or some situation, I've learned that I have to be courteous. I have to be gracious. I have to be sure of what I'm hearing from the Lord, that I hear right. Yes, all of that is true. But the bottom line is that I must obey and say what he tells me to say."

"I'm known for speaking very down-to-earth, very straight-forward, and very direct. So, let me tell you. Today, your life will change! It will never be the same!"

"You might say, *'Are you making that statement by faith, hoping that it comes to pass?'"*

"And I would say to you, 'Well, that may be your way, but it isn't mine.'"

"And you might persist, asking me, *'Why are you saying that?'*"

"Of course, I would tell you, 'Because of *who* I am. I'm a prophet.'"

"Your response, the one I usually get, might be, *'Okay. Well, you say you are, but...'*"

"And I would say to you, 'No, no, no, no, no! God has chosen every one of you. It's now about whether you will choose to walk in that which God has chosen for you. God has a plan for your life, and you need to get started on that plan, get on the pattern. In the Bible, you read about God's patterns. For everything that happens, God has a specific pattern. God gave a precise pattern to Moses, for example. He said, **'Be sure that you make everything according to the pattern I have shown you.'**[1] The question you must ask yourself is this. Have you discovered His pattern for you? If you have, are you following that pattern?"

"You know I didn't have any books to help me other than the Word of God. For me, that was and is my pattern. However, the thing is, until **you** know who **you** are, God can't use you. I'm an authority on what I know. Your pastor is an authority on what he knows. We're all that way, sharing what we know, sharing our lives—such as they are."

"Even the Lord Himself stood up, and when He read Isaiah—*'The Spirit of the Lord is on Me'*[2]—the people thought, 'Who is this guy? Where is he from? Who does he think he is?'"

"Jesus was, and is, THE authority on what He knows—which is everything. God showed me that. Although I am here to talk about the Lord Jesus, I can say I know a little bit about what it's like, about what He faced. Many didn't know who He was. Similarly, most don't know me, although I've been all over the world. I've given the word of the Lord to many of the great men of God, some of the men of God that have later come to this church."

"I'm sure many of you are thinking, *'Well, what exactly is the word of the Lord?'*"

"Scripture is His word revealed, at a specific time, through His Spirit. But God also has a fresh word for today, for you."

"You might say, *'Me?'* My response is, 'Sure!'"

"And so you might say, *'Will you give me a word from God?'* Sure, if He gives me one."

"You might also ask, *'Why?'*"

"And I would say to you, 'Because delivering God's word is what I do. That's ALL that I do. I don't have a church. No, no, no! I'm not an evangelist. This [speaking as a Prophet of God] is what I do."

"You're looking at me now, thinking, *'Is that right?'* And I say to you, 'Yeah, this is it. I found out what God wants ME to do, and then I do it. And He helps me and blesses me.'"

"You know you all have gifts. God has some wonderful gifts for you so that you might be able to function. You can't function without gifts from the Holy Spirit. I'm paraphrasing here, but that's what Jesus said. *'Don't leave. Don't get started without Him. You're going to need Him more than you know. As you go, you'll need the Holy Spirit.'* He gives gifts to us. If the Holy Spirit baptized you with His baptism, and you speak in another tongue, then He who is in you will quicken you. That quickening allows you to become another man, another woman. He's the One who enables you to change, to become like Him."

"I've been prophesying more than forty years now. I want to encourage you this morning that the Holy Spirit has sent me here to stir up you and the gift within you. Many of you are waiting for me to 'prove' myself, or do something. People are like that. They say, *'Well, let's see what he can do,'* as though they're ready to judge whether I am what I say I am, and that's all right."

"You all go from place to place listening to the men and women of God, and the gifting in their lives can be a great blessing. It inspires you. However, do you know what? There's gifting in YOU in the person of Jesus, the Christ in YOU! You may say, *'Well, what gift would that be that's in me?'"*

"Let me explain. If He called you to be a carpenter, what tools would you need to exercise your craft, your calling? Special tools made for cutting and shaping wood. If you were a mechanic, what would you use? Wrenches, spanners, and special tools to bring your skill forth. **The Lord will equip you with the necessary *'tools'* for the task that He assigns to you. Every one of you has an assignment on your life."**

"Are you sitting here today, wondering what those gifts are? Are you curious about whether you have certain giftings or not? If that's what you're thinking, then one of two things can be true. Either the gift is there, but it's so dried up or undeveloped, that it would seem as if it doesn't now exist. Or you don't have the gifting you think you have at all."

"Consider the gift in the life of an evangelist. I have a dear friend, Reinhard Bonnke. He is so expressive, so exuberant, so captivating when he's moving in his gifting. God made him that way! People get excited, of course, because of his reputation and his ministry. They're in awe of the things God does through him, and I'm sure, like many other people, some of you say, *'I want to be like Reinhard Bonnke. I want to be an evangelist. I want, I want, I want.'* Well, that's all right. You should desire to be an example to others. Some of you are saying you want to be like me. And I have to tell you that I doubt it."

"But then you might say, *"What's this all about?'* Well, I told you in the beginning. I'm here to stir up the gift within YOU. I know the Holy Spirit has sent me here to challenge you about YOUR gifts."

"You know, the gifts in my life are specific. Of necessity, as with any prophetic calling, they are the three gifts of revelation. These are the word of wisdom, the word of knowledge, and the discerning of spirits. And that last one is my best or strongest gift. I use that one to jiggle around through spiritual traffic. That's what it's for."

"And you might say, *'What's your word of knowledge?'* Well, it's His gifting given to me to know things that are and have been. And often it's to know something that's going on that nobody told you about. I can detect all of that through the Spirit. How? Well, it often works hand-in-hand with discerning of spirits. He did not give me gifts that I should judge or hurt anybody. The gifts are to heal, restore, encourage, and not to condemn or judge. Still, sometimes, if God tells you to say or do something, you must. That is often the word of wisdom. We all desire wisdom. Right? His Word says, **'Wisdom is the principal thing; get wisdom. And in all of your getting, get understanding.'**[3] I've sought them both my whole life. We all long for them. However, the *word of wisdom* is not what the Word of God is talking about in that passage. No, no, no. There is that unique, specific *word of wisdom* – not just His wisdom, but also the **word of wisdom**. Perhaps it is God saying, *'This is what I want you to do.'* You know, God gave you a specific plan. It may be that He tells you, *'No, you're not going to buy that building. It's this one over here.'"*

"And you may say, *'Is that really what the word of wisdom is?'* Sure. That's the word of wisdom. It's wonderful!"

"You may say, *'What about healing the sick?'* Oh, sure. Wouldn't it be great if you all could be like Benny Hinn, a vessel through which God heals the sick? But remember, it's the gift of God working in his life, **as the Spirit wills.**"

"You might say, *'What about Rodney Howard-Browne, the famous evangelist? The Spirit moves through him in a unique way?'* Well, did you know Rodney came to my meeting in South Africa when he was only eighteen years old? I called him out of the audience. 'You. Come here,' I said. I gave him the word of the Lord that day as the Lord directed. A specific word. It was wonderful, wonderful! It was God choosing to use me at that moment. I obeyed. I had no foreknowledge of what would become of him these many years later."

"Anyway, this morning, if you think you have merits, I'm glad you do. I do too. However, I know I am worthy only because of Him. Because of my obedience, I'm able to ask Him for what I want and need, and He gives it to me. I take Him at His word. He says through His word, **'This is the confidence we have in Him, that if we ask anything according to His will, He hears us. And if we know that He hears us, whatever we ask, we know that we have the petitions that we have asked of Him.'** "[4]

"Our focus this morning must be on Jesus. Although I've referred to myself and the gift in my life, don't focus on me. The Lord Jesus has justified me. I am godly in His sight, to the degree I am, only because of His righteousness. Now, I can do; I can be; I can speak. The Lord opens doors that no one can shut. I'm safe. I've been in countries where the police have to watch over you, but when God is with me, directing me, I'm safe. They can't touch me. It's not arrogance. It's confidence, in what He promised."

"You know, **there's something I always ask for whenever I stand up to speak for Him. I'm not inclined to know exactly what I'm going to say. What I always ask for is His Presence. I have to feel His Presence**, or I'm nervous. And, even when I feel His Presence, I might still appear to you to be a little apprehensive, unsure."

"You might say, *'Why? Is that a little lack of faith?'* No. Not at all. **I know all too well how our enemy can pervert things. I give the Word of God or the word *from* God, as He shows me that it applies in different situations and circumstances. In the mind of the person receiving that word, our enemy can cause confusion. Well, what is crucial to me is His Presence.** When He's with me, I'm always sure that what I say is what He is telling me to say. Then, at that moment, it doesn't matter what happens, what anybody thinks, what anybody feels. I know I'm okay. I'm at peace in His peace. I'm confident in His blessed assurance."

"We can, and too often do, strive to get the mind of the Lord, but we don't have to strive. It's so easy to understand when His Presence is in it. There's no confusion. There's no need to struggle. **He'll direct when He's in it. Ask him, 'Where do I go next?'** I must remember that my function is my gift **when I am obedient**, and likewise, yours is with each of you. He will reveal and bring forth that gift through you **when you are also obedient**. The Holy Spirit will lead you, guide you, teach you, and keep you out of danger, for He cares and knows about you. We have Him with us 24/7."

"God has told me major things over the years, important things. He told me about things that were about to happen. Some of the events had the potential to cause a great catastrophe in countries throughout the world. I've had very delicate situations where I've had to reveal things about to happen. Some were very controversial. I was very, very hesitant to speak about them publicly. It isn't that I would disobey the Lord, or that I'm not sure. But let me tell you what I've learned. When I hear anything from the Lord, I don't open my mouth. I don't run and start talking about it, intent on telling the whole world. Instead, I get on my face before the Lord to hear again from the Spirit, to be sure I understand Him right. And, if it has something to do with God's judgment, I beg God to be merciful, that it will NOT happen."

"Don't ever think less of, or misunderstand, His spoken word of prophecy, especially true when the spoken word of the Lord doesn't give the name, the date, or other specifics. That word is a word of exhortation given by the Spirit to help the body of Christ operate. Still, there are times when God NEEDS to give you the name and the date and the time and the place. That's how the Holy Spirit works. He worked that way in the Bible. Why wouldn't He work that way today?"

"God is moving by His Spirit. He's trying to reach those out there, outside these walls. He'll do it through you, just as He does through me. But **the only way it will ever happen is if you and I first recognize that God justifies the ungodly. And it's you and me that can be ungodly. Sometimes, there needs to be a reckoning in your life.** Are you as godly as others **think** you are, as you **feel** you are? Are you righteous in His sight because of allowing **His** righteousness to make you so? These you must ask of yourselves, and ask of God, **and then be willing to hear the truth.**"

"Above all else, remember John the Baptist's message. It was, *'Repent.'*[5] That's the way to fulfillment. The Lord Himself will clean you up. He will justify you, setting things right. He will change things. Then obedience is possible. Then His gifts will flow."

The guest speaker had finished his teaching about prophetic callings. He then pointed to a man in the audience, calling him to come forward and bring his wife with him. That man was me. I obeyed, but as I walked forward, I spoke to the Lord in my mind.

Why did You have him call me out, Lord? Are you going to use him to tell me something new? Or are You going to add to things You've already spoken about in the past?

When we had both reached the front of the sanctuary, the prophet stared at me for a few minutes before speaking. Finally, he posed a question to me.

"What is it that you want?"

"I want to know what God wants of me," I replied.

The prophet closed his eyes and spoke to heaven. "Lord, I thank You this morning for this man. I thank You for his life. I thank You for his testimony. And I ask today that the clarity of Your Word would come to him in such a way that he would be bold. Because, as You are showing me, Lord, the apprehension he feels at times comes as a result of uncertainty."

The Prophet paused for a moment, staring at me as I stood before him, as though he was puzzled about something. Then he once again addressed me.

"You have no position in this church? You're not an elder or anything, are you?"

"No," I responded.

"How long have you been coming to this church?"

"Ten years."

"How long have you two been married?"

"Thirty-three years," I said.

The Prophet paused, looked up to heaven for a few more moments, then the questions continued.

"The Lord is showing me something about Minnesota, and also New York. Are you from one of those places?"

"No. We have a daughter who went through ministry training in Minnesota. We also have a son who's currently living in New York?"

"You have a son in New York?"

"Yes."

Once again, the prophet stared at me without speaking. He appeared to be waiting for heaven to tell him what to say next.

"Who prophesied over you that you were a prophet?"

"Several people."

"Several people prophesied over you that you were a prophet? Do you believe that you are a prophet? You're not sure, are you, even though the Spirit Himself has told you many times that you are?"

"No, I'm not sure," I answered.

For the fifth time, the Prophet paused and looked heavenward. He then extended his hand forward, placing it on my head, and began speaking.

"Father, this morning, as I lay my hand on this man, I ask that You would give him Your favor. Let him be conscious of the knowledge of that which is within him. Let it spring forth and leap, and rise within him that he may know that it is You speaking. For this morning, the Lord would say unto thee—"

"Look at me, son! Look at me, son! The Lord would say unto thee, *'I have heard thy voice. And yeah, I have heard thy moaning and thy groaning, and I have heard thine anger and thy disappointment. My Spirit is within you. My son, and I've made you as a keyer instrument that will thresh. But you would say,* 'I cannot speak openly. I cannot speak openly because of my life...areas in my life. I can't control my eyes. I can't control my hearing. I can't control my emotions at times.' *But yeah,'* saith the Lord, *'I will purge thee this day, and thou shalt become another man. Thy sins are forgiven,'* saith the Lord, *'and that which is written in heaven about thee is now set. And from this day forward,'* saith the Lord, *'My Spirit shall start to work in thy belly. And He shall rise, even into thy throat. I shall loosen thy tongue, and yeah,'* saith the Lord, *'I will cause thy spirit to hear and understand the Word of the Lord. And when it cometh forth,'* saith the Lord, *'speak it. And surely,'* saith the Lord, *'the people shall remark and say*: "How knowest this man these things?"'"

The prophet continued speaking, *"'Thy wife hast influenced thee somewhat. She often tells thee what to do. Her love for thee has been strange but sincere. Her strength,'* saith the Lord, *'is in who she is. And by her prayerful intercession, she has kept thee, even when thou wast in places where thou should not have been. Therefore,'* saith the Lord, *'this morning, the mantle of the anointing is upon thee. And thou shalt stand bold and strong, and the word that thou shalt speak shall surely come to pass. And you shall see and know that I am with thee.'"*

It was many years later when the Lord taught me the second lesson in a different sort of way. It happened to be another early Sunday morning, and I, as usual, had arisen well before dawn. For several hours, I sat in my recliner, reading the last in a series of books on the life of William Branham. When I'd finished, the Holy Spirit spoke to me at length about what I'd read. He referred me to several passages of Scripture to read and note in my journal. He then explained how they were related to what I'd just read about William Branham.

When I'd finished that, I felt overcome with an unexplainable urgency. I told my wife I needed to get to our church's prayer room as soon as possible. I dressed and walked the three blocks to the church. When I arrived, I found only one other person in the prayer room. For an hour or so, I sat still with my eyes closed, focused on keeping my mind from wandering. I felt confident that the Spirit had something to say to me, although I wasn't quite sure what.

One by one, others entered the room, and the available seats began to fill. Scattered voices whispered prayers to the Lord or quietly worshipped. Some gathered in small groups, praying in their prayer language as the Spirit guided them. One of the groups, made up of four individuals, was standing near to where I was sitting. One man—my close friend and prayer partner—asked me to join them. None of the four stated any specific prayer request or direction, so I closed my eyes and prayed in tongues. No more than a minute later, the Spirit brought to my remembrance a time in my life some forty years earlier. I forced myself to focus as vivid scenes flashed through my mind. When the picture show ended, I stood there puzzled. I thought, *Why had it occurred?* The Spirit then filled my mind and heart with what He wanted me to comprehend. A moment later, the Spirit stopped speaking, and I felt someone tap me on my chest. I opened my eyes to find my friend's hand reaching out to touch me once more.

"The Spirit said, *'Give it,'*" he'd stated without hesitation.

I was uncertain, and asked the Lord in my mind, *What You showed me was something from my past. Did You mean for me to share it now?*

For a third time, my friend tapped my chest.

"The Lord said, *'Share what I showed you,'*" he urged.

As the others in the group stared at me expectantly, I began explaining.

"The Holy Spirit just flashed through my mind, in a minute or two of time, scenes from my distant past. I know it had to have been a multi-hour segment of my past, something that occurred more than forty years ago. At that point, I was twenty-one years old. I worked at Cincinnati Milacron in a department called Outside Diameter Grinding Run-Off."

"Dozens of men on a nearby assembly line worked as a team producing large grinding machines that weighed a ton or more. When they'd finished assembling a unit, they would hook it up to an overhead crane. The crane operator would then move it to our department. Our responsibility was to test the machine. We needed to make sure that the machine would do the job that the client had purchased it to perform. The first step was to grab a cart of over-sized test metal stock. We used the same type of metal the customer would be grinding in his factory. We hooked up the wiring and hydraulics. We'd fill the lower reservoir with water and cutting fluid. That acted as a coolant and lubricant in the grinding process. Next, we'd locate and mount the correctly sized grinding wheel. It had to have the perfect composition necessary to produce the final results desired."

"But the most important part of the whole process was the truing of the grinding wheel. This truing was a slow, meticulous process. We'd lock the industrial-diamond cutting bit into place. We then brought the grinding wheel up to speed, which always caused an initial vibration. That indicated the grinding wheel was out of round. We moved the diamond bit closer to the spinning grinding wheel a few millimeters at a time. Each pass of the bit across the face of the grinding wheel eliminated many not-so-obvious high spots on its surface. After finishing the truing process, the grinding wheel's surface would appear to be as smooth as glass. The coolant flowed over it unrestricted by imperfections. Then, and only then, was the test stock fed through the grinding wheel. When the end product matched the client's exact specifications, our job was almost complete."

"Finally, we would remove the trued wheel and diamond bit. We'd drain the cutting fluid, and disconnect the wiring and hydraulic system. Last, we'd power wash and air-dry the machine, and then strap everything onto an oak pallet for shipment to the customer."

"The Lord showed me that whole process again a few minutes ago," I continued explaining. "He then correlated what I was familiar with about that process to how he prepares one of His children for service."

"The Holy Spirit said He *'assembles'* us, knitting us together in our mother's womb. He forms each of us to one day fulfill that task, which He knows awaits us. The Spirit **wires** us with power sufficient to meet the demand which the Father intends to place upon us. He then **fills** us with His living water and anointing—the **coolant and cutting fluid** of the Spirit. This infilling allows us to endure the constant pressure without burning out under stress. He equips us with the necessary abilities, gifting, and strength, which is the heavenly **composition** required for the desired results. At that point, the Spirit **trues** us. His explanation compared this to the diamond truing the grinding wheel. His **truing** removes our imperfections—SELF. He eliminates our high spots—arrogance, pride, vanity, and the need to control."

"When He's finished His perfect work in us, He looks at us. We will have then become like the glass-smooth grinding wheel. In our trued and perfected "face" He is then able to see His reflection. Only then can He use us, certain that we can produce that which the Father has ordered."

"Additionally, He assured me, interaction with the world wears on us, just as the grinding wheel's interaction with the raw metal stock wears on it. Therefore, occasional, ongoing truing is necessary to maintain the final quality. Accordingly, the Holy Spirit will repeatedly bring us back to His truing process. This 'regular truing' maintains *us* at a level of faultless finish, which is what He requires of us to bring forth His perfect work."

As we were driving home from church, I shared with my wife what happened in the prayer room. That's when the Spirit spoke once more, this time through her.

"The Lord said to tell you to sit down immediately when we get home and write down what He showed you and spoke through you. As you do, He will help you to recall every detail. The comparison He showed you is vital for you to remember and teach to others."

After I'd finished writing it out, the Spirit addressed me about what I'd written.

"Son, this is an essential lesson that could benefit any who call themselves Mine. However, for those I entrust with the responsibility of delivering My words, this is **VITAL**. There is a necessity that you learn and never forget what I revealed to and through you today. There is one final thing I want you to remember. **When troubles come your way, understand, and consider this. It is NOT necessarily your enemy stirring things up. <u>First and always</u>, consider if the grinding wheel is simply in need of truing.**"

A few weeks later, the Holy Spirit referred me back to a particular group of pages in one of my oldest journals.

"In these pages, you will find a third valuable lesson. This one I explained in detail in the past, as you can see from your notes. Now I need you to review and understand once more what I taught you."

I read the many Scriptures that He had referenced, as well as the copious notes related to them. The most significant part of these I'd definitely forgotten. In the original records, the Lord had led me to various places in the Bible where it described an *ambassador,* envoy, or messenger. He'd then referred me to my Strong's concordance for alternate meanings for the same Hebrew and Greek words. These words meant so much more than *"ambassador; envoy; messenger."* They also translated as *"herald; hinge; pivot; shaft or pin upon which something turns."*

At this point, the Holy Spirit began elaborating on what He'd shown me in the past.

"There are **two guiding principles** *upon which you, as My servant, must always act and move when representing Me.* **First, your confidence must rest in Me alone. Second, your presentation must always be a truthful representation of Me, and Me alone.**"

I thought about what He'd said. The principles seemed very basic, very easy to understand, but He wasn't through speaking.

"My apostles were heaven-appointed 'sent forth' ones. Study My Word. You will see this. Their arrival would always **'bring health'**[6] *and healing to those to whom My Spirit sent them. They brought health to the body, soul, and spirit through their words, their actions, and their very presence. As an envoy of Christ, the message they boldly and confidently carried never varied. No matter where I send you, as one sent forth, your words, actions, and presence should do the same. My Spirit's desire is always one of reconciliation, healing, and love."*

"Finally, as you go forth, you do so as My ambassador. When you arrive, the power and authority of My kingdom, which you represent, comes on the scene with you. **Remember this always!** Go with confidence! Expect that there will be times and situations when your words—**as they originate from My heart**—will shake up situations that you encounter. Know also that your very presence—**as I move in and through you by My Spirit**—will change the environment into which I send you. In these instances, your absolute obedience is essential. That is what will allow Me to use you as My 'hinge' to open up situations that Satan held closed. Likewise, through you, I will also close those passageways through which Satan has found an entrance."

Everything Matters, However...

For weeks on end, I could not write this—what the Holy Spirit said was to be the final chapter. The truth is I didn't know what He wanted, and I'd asked many times.

I'd invested years, and many tears, struggling through the previous twenty-six chapters. I was not about to put together what I believed to be a proper concluding chapter. Still, the Holy Spirit did not seem eager to speak.

At one point, He began dropping little hints—a single word, a short phrase, and even a question. Yet, no further explanation followed. It reminded me of sporadic drops of rain falling from a cloudless sky.

Four weeks later, without any notice, His voice came through loud and clear.

"Will you give Me your undivided attention for a while, so I may enlighten you as to how these pieces all fit together?"

His words made me realize that I had once again allowed other activities and thoughts to pull my focus off Him. "Yes, Lord," I said.

"I have repeatedly emphasized two foundational principles over our many years of conversing. All who desire to draw near and learn from Me must learn these well. The first principle is...

EVERYTHING MATTERS!"

"Do you recall," the Lord asked, *"the initial word I spoke to you on this issue four weeks ago?"*

Instantly, I knew the moment to which He was referring. "Yes! Out of nowhere, I heard You say, *'Yield.'* I wondered at first if it had been my imagination," I replied. "An hour or so later, You repeated it. My mind searched for ways that I was possibly not yielding to Your instruction and guidance. As time passed with no further explanation from You, I was even more puzzled."

"To your credit, you didn't give in to the spirit of Self-Condemnation that began to harass your mind."

"I couldn't think of, or see, where I had fallen short with You, Lord," I said. "I felt peaceful about the whole thing."

"That's the sign of a character guided, once again, by Me," He stated. *"I saw further evidence of this when I spoke to you three days later."*

"I remember! You said, *'Yield is a funny word.'* When I heard that, I laughed. I'm not sure why. It was as though you were teasing me with just enough to get my attention, but, once again, there was no explanation."

"I was leading, son, and waiting to see if you would follow," He said.

"I have to admit, I thought long and hard about Your statement, Lord. I looked the word up in the concordance. Four more days passed, then You spoke again about this."

"Yes, son, you did what most are prone to do. You took something fundamental and made it complicated. You analyzed what I said, as though there was some hidden treasure in my statement. It was quite simple. You realized this when I said...

'There can be no yield if you're unwilling to yield.'"

*"Son, I encourage you to reserve more time each day to spend in intimacy with Me. Make an effort, even if it's only a few minutes more today than yesterday. **Every minute of your existence matters!** However, do not just use these precious extra moments to study My word, or to talk to Me about your most pressing concern. Instead, constrain your flesh and soul. Be still before Me. Allow My Spirit to commune with yours. In this, you will find richness unattainable in any other way."*

*"Believe Me when I tell you, son. **There is no limit to what you may learn and experience in your lifetime. The key is subordinating your plans for each day to Mine. Give yourself time and room to draw closer to Me. In doing so, you will discover My 'divine' purpose. I promise you this. Mine will be far more rewarding than anything you could have hoped for or imagined.**"*

Four days later, the Holy Spirit interrupted my thoughts again. He caused me to recall an event that had occurred eighteen years earlier.

It had been about nine in the evening. I had been driving home after attending the mid-week service at our church. My wife and three older children had all been bedridden with illness. Therefore, my youngest daughter and I had gone to church without them. As we rode along that evening, this eight-year-old girl had begun asking me questions. These were not random and general questions. They told me that she had been thinking deeply about Jesus.

When I had pulled the car into our driveway, I'd turned off the motor, and sat there with her for a minute in quiet. Holding her little hand in mine, I'd explained as best I could how much God loved her. Without getting too graphic, I told her what it meant for Him to have died on the cross. "He did it so one day our whole family could be in heaven with Him," I'd said.

Thinking back now, I recall how she'd sat very still, staring straight ahead. The Voice of the Lord had prompted me at that moment to lead her to give her heart to Him. I'd paused while wondering if she was too young to understand what being "born again" meant. Once more, the Lord had spoken to my heart.

"*Keep it simple, son. She is a child, with a child's eagerness and willingness to believe, just as you had at her age. Your heart then was as pure and sweet as hers is now. It was at this age that you began wondering about Me. There was no one available then to help you cross the threshold into My waiting arms. If you join with Me in completing this work, your reward will be seeing her spirit, heart, and future in My hands.*"

Obeying the Lord, I'd watched in awe while my daughter's gentle spirit became one with the Holy Spirit. Her tears spilled forth from joy-filled eyes as she looked up at me, smiled, and said, "Jesus just talked to me, daddy!"

After allowing me a few minutes to recall and revel in that memory, the Holy Spirit continued. He spoke of another point of connection between her spirit and mine in the years that followed.

"*Son, do you recall four years later when she'd severely sprained her ankle. It had swollen to the size of a small melon. Do you remember how you looked beyond the physical evidence that your eyes saw? I allowed you to see things as I saw them. You became angry with Satan. You refused to accept what your physical eyes said was the reality of the situation. Instead, you took off the air cast that the doctor in the emergency room had put on her. You coated her ankle with olive oil, and then you called everyone else in your home to join you in praying for her. You didn't want any doubt hindering the focus of you or your family, so you instructed everyone to lay hands on her ankle and pray only in their spirit languages. You spoke with confidence and a bold authority, and they followed.*"

"*Several minutes later, you stopped praying, although there was no direct evidence of healing. Nevertheless, you felt a leading in your spirit that I heard your prayers and that I had been faithful to do what My Word declared. Standing on your faith in Me, you took your daughter's hands and encouraged her to walk. You told her to step forth on the injured foot. At that moment, her eyes watched yours. Her spirit was in unity with your faith and Mine. You took several quick steps backward, and she followed without hesitating. Son, will you ever forget her wide-eyed reaction? Do you remember her joyful exuberance when she realized that the pain was gone and her ankle had returned to normal?*"

"*Listen carefully to Me now, son,*" the Lord continued. "*What occurred that day was a direct result of your obedience years earlier. When you helped your daughter* move into union with Me, her heart and spirit also melded with yours. Since that day, the loving-kindness that flows like a deep river from her spirit has been like a magnet. It draws thousands to Me. Everything she does to advance My kingdom accumulates a great reward for her in heaven. **It also accumulates a similar reward for you.** Your one unquestioning act of obedience that day in the car changed everything. It will continue to have far-reaching ramifications. You will not begin to know or understand this until the day you stand before My throne."

The Holy Spirit paused as an understanding of what He had explained overwhelmed me. I sat for several minutes more without responding, as wave after wave of joy engulfed my soul. He then spoke again.

"Do you realize how deeply your son loves you, how he watches you and models his actions after yours? For many years, you took him with you to the Full Gospel breakfast functions, as I encouraged you to do. I know that you questioned this many times in your mind. You worried about it being too much for a ten-year-old boy. Still, you had no way of knowing how much his spirit would absorb by association with those godly men. For him, the hundreds of testimonies he heard were like a dry sponge submerged in a bucket of water."

"Think back to a few weeks after your son's twelfth birthday when the tornado touched down very near to your home. You had just finished reading Pat Robertson's autobiography—'Shout It From The Housetops.' He told of a hurricane which he withstood by faith in My Word—a violent whirlwind that threatened to destroy the work I had led him to establish. His book caused your level of belief in My faithfulness to uphold My Word to reach a new plateau. That day, as the tornado drew closer to your property, you stood at the large picture window in your living room. Looking out at the eerie sky, you watched the clouds swirling overhead. The trees were bending and breaking before your eyes. As a faith unlike anything you'd ever before experienced arose in your spirit, you determined to trust that what I did for Pat, I would do for you. With a loud voice, you rebuked the storm and the tornado in My name. As you did, your enemy bombarded your mind with thoughts of how laughable your efforts were. Those demons made you recall how the media had ridiculed Pat when he testified to his actions. Your enemy urged you repeatedly to flee to a safe place, to cower while the storm had its way. Instead, you allowed My faith to arise within you. You watched as the winds abruptly stopped and the sky cleared in response to your command. It thrilled your heart to see the immediate result of your faith in Me. However, it thrilled My heart, even more, to see your son standing beside you through it all. His hand was gripping yours, as he joined you in coming against the work of Satan. He prayed with confidence using his recently acquired prayer language, and he boldly and confidently rebuked Satan in My name—just as he observed you doing."

Everything Matter, However…

"Son, you obeyed years earlier when I urged you to begin taking your son to those Full Gospel functions. As a result, you were able to rejoice together with him years later. Your **COMBINED** faith and actions altered the path of the storm that day. Damage to your property was averted, unlike other properties around yours. You and those other godly men had a significant effect upon your son's spirit at a young age. As a result, his faith in My Word, and in Me, is robust to this day. Once again, My son, I tell you…

EVERYTHING MATTERS!

Several more days had passed before the Holy Spirit came back to this subject.

"Listen carefully and consider well what I am about to say to you. Permit Me to enlighten you even further on how this first principle has played out in your life."

"I mentioned before a special moment in your and your family's lives. That day, you and your wife committed to participate with My missionary in his efforts. I had challenged him to put a copy of the New Testament into the hands of every family in his hometown, a large city in Africa. This undertaking was a daunting task at first. He sought My wisdom about this and followed My direction. With the help and financial support of thousands of families like yours, he was able to succeed. It took many years, but he did not waver. Your part of the outreach was to pack, label, and mail the New Testaments. He provided you with labels for everyone listed on the two telephone directory pages that he gave you. Do you recall the fun that the six of you had while packing the items? You all struggled, trying your best to pronounce the names and addresses. And together, your family prayed over the packages before taking them to the post office."

"For you and your wife, that was a large financial investment in a people and town that you would never see. Do you recall how many times you thought about that project over the next few years? You wondered if anything ever came of it. Eventually, you forgot about it, until now, when I brought it again to your mind."

"So many times through the years, I watched as you looked back and questioned your efforts in your mind and heart. You wondered if any of the many things you have done in the past had any real effect, importance, or lasting value. Many times, you donated a large amount of your time and money into that which I set before you and your family. You did so with a pure heart and a genuine desire to help others. Years later, you struggled to meet the needs of a growing family, as well as the demands of your creditors. It was then that your enemies reminded you of all of the money you 'foolishly' gave away. They pointed out how that money could have prevented the lean times."

"Let me assure you now, son," He declared. "You cannot even begin to calculate the impact that those mailed Bibles had. It changed many of the families that received them. That carried over to their following and preceding generations. Many of their relatives and friends benefitted. Their churches and communities, and their country as a whole were forever changed. Granted, some threw them away in anger. Nonetheless, many of these were later found and read. They touched individuals you had no intention of reaching. When My Spirit, acting through you, sends forth My Word, trust Me, son, it **NEVER** returns void! So, please understand and know, once again, that...

EVERYTHING MATTERS!

† † †

Later that same day, the Holy Spirit came back to another incident about our son.

"A couple of weeks ago, your son told you about his recent visit with a family friend in Broken Arrow, Oklahoma. What he said surprised you. You and your wife had repeatedly blessed this young man's parents in the past. You strongly encouraged his dad to pursue God's calling on his life to be a pastor. After much prayer, the dad and mom both did so. They moved themselves and their three sons to Oklahoma to attend Rhema Bible College. Their second son was your son's long-time friend. When that son graduated from high school, he also chose to attend Rhema. After graduation, he sought Me in prayer for direction about what type of ministry to pursue. When he and your son had lunch two weeks ago, that young man said he knew his calling was to be something other than a pastor in a church."

"He then told your son, 'One day I was praying to the Lord for direction about that. He reminded me of something that happened at a time when I was much younger. Our family had moved here to Broken Arrow, and we were hurting financially for months. It was obvious that my folks were worried sick about it. They were way behind on the bills and had just enough to cover the next month's rent that was due in a few days. They had begun questioning God about why they were always struggling, asking Him for an undeniable sign that they were truly following His will for their lives.'"

"That afternoon, my folks picked my brothers and me up from school, and we headed home. When we arrived, there was a small mountain of boxes stacked on our porch, blocking our front door. UPS had delivered them earlier that afternoon, and a neighbor said she had signed for them. They were all from your parents. We hauled them inside and began opening them. They were full of a wide variety of groceries, and a word processor, which my mom and dad desperately needed for school, and an envelope with money in it. My parents broke down crying, thanking the Lord for answering their prayers. What your parents had no way of knowing was that our kitchen cabinets were empty, and our family only had a few dollars left. My folks had prayed at length the night before with my two brothers and me, telling God how much we needed the basics like food and gas money. My dad said the Holy Spirit clearly spoke to his heart telling him to trust the Lord—**and the next day the boxes arrived.**'"

"Now, let me explain something to you, My son. It would have been far easier and much less expensive for you and your wife to have only sent a check to them. Even so, you were obedient to send the physical items that I directed. I desired to bless them with those EXACT items for which they petitioned Me. It moved their hearts and souls to see their prayer request filled to the smallest detail, and without knowing it, you included some of their favorite foods. The best part for **them** was discovering **HOW** I had fulfilled their prayer request. It came through friends from across the country. It came through someone who could only have heard of this need and request from My Holy Spirit. Most of all, it amazed them that I had already put things into motion **long before** they ever began petitioning Me, which allowed them to receive it the day they needed it."

"As your son finished telling you, 'Dad, he said he never forgot what you and mom did for their family that day. He said when the Holy Spirit brought that memory back to his conscious mind, there was no doubt in his mind that it was the answer to his prayer, and he had absolute peace about it. He said he'd finally found what God wanted him to do. What you and mom did for his family that day became his inspiration. Now, he's doing something similar, helping others on an even larger scale.'"

"Are you beginning to understand, My son? You have no concept of the long-term effect that such a seemingly minor act of obedience may have. As I have said many times now to you...

EVERYTHING MATTERS!

Several days later, the Spirit spoke once more. He picked up right where He had stopped.

"Son, let Me tell you now about three times of divine intervention in your eldest daughter's life. They appeared unrelated, and you could have too easily overlooked the significance of them. Even so, each played a crucial part in her becoming the person she is today. Each still guides her thoughts and actions to this day."

"Do you remember how upset she was with you that one summer in junior high? You forbid her to continue reading young adult books," the Lord said. "Instead, you placed in her hands a lengthier adult classic to read. You saw in her an incredible potential that she was not yet able to see. The first book you gave her remained on her dresser for weeks. With an obvious stubbornness, she resisted your request. When curiosity had finally gotten the better of her, she'd picked it up and started to read. A *few hours later, she had finished it. She then came to you to tell you how incredible the story was. She's voiced many times through the years how much she'd enjoyed that book. She also expressed how thankful she was to you for having urged her to read it. Son, without you even realizing what had occurred, My Spirit guided your actions. He encouraged you to introduce her to certain books. Yes, this grew her vocabulary. More so, it broadened her outlook on life, on the world, and many other things she'd not yet come to think about or consider. Most importantly, though, it shaped within her a heart of compassion for the hurting, the homeless, the abused, and the forsaken. These were the very topics that were the basis of many of the stories she'd read."*

*"What about in high school? You insisted she take at least one non-traditional class. You suggested one that would challenge her in ways she did not expect. Several weeks into that Mechanical Drawing class, she was ready to quit. She was the only girl in the class. In her mind, the class was **boring**, as she expressed to you repeatedly, often with anger and resentment. She was confident that what she was being **forced** to learn would be of no value in the '**real**' world. Through your bedience to My leading in this matter, My Spirit was able to direct her path, with an intended purpose in mind. Many years later, she spoke with such conviction about her amazement at how the training received in that class affected her. 'It made it possible for me, to this day, to see things and situations from different perspectives,' she had said." I can see past the obvious. Things I otherwise would have overlooked, I now see."*

"Last, but not least, was the time she called you from Bible College. She asked you to come and pick her up and bring her home," the Lord added. *"Frustration had overcome her. She wanted to give up on her training there. She expressed uncertainty about having made the right choice when choosing that vocation. Day after day, she called many times per day. Each time she called, you asked her the same question, which I told you to ask her—'**What did the Holy Spirit tell you?**' At first, it irritated her. Over the days that followed, her growing anger and resentment were evident. The conversation on her calls progressed from asking, to demanding, and finally to begging you to come and get her. Still, My son, you and your wife both had prayed about the situation.* **You were obedient to My directions and held firm to what My Spirit told you** *to tell her. Because of your obedience, she finally gave in and did as you suggested. She isolated herself in her room and eliminated all distractions. For the first time, she waited to hear My voice. It was a mere fifteen minutes later when she called back. She meekly, humbly and, yet, confidently, told you that I spoke to her, and she was staying where she was.* **Through this, your daughter learned the importance of patience. She learned to see a thing through to its conclusion once she commits to it. She also learned the most important lesson by experience. She now KNOWS how to wait upon Me in stillness, and understands that I am always ready and willing to communicate with her.**"

"Each of these incidents grew her character in significant ways. That growth continues to bless her and others to this day. It will continue to affect the shaping of her character in the years ahead. You could have acquiesced to her willful demands. In doing so, you would have forfeited your responsibility to guide her. She may never have had the opportunity to meet her husband, who I chose to complete her. Together, they have been a blessing to thousands that they have ministered to over the last twenty years. My son, I tell you again...

EVERYTHING MATTERS!"

✝ ✝ ✝

Three more weeks had passed. I happened to be thinking about what the Holy Spirit had revealed to me about three of my children. I wondered why He had said nothing about our second child. Right at that moment, as though anticipating my thoughts, He began talking about her.

"As important as what happened with your other three children, is what occurred with your second daughter."

"I blessed her with a heart full of joy that easily draws others to her and, in turn, to Me. Nevertheless, before she had learned to wait upon My Spirit, two other forces guided her thoughts and actions. The first of these was her desire for love as a young woman. The second was her perceived need to find that special someone with whom she could spend the rest of her days. This preoccupation led to several emotionally painful events—multiple seasons of relationships formed and then broken."

"Son, it took great courage on your part to speak into her life spiritually at those times. You encouraged her to wait for the right young man. There were periods of great anger and hurt as she rebelled against what she saw as your desire to control her. After school, she moved far away, with the idea of making her own life decisions without your input. You and your wife never stopped praying for her. The day came when she was certain that she had finally found the right young man. However, his abusive nature and actions proved otherwise. Despite the pain she bore, your daughter did everything possible not to let you and her mother know what had happened. Finally came the day I prompted you and your wife to drive, unannounced, to where she was living. I instructed you to pack her up and move her home. She was furious. Even so, she respected you enough to hear what I told you to say to her, and then to obey. For weeks on end, she moped around your home. She cried day and night, and started arguments with you about interfering in her life."

"After thirty days, she finally heard My voice and allowed Me to heal her heart and emotions. Her spirit and soul found much-needed peace. Only then was she in a position to see, and welcome, the young man who I had always intended to be her earthly mate. Now, with both of them united in soul and spirit, in union with My Spirit, they are a source of tremendous blessing. They've touched thousands, and will continue to do so in the years to come."

"My son, as with your other children, your willingness to obey Me was critical. Each time, there was a real possibility of permanently alienating your daughter. Your unquestioning response made way for Me to complete the Father's desire for her life. Again, son, I emphasize to you that...

EVERYTHING MATTERS!"

"Think back with me now to the day, not so long ago, when I prompted one of your wife's co-workers to approach her. She asked if you and your wife would come to the hospital and pray for her dad. The man was in a coma and had been completely unresponsive for four weeks. Your wife knew the daughter and her mom, but neither of you had ever met her dad. When the two of you entered his hospital room, you became very concerned. Not only were the wife and one daughter there, but so also were the other adult children and their spouses. They were waiting for the doctor to remove all medical assistance. That night was to be everyone's final goodbye. You both greeted his wife and then asked her to join you and your wife in asking the Father in Heaven to bring her husband out of the coma, completely healed. Through My Spirit, you rightly discerned that Doubt and Unbelief filled the room in the presence of the others. No one, other than the daughter with whom your wife worked, offered to join you, your wife, and the man's wife in that time of prayer. The others had already decided in their hearts that his situation was hopeless. They awaited his last breath."

"Do you remember asking Me in your heart, at that moment, how to proceed? You thought I would tell you to anoint him with oil and pray a quick prayer of faith over him," the Lord reminded me. "However, I knew he could still hear the conversation in that room. I also knew that there was a need to stir up hope in his spirit so that faith might take root and spring forth. Therefore, I directed you to place your hand gently over the region of his heart and to begin testifying to him. You obediently spoke aloud, telling him of all the times I was faithful to heal you and your family. You told him of many believers and non-believers to whom I poured out My healing presence through you and your wife. You later paused and then continued, when you heard my prompting to tell him of the many other testimonies of healing, most of which you had read or heard over the years. I know what a struggle that was, son. Enemy voices assailed your mind. Insanity and Ridicule tormented you and laughed at your actions. Nevertheless, you persisted in faith. You concluded your time there by following My last request. You *prayed aloud over the man in your prayer language, with a boldness that came from Me, until I told you to stop. You did so, even though you were uncertain why, or what it was that you were saying."*

*"You felt no special anointing or response as you testified and prayed for more than one hour, obeying My direction. Finally, after hugging the wife and daughter, you departed late in the evening. When you left, there was still no evidence that anything had happened. Very early the following morning, the daughter called your wife with exciting news. Within a few hours after the two of you left that room, her father came out of the coma. He sat up and asked for something to eat. Still, it was his next words that affected every member of that family in a way they could not deny or explain away. They were words that many of them will **NEVER** forget."*

"He said to his wife, 'Who was it who had his hand on my chest? When he put it there, it felt like my whole body was on fire!'"

*"My son, even as you struggled to ignore Doubt and Intimidation, My Spirit moved. Your obedience made it possible for Me to heal that man. Yes! I am well aware of how confused and distraught you became when you received word that the man had died of a completely unrelated cause only two days later. Know this, My son! It was his time to come home to an eternity with Me. However, through the obedience of you and your wife, I was able to stir the hearts and challenge the beliefs of every other person in that room. **That** was the mission! **That** was the goal, and your obedience brought it to pass. Those few moments in time are still affecting that family more than seven years later and will continue to do so throughout their lifetimes. What they witnessed in those few hours will be thought of more and more frequently as each of them draws nearer to their final breath."*

"I hope I've made it clear enough to you at this point. ***You may not understand it. You may not see tangible results in your lifetime.*** *Even so, the inescapable truth is that **EVERY** thought and word, **EVERY** action and reaction, is vital. **EVERY** decision—to obey, or disobey, or to remain neutral and non-committal—is critical. They have an effect on circumstances and lives, now and in the future, both yours and others.** *For this reason, I will never stop reminding you that...*

EVERYTHING MATTERS!"

Again, only a few days later, the Holy Spirit spoke to me early one morning.

"Do you recall the day, many years ago, when you helped to move your in-law's refrigerator early one Saturday and injured your back in the process? The following morning, you could barely get out of bed. When you and your family went to church that morning, you were in severe pain. Do you remember how you sat through worship

because it was too painful to stand? As you did, I heard you repeatedly begging Me in your mind to heal your back. It was only a few minutes later, when I prompted the pastor to delay his sermon. Instead, he called for 'the person who needs his back healed.' You went forward immediately. The pastor lightly touched his finger to your forehead and prayed for you. In the next moment, you felt a hand shove your spine into its proper position. Your back straightened, and you abruptly stood upright. I healed you and removed your pain. Do you recall how you quickly you looked behind you to see whose hand it was that had been on your back, only to find no one there? You realized that it was I who had fixed your back, didn't you?"

"I'll never forget that day, Lord. A wave of chills passed up and down my limbs as I realized what occurred at that moment."

"Do you also recall the day you stood facing the corner of the prayer room at your current church? You couldn't keep from crying because of the severe pain in your shoulder. You had fallen on the ice and torn your rotator cuff. For days, you sat propped up in bed each night, trying but failing to sleep. Each time you nodded off, your body slid down off the pillows, and you jerked awake. Shooting pains racked your body night after night. You begged Me to heal you and were extremely frustrated because it hadn't occurred. However, that morning in the church prayer room, I answered you. I said, 'Raise the injured arm high and wave it back and forth in worship to Me.' Do you remember how you very slowly lifted it despite the burst of pain? **Then everything changed, in a moment.** You found that you could wave your arm exuberantly because I was faithful to heal you once more."

"Yes, Holy Spirit! I was so exhausted and in so much pain! I desperately needed You, and You came through again. Thank You, Lord!"

"Do you further recall the day at your office, just a couple of months ago? You were talking with a client on the phone, and I interrupted your thoughts."

"Absolutely! I heard You so clearly say, '*I want to heal Thomas.*' Your statement surprised me. I didn't expect to hear from You, and even more so **what** I heard you say—especially while I was on the phone with a customer. You said it in almost a casual way. Thomas was standing across the aisle from me at his desk. He was always standing because he was in such pain that he couldn't sit for any length of time."

"Yes, and your first thoughts were, 'What will he think if I tell him what I just heard? Does he even believe in God?'"

"Lord, he said that he'd experienced a devastating accident. It occurred when he was in the paratroopers many years earlier. His main parachute failed to open on a jump he had made. The secondary chute hadn't activated in time to soften the impact. He'd broken most of the bones in his back when he hit the ground. They put him back together, and he was in the hospital for a long time. I know he has overwhelming pain every day of his life and has been on heavy doses of pain pills since then. When you spoke to me, I told him what you said, and offered to pray for him. He said he wanted to think about it, and that was the end of the conversation."

"That night, I showed you the severity of his situation. It was the reason for his first wife to leave him, and it depressed him to think about the reality of a pain-filled future."

"Holy Spirit, I remember the next morning when he came into the office, he acted withdrawn all day long. Right before it was time for him to leave for the day, he walked up to me and said one word: "Yes." I didn't hesitate. I put my hand on his shoulder and just thanked You for healing him and blessing him. I asked You to make him acutely aware of Your love for him. That's all! It was a short prayer, after which he left without saying a word. The next morning, he came in with a BIG smile on his face. I had never before seen him smile, Lord. He walked up to me and said, "It worked! There's no pain!" He then bent over and touched his toes and twisted his torso left and right. Since that day, he's acted like a different person— joyful, peaceful, and full of energy!"

"Yes, My son, he has. However, I want you to understand the reason **WHY** *My healing readily manifested in all three situations. It was because someone was* **DESPERATE**. *When you, or anyone, is desperate enough that you look to Me,* **and Me alone**, *to meet the need, I am always faithful to do so. That desperation, which causes you to trust me to fulfill your hope, allows My anointing to flow."*

"Do you want more of My Presence? Do you want to experience the endless flow of My anointing in your life? Ask me, from a sincere heart, to make you desperate, **EXPECT** *it to happen, and welcome it!* **Your obedience and the level of your expectation is vital!** *This revelation is just one more example of how…*

EVERYTHING MATTERS!"

Late one evening, the Holy Spirit interrupted what I was doing. He told me that He wanted to continue where we had left off in this last chapter.

"Do you recall when I explained for you the difference between being an EXAMPLE and an ENSAMPLE, and why I guided the KJV translators to use that specific word?"

"Yes, Lord," I replied. "I wrote in my journal the words You used to define the word EXAMPLE. It was…

'Someone or something set before others as a guide, pattern, option or choice—which others may, or may not, choose to follow.'

"You emphasized that this was the ***passive*** form. You then had me write down Your definition for ENSAMPLE. It was…

'That which strikes a blow or makes a mark, impacting, affecting or changing beyond the surface, permanently altering that with which it comes into contact.'

"My son, an **'ensample,'** will always cause two things. The first is a definite impression and a lasting relationship. The second is an absolute, identifiable change. That which an 'ensample' encounters, forever after finds its identification, references, and indices permanently altered. From that moment on, the world associates its relationship **TO**, and often **BY** the very name of, whatever (or whoever) impacted it. **For this reason, those in a relationship with Christ are known to the world as Christians.**"

"You emphasized that this was the *active* form, Holy Spirit. You then referred me to images of manufacturer and designer marks. You explained how many became synonymous with dynasties or periods of history. Others identified a particular craftsman or manufacturer who designed and produced them."

"Exactly. When My Word is available for men and women to follow, it is an EXAMPLE, but it is **passive**. It contains the "potential" for life, awaiting an opportunity to grow in fertile soil. With some, however, My Word makes a profound impact, transforming the one with whom it has come into contact. It has then fulfilled a higher purpose as an ENSAMPLE. It has shown itself to be *active*. It lives! **It's full of realized and yet-to-be-realized potential**. Never forget this, son! Be forever *active*! Be an **ENSAMPLE!**"

The following morning, the Holy Spirit woke me early and began speaking to me as I lay in bed listening.

"Son, this morning, I need your undivided attention. It is not enough that you understand what I explain. **You must live with an ever-present awareness of how any single action, thought, or word affects everyone and everything else. It affects at that moment, but the ongoing repercussions are also continually expanding across space and time, creating an ever-increasing sphere of influence.**" The Lord then strongly emphasized to me, **"This is a CONSTANT, and a constant holds whether your actions, thoughts, and words are a positive or a negative influence."**

"In this final chapter, I stated that there are two foundational principles. All who desire to draw near and learn from Me must never forget them. I have gone to great length to reveal to you the first principle. I spoke of its importance, and its continuing effect on you and others you encounter. I illustrated, as well, its effect on individuals that you may never personally meet. Nevertheless, it's the **second** principle that is the **"keystone"** upon which all else depends. Let me explain."

With the utterance of those final words by the Lord, something changed. I felt the Holy Spirit infusing my conscious mind with a specific scene. I recalled an incident that occurred the first summer after we had moved into our home in the country.

Our property was twenty minutes from the nearest Interstate highway. It also was positioned ten-minutes equidistant from three small communities. Our closest neighbor was a significant distance away. No longer would we have to tolerate a neighbor's excessively loud music or television. We enjoyed the cool breezes that swept across the fields each evening and left our windows open without concern about outside noises disturbing our sleep. We welcomed the lack of noise from cars, buses, emergency vehicles, and planes.

When we informed our children that we were moving out of the city, they were eager. They had no concept of what it would be like to live in the country. Even so, they quickly adapted and made new friends. They familiarized themselves with the area. They explored our three acres of yard and wooded area, as well as many of the surrounding farms and trees.

My employment at the time required me to leave home before the rest of the family was awake. Each evening of that first summer, I arrived home at dusk. My children listened for the sound of my car turning into our gravel driveway. On hearing it, they would jump to their feet to look outside and confirm that it was me. An excited yell to their mom followed, declaring, "Daddy's here!"

This 'reception' was the scene that the Holy Spirit brought alive in my mind. Afterward, He spoke to me about what I was seeing.

"Son, didn't it bless your heart to hear your young children call out like that each time you arrived home? Didn't you enjoy watching them burst through the doorway, eager to meet you as you got out of the car?"

"Yes, Lord. It made me feel happy to know they were waiting for me to appear. They were usually eager to share the events of their day with me," I replied. My thoughts lingered in the sweet memories of those days.

"Son, We are no different. It thrills Us when you suddenly become aware of Our Presence. We are delighted when Our arrival triggers a similar joyful response, and look forward to our time spent with you, as you share your heart with Us."

"What happened when your children outgrew that phase? How did you feel when they no longer seemed to be as joyful about your return or your presence? Didn't it sadden you, son? They each started aging, and their interests changed. They grew more and more distracted or caught up with the things of the world. Didn't it leave you feeling somewhat forsaken? Didn't it make you long for a return to those earlier days? Didn't you fondly recall their childhood when they were so eager to hug your neck?

Didn't you wish for the intoxicating joy of their voices filling your ears and bringing a big smile to your face? Isn't this what you and your wife now cherish so much about the time you spend with your youngest grandchildren?"

"Think about it, son," the Lord continued. ***If We created you in Our image and likeness, wouldn't it make sense that We would likewise react the same way? Wouldn't we long for that type of continual response from you as Our child? How about when you find your satisfaction, amusement, or joy in the things of the world? Is it unreasonable for Us to be jealous, or to long for your return to your former way? After all, We did create you for Our pleasure. Should it be so disconcerting that We would desire for you to dwell in Our presence continually?"***

"In conclusion, always remember this. Although I've extensively elaborated on the first principle, it is the second principle, the keystone, upon which everything else depends, and that second principle is...

NOTHING MATTERS AS MUCH AS YOUR INTIMACY WITH US!"

"As you've learned through experience, it isn't difficult in the least to draw near and learn from Us. Set aside your reservations and personal aspirations. Let your fascination and preoccupation with the world, and all it has to offer, rest. Humble yourself and become, once again, as a little child. Listen eagerly for **Our** footsteps. Then, when you hear Us approaching, you will be able to rejoice at Our presence. Son, I will **never** tire of hearing you cry out without hesitation or embarrassment...

'Daddy's here!'"

Burden-Lifting Revelation

After all of the years of interaction with the Holy Spirit (described in detail in the previous chapters) that culminated in five years invested in the writing, formatting, and release of this book, I suddenly found myself struggling to understand what the Lord expected me to do next. More and more often, I reviewed the many lessons that the Spirit had revealed to me, including the many I shared in this book.

As time passed, I regularly wondered why I had heard nothing more about all that the Holy Spirit revealed to me in Colorado. This puzzlement increased when some of those who had read this book periodically asked for an update on further events, and I had nothing more to tell them.

In late 2015, a guest speaker, Tracy Stewart, spoke to our church body. When I heard her at that time, her message was one I would not soon forget. Therefore, when my pastor announced that Tracy was again returning, on October 21-23, 2017, I made a point of attending both the Friday evening and Saturday evening services. God's messages through her in both services were a huge blessing. On Sunday morning, I had planned to go to the second service, as my wife and I usually did. However, the Holy Spirit woke me up at three in the morning and began talking to me. He explicitly stated that He wanted me to go to the first AND second services. My wife slept in, with plans to meet me at church for the later service, while I went by myself to the earlier service.

Tracy spoke in great depth this time about holding patterns. She reiterated what her husband, James, had explained to her, from the perspective of the long-term pilot and flight instructor—which he was—about their use by Air Traffic Control facilities. Tracy then revealed how the Spirit had spoken to her, correlating that understanding from her husband with how our Heavenly Father operates.

After that service ended, I asked Tracy if she would pray for me, explaining that I felt I was in what amounted to a 17-year holding pattern. She asked me to sit down and briefly explain. The 2-minute summary I gave her included my obedience to God regarding the trip to Colorado and adding that many things had occurred since then to reinforce that experience as having been real. I told her that after years of interaction, it seemed now like nothing was happening, that the Spirit stopped talking about everything related to it. I related how I became VERY frustrated, somewhat depressed, and truly began questioning everything I *thought* I had experienced, seen, and heard.

What I hadn't told her was that two weeks before her arrival at Heritage this time, my close friend and prayer partner had gone out of his way to say to me that I needed to be listening carefully because the Spirit wanted to say something to me. I prayed and focused for days, but heard nothing. A week later, while we were both praying in Heritage's Prayer Room before that week's service, he again said the same thing, with even more urgency. Still, he did not elaborate. Despite my renewed focus attempting to hear whatever it might be that the Lord wanted to say to me, I heard nothing.

A few days later, just before Tracy's arrival this second time, my wife was reading the Word and praying, after which she told me a message from the Lord.

"The Holy Spirit said there is a place you need to go, and you need to leave the end of this month (nine days later). You need to stop letting things distract you, get quieter, and hear Him."

† † †

As I indicated, I obeyed the Spirit's leading and went to the first service. As Tracy and I sat there after that first service, she prayed for me. I then went to the prayer room while awaiting the second service. My close friend and prayer partner was in the prayer room when I entered, so I sat down next to him. He reached out to take hold of my hand that we might pray together. The moment our hands touched, the Holy Spirit spoke to me in an unmistakably clear Voice.

"You need to return to Fort Collins, Colorado, at the end of this month. Make your hotel arrangements immediately. When you arrive there, we'll pick up where we left off **SEVENTEEN YEARS AGO.***"*

I thought I imagined it, possibly influenced by the fact that I had just finished talking to Tracy Stewart minutes earlier about NOT hearing from God.

I opened my eyes to find my friend looking at me with a smile on his face. He said, "He just told you, didn't He?"

I replied as a question, "I'm supposed to return to Fort Collins at the end of the month?"

He shook his head and said, "Yep. And He wanted you to hear it for yourself so that you couldn't deny it."

Leaving the prayer room, I went out to the sanctuary for the second service. As I sat next to my wife, I whispered in her ear what had just occurred. She smiled and shook her head in the affirmative.

I made the reservations right after church, began fasting once more, and left on the morning of the 31st for the long two-day drive, as He had directed—and precisely as He had told me to do seventeen years earlier. On the first day, I drove for ten hours while worshipping non-stop. For the second eleven-hour day of driving, the Lord told me to listen to my digital Bible. As I did, I periodically felt an urgency to pray in the spirit.

That you might more fully understand what occurred next, I am momentarily jumping forward in time to when I had returned home from the trip to Colorado, at which point the Lord urged me repeatedly to call Pastor Cleddie and set a time to meet with him to talk. The Holy Spirit told me specifically to tell my pastor ahead of time that this was NOT a request for counseling, and He did NOT want us to meet at a restaurant where we both might be distracted. Instead, He said to ask my pastor if we could sit in his parlor, undisturbed, and talk. Thursday evening, I reached him, and we planned to meet the following morning, which we did for about 2 hours.

The Holy Spirit guided me as to exactly what he wanted me to talk about and say to my pastor. When I had finished, Pastor said he was pleased about what I had revealed, and he then told me why. As we ended our time together, he asked if I would take 20-25 minutes at that evening's River Service to tell everyone present what God had revealed to me—just as I'd shared it with him. What now follows is much of what I shared that evening.

Back in Colorado, the previous week, three days of frustratingly quiet time crept by as I paced the floor in that hotel room. I had heard nothing from the Holy Spirit since arriving, and I did not feel His Presence.

Then suddenly EVERYTHING changed, as He made Himself and His purpose for my being there known, speaking to me in a loud and distinctive Voice.

"You don't have the faintest idea of what is now occurring, and for many decades before this moment has been occurring, in your life. Do you, son?"

Uncertain as to what He expected me to say to such a statement, I hesitated for the longest time before replying, "I thought I did. At some point, though, everything died off. I admit to You, Lord, that I did not then, and still do not understand why. Did I do something wrong, or NOT do something that I was supposed to do?"

"Not at all, son. As I explained to you in great depth many years ago, everything must be in the Father's perfect timing. Think back now to a time in your life nearly twenty-three years ago."

When He said that, I found myself instantly recalling a series of events from the period to which He referred.

"What petition did you continuously bring before Me for more than SIX years, son?"

Instantly, I knew what He meant. "I begged You to please change me, free me, and do whatever was necessary to make me into a vessel that You would be pleased to use in any way You desired."

"Exactly! Son, I heard the absolute sincerity of your heart-cry and started THAT MOMENT on My plan to do what you requested. Allow Me now to help you recall the

sequence of events that occurred **after** that day, which are still playing out even to this moment. Do you remember the book I had you buy?"

"Wow! I just recalled that. I was driving up the Interstate to a sales appointment, running late, and you spoke so clearly, directing me to take the next exit, rather than the one I needed to take for my appointment. You sent me to Berean Christian Book Store, a short way off the exit ramp. I walked around inside, wondering why I was there, constantly looking at my watch, worrying about being late. Confused about what You wanted, I stopped in one aisle and stared. There before me was the book *Rees Howells, Intercessor*. You told me to buy it and read it. I finished it about a week later, having highlighted and underlined much of it. I thought about it a lot. But I wasn't sure I wanted to be THAT kind of vessel!"

"Eight months later, I caused your path and Byron Huff's path to meet, son. That was the next vital step in My plan. A few months after that, despite your many years invested in Full Gospel Business Men's Fellowship, I directed you to step away from it. Furthermore, I instructed you and Byron to work together to start a Saturday morning Men's Prayer & Discipleship group."

"Yes, Lord! And a few months after that, You told me to buy 20 copies of the book *Rees Howells, Intercessor,* and to give a copy to each of the men who remained as part of the prayer group, which I did."

"The men's prayer group grew to be challenging and exciting, Lord, and my entire focus was on those Saturday mornings. About one year after initially reading that book, I heard you clearly say, 'Read *Rees Howells, Intercessor* again, son.' EVERY year after that, almost like clockwork, you said the same thing."

"Yes, son, I did. There was a purpose to what I requested, and it was a necessary part of the plan the Father has set in motion."

"I remember the fifth consecutive year of Your request. I was perturbed and questioned why I needed to read it again. However, all You did was repeat Your request, so I obeyed. After that, you sent me to the Brownsville Revival for a week. When I got home, you told me to return there immediately, but this time to take my entire family. I'd barely returned home a week later with the family than I left again to participate in evangelistic outreach to Argentina for three weeks, as You insisted that I do."

"Yes, son. And what happened after you returned home from Argentina?"

I thought about His question for quite a while until He finally interrupted my thoughts, saying, "Son, I **KNOW** the truth. It's about time that **you** acknowledge to yourself this very truth that has puzzled you all these years."

"You told me to read that book for the eighth time, and I told you I knew the book by heart. I'm sorry, Lord."

"The point, son, was that you READ the book **seven** times, but you had learned NONE of the valuable lessons that Rees learned, which transformed his spirit, soul,

Burden-Lifting Revelation

and future. To this day, you can quote large sections of the book. Still, you applied little of it to your own life, which would have allowed you to begin the process of TRANSFORMATION. Therefore, **to fulfill the desire of your heart, <u>and to be true to My word to give you what you so persistently petitioned Me for</u>**, I had to make some moves in your life."

"What moves?"

"Immediately after returning from Argentina—but a while before you read the book for the eighth time—what happened to YOU?"

Suddenly, my mind and heart saw the truth to which He was referring, and the reality of it was quite painful. Hesitantly, I responded.

"I lost all desire to sell. Before that trip, I was one of the top sales reps in the nation for our company, making major dollars. I had received a tremendous amount of praise, awards, and trips for Patti and me to go to resorts throughout the USA and the islands. Everything then fell apart. Customers canceled one after another and I could not understand why, or salvage them. I was doing what I had always done to succeed. I began working longer and longer hours, and it seemed as though the harder I worked, the more it all fell apart. Our company then sold out to an overseas firm, and the new management eliminated my account manager position. Everything I turned to after that started well then died. I was getting desperate, and my wife was getting panicky. I ended up losing everything, Lord. I felt horrible, ashamed, embarrassed. I felt like a loser and worthless to my wife when we lost the home that she had come to love. I thought about it constantly, and I still couldn't understand what happened or how."

"Son of My heart, the first three lessons I taught Rees, near the beginning of the book, were **VITAL** to him becoming what he became. You read it – SEVEN TIMES – and NEVER considered voluntarily applying those same lessons to your own life. Therefore, I began moving to bring about that transformation."

"The first thing I did **FOR** you—not **TO** you—was what I did **FOR** Rees. *I touched your AMBITION*. The super, self-confident attitude steadily diminished. Why? <u>**If you are to be a vessel that I inhabit and work through powerfully, there can be not one trace of personal ambition.**</u> Next, **I touched your PRIDE**. Suddenly, the 'star' fell from prominence, didn't you? Before very long, few in the company continued to hold you in high esteem as they had. Many shied away from even associating with you, and then the new owners eliminated the very position that you gloried in, identified with, and about which you were so proud. In doing this **FOR** you, you became somewhat like Christ Himself—'a man of NO reputation, and despised.' Why did I do this **FOR** you? <u>**If you are to be My vessel, there will be NOTHING for you to be proud of, because ALL glory must belong to Me. Those drawn to the Father will be because of My reputation, not your own.**</u> Later, when you fought so vigorously to try to regain what you had lost to that point, I went even further. *I caused your money to diminish—*

substantially and rapidly. Why did I do this FOR you? Once again, to be a vessel of Mine means it will no longer be about YOUR ability to meet your or your family's needs. As with Rees Howells, when he fully surrendered to Me, you will have NO SAY about your provision. You will be a branch grafted into the Vine, and the branch gets NOTHING. It serves as a conduit of supply to bring forth fruit for my Kingdom."

"All of this was YOU? I didn't do anything wrong?"

"Yes, son. It was I, your Lord and Savior. You asked Me to do whatever it takes. That is exactly what I have done and am continuing to do."

At this point, I was a crying mess. The Holy Spirit next told me to call my wife and explain to her what He had just explained to me. When she answered, she knew I had been crying. As calmly as I could, I explained what the Lord had revealed. Her reaction stunned me! She was HAPPY and okay with it. That blew me away! She said that the Lord had already told her, but the Lord wanted to reveal it to me Himself. In my saying it to her, though, it was as if a HUGE burden and guilt lifted off my shoulders. After hanging up, the Holy Spirit spoke to me once more.

"When I told you to come here to Fort Collins this time, I told you only to bring your Bible, and to buy a fresh copy of Rees Howells, Intercessor. Open it up now and begin reading it."

Thirty minutes or so later, the Spirit interrupted me with a question.

"That sentence you just read – have you ever noticed it before?"

I read it again and then stared at it. It was the fourth lesson the Spirit of God spoke about to Rees. That subject was **SANCTIFICATION**. It seemed basic. I knew it meant *making holy or set apart*. So, I guess it was because I thought I understood it, that I passed right over it every time I read it. The Spirit then confirmed my thoughts.

*"Son, you don't begin to understand the multitude of meanings or ramifications of the word SANCTIFICATION. First of all, **SANCTIFICATION has NOTHING to do with you. It is ALL about what I do to the vessel to make it a fitting and pure habitation for Me. It is not about you cleaning up your act. Once you confess your sins and repent, then it is also not about SIN, which Jesus atoned for with His shed blood. From that point forward, it is all about SELF. Had you read this book the previous eight times from that perspective, you would understand that EVERYTHING ELSE that I taught Rees Howells, and did FOR him, was a systematic process of purging the vessel of all trace of SELF.** The remaining 260 pages of that book are one lesson after another, presented, learned, and lived out. Every lesson was another facet of sanctification, of Me purging or sanctifying the vessel, that I might indwell him in an increasingly deeper and greater way. Similarly, I want to do this FOR you if you will allow Me."*

After relating the above to that Friday night crowd, I also explained one additional thing that the Holy Spirit pointed out to me, which He said I misunderstood.

"In a recent conversation with my close friend and prayer partner," I told the crowd, "I told him how much I enjoyed praying together with him all of these years and how I appreciated his dedication as an intercessor. However, I had also laughingly finished up by saying, 'You know, though, that unlike you, I'm not **called** to be an intercessor.' In Colorado, the Spirit reminded me of that conversation, and said, *'Anyone who desires to be a purified, mightily-used vessel for Me must be, first and foremost, a genuine, dedicated intercessor.'"*

After I finished speaking with the body at Heritage, my pastor thanked me and then said to everyone in attendance that night that our church body desperately needed to hear what I had just finished speaking. He explained that there were MANY in our church in the same position I had found myself, and they have been for years, with no understanding as to why. Meanwhile, like me, they repeatedly question in their hearts whether anything is still happening, "as if God has somehow forgotten about them."

In the remaining days in that Colorado hotel room, the Spirit of God spoke to me about many other subjects. In each instance, the Spirit spoke as a storyteller, just as Jesus did when He ministered and taught the masses. Every "story," however, in some way, was related to or taken from events in my past. Each also emphasized specific shortcomings in my life and spiritual walk that needed correction.

In the first instance, He spoke directly to a particular point when He said, *"Those who are used by Me in a mighty way possess no more anointing, gifting, or fullness of My Spirit than any other man or woman. The difference is the individual's willingness to totally, genuinely die to SELF, and then to walk out what I have called them to do or be. Even with these,* **NONE were able, in their knowledge, understanding, strength, and determination, to come up to it.** *As I showed you with Rees Howells, those who sought the Lord and were willing to surrender to the working of My Spirit,* **moved beyond themselves**. *As they diminished, the Spirit of the Lord increased, and that which was both unthinkable and unattainable became a reality, step-by-step.* **This type of death and resurrection is NOT a learned transformation. It is an intentional devaluation, a debasing of what is considered by the world to be of great value, that He who became least may establish in you that which is of a far greater, lasting value.***"*

In another instance, He further clarified a specific point when He said, *"Son, don't put pressure on yourself that I didn't put on you. I DON'T want you to come up to the point where you finally believe that what I am detailing out is something exciting in which you'd like to be a part.* **What I need is for you to reach such a point of desperation wherein your spirit longs to be submitted and fulfilled, even though you know, in your flesh and soul, that you aren't, in your strength, able to surrender.** *As with Rees Howells, and many others, I am waiting for your ever-growing love for Me, and your desire to please Me, to tip the scales enough that you would find yourself willing to be made willing—WITHOUT knowing what comes next, or what your final surrender in a given area will all entail."*

There were two specific lessons, though, that He urged me to note in exact detail in my journal, and later told me to include here. Those two lessons follow.

"Shaken, <u>AND</u> Stirred"

Having watched a few action movies over the years, I am familiar with some of Hollywood's film productions of the many James Bond books written by Ian Fleming. Although numerous men have played the starring role, in each new book brought to life on the big screen the directors have been careful not to alter the character's well-known persona— retaining his memorable mannerisms, catchphrases, and carefully-crafted image as the fictional British MI6 agent known as '007.'

The phrase most uniquely identifiable from all James Bond films is the character's precise way of introducing himself when meeting anyone for the first time. His standard introduction was "Bond. James Bond." That unique trait also included his shaking the person's hand while focusing on their eyes. The repetition of his last name was an intentional effort to cause others to recall it easily the next time they met.

Sean Connery was the initial actor to deliver this line as he played the part of Bond in the first movie, *Dr. No,* released in 1962. That introduction became a standard in all future James Bond films.

The second most memorable line that the character voices is a short, but precise explanation of how he (Bond) wants his martini made. Bartender training instructs that the mixed ingredients for a classic martini are to be 'poured over a glass of chipped ice, which is then stirred and stirred, and stirred again until the martini is deeply chilled when presented to the patron to drink.' Nevertheless, in the third James Bond film, *Goldfinger,* released in 1964, the James Bond character (once again played by Sean Connery), asks for his martini to be "shaken, not stirred." Like his introduction, these words have also become readily identifiable with the James Bond persona in all future '007' films.

Although I had read the above facts at some point in my distant past, something occurred while I was in that Colorado hotel room this time that puzzled me. While praying, walking back and forth in the room, I suddenly heard words spoken in a loud voice: *"Shaken, AND Stirred."* I admit that I was, and still am, uncertain as to whether those words were audible or spoken only to my spirit being. I recognized the voice as being the Holy Spirits. Even so, when that very scene from *Goldfinger* suddenly came to the forefront of my mind at the hearing of those words, I was confused. With clarity, I recalled seeing that movie in 1970 at a military base in California, and could even 'see' the very theater seat I sat in that day. As I pondered on it further, something bothered me about what I was seeing and hearing. It then came to me! I was positive that the words from the film were different from those spoken by the Holy Spirit. While dwelling on this, I waited on the Lord, hoping for clarification.

No immediate verbal explanation came from the Spirit. Instead, the *'picture'* in my mind suddenly changed from one of Sean Connery (in the role of James Bond) to an image of two large hands firmly taking hold of and vigorously shaking, the shoulders of a man. The intense thought that came to me at that moment was **'someone is being shaken out of their comfort zone'**—except it did not end there.

A moment later, the film scene returned, accompanied by this detailed explanation from the Holy Spirit, which He then told me to write down.

*"Son, most individuals want things the way they want them, just as they portray this movie character. They want things one way or the other, but not both, not uncertain or indeterminate. They want everything **under control**. When something contradictory to what they want unexpectedly shakes their world, most react by striving to overcome it, **to quickly bring things under their control again**, back to the way to which they have become accustomed."*

*"On a different note, most individuals never come to realize that some things, which they have readily and unquestioningly learned to accept as truth, are **craftily formulated and highly promoted untruth**. One such lie is that man was created and expected to be the master of his destiny."*

*"Because of a predisposition to believe that lie, it is incomprehensible to many, and uncomfortable for most to even consider, that He who is the Source of perfect peace, and both establishes and maintains divine order, would intentionally shake their world. What they fail to understand is that the Spirit **purposefully** allows such shaking to induce cracks in their carefully self-created and self-controlled world."*

"Once this misunderstood chaos penetrates the deepest part of their being and existence—often leaving them feeling helpless and uncertain—they will finally be positioned for the Spirit of God to begin the 'reconstruction' that He knows must occur."

That which He begins, He is always faithful to complete—bringing forth a new creation with a **transformed** soul or (self) nature."

"Yet, even then, the decision as to whether or not this occurs rests with the individual. In their uncertainty and insecurity, will they revert to striving to restore their world to what they believed to be 'ordered'? Or will they finally acknowledge their own far deeper, previously ignored need that only I, their Creator, can fulfill?"

"Will they allow Me to help them understand that I have both **shaken their world AND stirred them deeply** for a reason? Will they permit their soul and spirit to rest in My hands while their Creator—who is also the Divine Potter—reshapes the 'clay' of their existence? Will they trust Me to bring them through the necessary Fire to make them into the purposeful vessel that the Creator always desired them to be? Will they then trust the Heavenly Father to place them back in My hands, where He knows they will find their greatest fulfillment?"

"Even though that which I've spoken from My heart applies to you, son, as well as to all humanity, only one thing should truly matter to each person. **'DOES THIS APPLY TO ME, AND IF SO, HOW?'"**

"As time truly draws ever shorter, My Spirit pleads with each of you to finally be honest with yourself about how **YOU** would answer the following questions."

"Are **YOU** willing to surrender **YOUR** will and **YOUR** ways, allowing the Spirit of Christ to lead you to **YOUR** greatest possible fulfillment? If not, have you thought carefully and truthfully about WHAT it is that is holding you back?"

"Is it because you insist on having what **you** want, the way **you** want it? Have you grown accustomed to, and even satisfied with your life as it currently is? Do you intentionally ignore that small voice within that tells you that life is about more than SELF and that you were born for a far greater reason and purpose than you have ever considered?"

"Finally, if none of these questions move your heart or stir your mind, **is it possibly because you are holding on so tightly to the reins of control in your life**? If so, are you so sure of your ability to handle whatever may disturb the world that you have created? In your eagerness to be the captain of your soul, are you even aware that **YOU are, by your very actions**, SELF-identifying with the Bond character's famous words, confidently replying without hesitation to anyone's inquiry (as he did), that **YOUR** preference continues to be: **'Shaken, NOT stirred'?"**

Spirit-Determined Focus

While taking a break from reading my Bible on my last day in Colorado, I stood before the window of the hotel room I was staying in at the time. I looked at the homes in the distance and the mountains beyond them. A question came to mind to ask the Lord, and the following conversation ensued. Afterward, He told me to make a note of it, and to think about it regularly.

"Lord, You've insisted that I repeatedly return to this same place. What is so special to You about Fort Collins, Colorado?"

"There are lessons that you still need to learn, son, and isolating you here allows you to listen to what I need you to hear and understand. What did you see while standing here at the window?"

"I was gazing out the window, not focused on any particular thing, waiting for You to respond. Is there something that I should be seeing?"

"What did you see?"

I hesitated and thought carefully before responding. "As I was staring in a daze, I vaguely saw the tree outside the window, although I wasn't looking at the tree. Through its nearly bare branches, I saw the storage building at the rear of the hotel parking lot. Beyond that is the tram roadway, the railroad tracks, the path for walking and bicycling, quite a few houses, and finally the mountains."

"Did you SEE the glass in the window, or the framework simulating panels in the glass?"

"I didn't think about them."

"Did you SEE the many seed pods still clinging to the tree branches?"

"Just for a moment, but I didn't focus on them."

"Did you note how each seed in those seed pods I separately encased and protected?"

I stared at them a moment, then replied, "Not until You just now mentioned it."

"You did, however, notice how overgrown the grass and weeds are on either side of the fence separating the train track from the walking path, and wondered why it was allowed to become like that, didn't you?"

"Yes."

"You also thought about and judged the condition of several houses within your view that need extensive repair. Isn't that true?"

"Yes, but what are You trying to show me, Holy Spirit? I don't understand."

*"Did you think about ALL of the homes visible beyond the walking path? Not the houses, son, but the HOMES—made so by the families in those structures that made the houses their homes. Did you even, for a moment, wonder **who** might be living there? Did you consider what areas and peoples of this city and county they interact with, and*

whether or not any of them know Me? Did you spend one minute considering their lives, hopes, dreams, disappointments, hurts, sufferings, or needs?"

"No, Lord. I honestly can't say that I did."

"Exactly. You ask Me what is so special about this city. **You are looking right at it and not seeing it**, son. What I am trying to show you is that you, like most people, see what you **focus on** or **WANT to see**—just as you did each of the many times that you read the book on Rees Howells."

"Listen carefully now while I explain what I want you to understand. I, the Lord, created the human eye to be a literal window to the individual's soul. That is the incredible beauty of the eye. It both takes in and sends out. It allows your soul to gather in all that it observes. It is capable of focusing on incalculable numbers of planes, distances, levels, and objects. It can observe millions of things in a single glance. However, the mind, which is part of your soul, determines **where** the eye should and should not focus. In other words, **YOU, and you alone, choose what you will and will not see.** Do you understand?"

"Yes."

"When looking out this window, your **focus** determines WHAT you see. However, son, **your PERSPECTIVE, at that moment, determines HOW YOU PERCEIVE WHAT YOU ARE SEEING**. When you looked at the homes, those individuals walking or riding on the path, or even those on the tram when it passes, you noticed people. However, I see each person as a soul that I desperately long to reach."

"Why is this city important to Me? Because it is perfectly representative of all cities. **I see this as a community of souls worth saving**, while you, and most others, see only a busy, rapidly-expanding metropolis full of people hurrying here and there."

"When you allow Me to guide your study of My Word, don't you invariably 'discover' previously unnoticed nuances or meanings? In like manner, **I desire that My children would genuinely see with a Spirit-led insight what their eyes are observing in this world. That occurs ONLY when My Spirit is permitted to move through an individual's spirit to sensitize their soul, allowing them to see what and as I see.**"

"**Truly**, you **ARE** in control. You choose WHAT to see or not see. Nevertheless, when you sincerely ask Me to direct your spirit and soul, thoughts, and vision, you will **ALWAYS** see with new eyes, guided by My understanding and the mind of Christ. That which I show you will displace anything else that otherwise would have captured your attention. This **SPIRIT-DETERMINED FOCUS** is vital in these final days before My return—in you, and all my children—to prevent any of My children from carelessly or callously overlooking a single soul."

Scripture, Book & Song References

Acknowledging the 'I' in Sin: (All references in this chapter are from the NKJV)
1. Rev. 3:19
2. Heb. 12:5-6
3. Ps. 118:8
4. Prov. 3:26
5. Ps. 107:9
6. Prov. 3:5-7
7. Phil. 4:19
8. Heb. 10:23
9. Eph. 6:12
10. Heb. 12:2
11. Heb. 12:2
12. Heb. 12:2
13. Heb. 12:2

Learning to War:
1. Romans 13:1 (NKJV)

Called Away:
1. 1 Pet. 3:15 (HCSB)
2. 2 Cor. 1:22 (NIV)
3. 2 Tim. 2:19 (NIV)
4. 2 Tim. 2:22 (NIV)
5. Eph. 4:30 (KJV)
6. Rom. 7:15-20 (TNIV)
7. Rom. 7:21-25 (TNIV)
8. Eph. 5:8-11 (NKJV)
9. Rom. 7:24b (TNIV)
10. Rom. 7:25 ((TNIV)
11. Matt. 13:15 (NKJV)
12. Matt. 13:15 (NKJV)
13. Phil. 4:8-9 (NKJV)
14. Matt. 11:29 (NKJV)
15. Ps. 46:10 (NKJV)
16. 2 Cor. 10:5 (NIV)
17. 2 Cor. 10:5 (NIV)
18. 2 Sam. 22:5-20 (NKJV)
19. Rom. 5:17 (TNIV)
20. 2 Cor. 5:17 (NKJV)
21. John 8:36 (NKJV)
22. 2 Tim. 1:7 (NKJV)
23. Heb. 13:5 (NKJV)
24. Acts 13:22 (NKJV)
25. Jer. 31:34 (NKJV)
26. Lam. 3:23 (NKJV)

Facing the Truth:
1. Eph. 5:8-11 (NKJV)
2. Luke 10:19 (NIV)
3. Eph. 5:2 (NKJV)

After-Effects:
1. Ps. 34:4-6 (NIV)
2. Eph. 6:13 (NKJV)

Gone Away Backward:
1 - 4. Is. 1:4b (KJV)

Let Me Re-Mind You: (Ref. # 1–7 are from the KJV; Ref. # 8 is from the NKJV)
1 - 6. James 1:5-8
7. James 1:22-25
8. Prov. 3:5-6

Positioned to See:
1. Prov. 15:22 (NKJV)

Evidence of Love: (All references in this chapter are from the NKJV)
1. Luke 7:7b-8
2. Luke 7:8
3. Luke 8:16

Spirit of Reconciliation: Grace to Forgive:
1. John 10:27 (NKJV)

If You Would Be My Voice:
1. Heb. 8:5b (NLT)
2. Luke 4:18 (NIV)
3. Prov. 4:7 (NKJV)
4. 1 John 5:14-15 (NKJV)
5. Matt. 3:2 (NKJV)
6. Prov. 13:17 (NKJV)

B-1: _Intercessory Prayer_; Dutch Sheets; © 2008 Bethany House Publishers
B-2: _Kickin' Devil Hiney_; Eastman Curtis; © 1997 Harrison House
S-1: _More Of You, Lord_; Eric Nuzum & Chris Springer; © 1999 Integrity's Hosanna! Music
S-2: _Your Love Is Extravagant_; Darrell Evans; © 1998 Integrity's Hosanna! Music
S-3: _Hungry_; © 1999 Vineyard Songs (UK/Eire)
S-4: _You Are A Holy God_; Brian Duane & Kathryn Scott; © 1999 Vineyard Songs (UK/Eire)
S-5: _Breathe_; Marie Barnett; © 1995 Mercy/Vineyard Publishing
S-6: _Thy Throne, Oh God_; The Maranatha! Singers; © 1991 Maranatha! Music
S-7: _My Deliverer_ © 1999 Calvary Temple of Indianapolis Praise Choir

About the Author

Born and raised in Cincinnati, Ohio and the surrounding area, John and his wife are long-time members of Heritage Fellowship, located in Florence, Kentucky. John also was a member of Full Gospel Business Men's Fellowship International for more than two decades. During that time, he served in various capacities, including ten years as a chapter officer, the last two as chapter president. John also participated in ministry outreach to prisoners in nearby state and county prisons. In his later years with the organization, he traveled to numerous chapters in the Midwestern USA, testifying and ministering as a guest speaker.

Directed by the Holy Spirit, John co-founded a prayer and discipleship group for men that met for 4-5 hours every Saturday morning. More than twenty-five years later, some in that group still regularly meet for prayer.

At one point, John underwent personal deliverance in obedience to the Holy Spirit at a church located five hours north of his hometown. Later, he trained with that same church body to minister Spirit-led deliverance to others. For seven years, John joined in with that church body ministering at their quarterly conferences. He and his wife also brought dozens of couples and individuals from their home church and city to those conferences. Back in his hometown, he later trained other men to work in cooperation with the Holy Spirit as part of a local deliverance ministry team. Together, these men applied what they had learned, helping many to be set free. Details of these occurrences are in this book.

After being ordained as a minister in 2010 under the auspices of Church Growth International of the Americas (CGIA), John and his wife began working as a team, praying for the sick and dying, in local hospitals, nursing homes, and wherever the Holy Spirit directed them.

As the Spirit of the Lord moved on them and through them, they and their children have experienced many miracles and healings, personally, and as the Lord's vessel of hope to others. At the Lord's encouragement, they continue regularly to pray for and reach out to those in need. Through their obedience, many have come to know Jesus as their personal Savior, Healer, and Deliverer.

Now retired, John continues to write nonfiction and fiction books and articles, attempting to fulfill God's call on his life to be a "writer with a ready pen," putting into words what the Spirit of the Living God is laying upon his heart.